The African-American Military Experience in the Civil War

An Annotated Bibliography
of
Selected Articles

Jerome Liddy

HERITAGE BOOKS
2018

HERITAGE BOOKS

AN IMPRINT OF HERITAGE BOOKS, INC.

Books, CDs, and more—Worldwide

For our listing of thousands of titles see our website
at
www.HeritageBooks.com

Published 2018 by
HERITAGE BOOKS, INC.
Publishing Division
5810 Ruatan Street
Berwyn Heights, Md. 20740

International Standard Book Number
Paperbound: 978-0-7884-5809-5

IN MEMORY OF:

Hugh Liddy
Company D, 5th Ohio Infantry
Born in Ireland
Killed in action before Atlanta on August 3, 1864

Anthony Liddy
Company H, 10th Massachusetts Infantry
Born in Ireland
Killed in action before Cold Harbor, June 5, 1864

Patrick Liddy
Company F, 155th New York Infantry
Born in Ireland
Critically wounded at Cold Harbor on June 3, 1864
Passed away at
Finley Army Hospital, Washington, DC
June 22, 1864

CONTENTS

ACKNOWLEDGEMENTS

I would like to thank a number of people for their help in the writing of this book and in particular Dr. John C. Gruesser of Kean University, Union, New Jersey. John was instrumental in the earliest development of this project. I would also like to thank those unidentified New Jersey librarians who graciously assisted me in my searches at the Harry A. Sprague Library, Montclair State University, the Alexander Library at Rutgers University, and the Firestone Library, Princeton University. I am particularly grateful to the efforts of Helen V. Beckert, Reference Librarian at the Glen Ridge Pubic Library, Glen Ride, New Jersey for her diligent and relentless pursuit of numerous hard to find articles. No matter how obscure the periodical, or how small its circulation, Helen would track it down with both humor and a smile. I am deeply indebted to Helen for her assistance. I would also like to thank a friend of many years, Alan Rosenfeld, for his perceptive comments and suggested changes. I would also like to thank my daughter Mary Ellen for her extraordinary computer skills and, lastly, I would like to thank my wife for enduring those seemingly endless hours of proofreading. I'm really glad I returned that umbrella so many years ago.

CHAPTER ONE
INTRODUCTION

Prior to the early 1950s, the military role played by African-American soldiers and sailors in the American Civil War, and their contribution to eventual Union victory, was, with pitifully few exceptions, either misrepresented, ignored, demeaned, distorted, or misunderstood by most American historians. For example, in a popular history of the Union campaign in the Mississippi Valley published in 1901 and written by John Fiske, at that time a greatly admired American philosopher, evolutionist, and historian, the role played by African-American soldiers in the campaign is never acknowledged, either directly or indirectly. Fiske completely ignores the unsuccessful May 27, 1863 assault by two black Union regiments on the Confederate entrenchments along the Mississippi River at Fort Hudson, Louisiana, the first officially sanctioned use of organized units of black troops in Civil War combat. Likewise, he fails to acknowledge the brutal slugging match between Confederate forces and several newly organized and ill-equipped Union regiments of former slaves, which occurred barely ten days later further upriver at Milliken's Bend. And the only mention of Fort Pillow, the scene of the Civil War's most notorious racial atrocity in which an incredible 64% of the black garrison was killed, is not to the massacre itself, but the fort's position on the bluffs overlooking the Mississippi River and its subsequent abandonment by Confederate forces in mid-1862.

The contribution of African-Americans to Union victory, when not ignored was all too often ridiculed. In a well-received and popular 1928 biography of Ulysses S. Grant, the historian W. E. Woodward declared that "American negroes are the only people in the world, as far as I know, that ever became free without any effort of their own ... They twanged banjos around the railroad stations, sang melodious spirituals, and believed that some Yankee would come along and give each of them forty acres of land and a mule." As soldiers, according to Woodward, they did not favorably impress most senior army officers. "Sherman considered them a joke, and Grant usually kept them in the rear." Herbert Aptheker, an avowed Marxist writer and historian, observed in 1951 that the reason for this viewpoint regarding African-Americans and African-American soldiers was painfully simple: "A Jim Crow society breeds and needs a Jim Crow historiography." At the time more than a few historians were outraged by Aptheker's comment, dismissing his statement as abrasive and politically motivated. Others, including the historian Dudley T. Cornish, author of a groundbreaking study of African-American soldiers in the Civil War, sadly remarked that the observation was fundamentally true.

Between 1865 and the early 1950s, American history by and large – with only a handful of exceptions – consciously ignored the fact that during the Civil War nearly 200,000 African-

Americans served in the Union army and navy, that as soldiers they participated in 449 engagements, 39 of which are listed as major battles, that approximately 37,000 lost their lives in the conflict, and that in April 1865 more than one in ten soldiers in the Union army were black men in blue uniforms. In proportion to population more African-Americans may have fought for the Union than did their white contemporaries. Organizationally African-American soldiers, serving in segregated army units commanded by white officers, contributed – in the last two years of the conflict – 120 infantry regiments, 12 heavy artillery regiments, ten batteries of light artillery, and seven cavalry regiments to the Union war effort. These facts, and their social, racial, and political implications for what Lincoln termed the Republic's "mystic chords of memory," were by consensus later erased from national consciousness. As late as 1943, the black historian W.E.B. DuBois could write, without fear of contradiction, that the important part played by African-Americans in the Civil War, and the public recollection of that memory, "had been intentionally and systematically played down until today it is not simply neglected but nearly forgotten."

DuBois' comment regarding public recollection of the Civil War and its impact on the subsequent writing of American history, relates not only to the immediate recollection of the war, but to how that recollection was subsequently interpreted, internalized, and shaped by post-war generations into a coherent and socially acceptable representation of the past. According to David W. Blight, in his award-wining and thought-provoking 2001 book *Race and Reunion: the Civil War in American Memory*, several competing visions for interpreting and remembering the turmoil of the Civil War initially contended for national dominance in the decades immediately following the war.

The first and earliest was the idea of national reconciliation through carefully selected historical memory. In this vision of Civil War interpretation and public memory, both sides sought to justify the awful brutality of a divisive war by celebrating the battlefield valor of Billy Yank and Johnny Reb in a carefully choreographed dance of reconciliation and reunion. In this nostalgic interpretation of the past, both North and South were right, neither side was wrong; both sides were equally honorable and both sides fought for principles they believed just and worthy of defense. This interpretation, and its impact on defining and shaping emerging public memory, was later incorporated into a Southern white supremacist vision with its emphasis on the dashing cavalier, the old plantation home, the nobility of Lee and his lieutenants, the romance of the Lost Cause, the affectionate slave master, and the destructive social and political consequences of mainly Northern troublemakers who, motivated solely by self-interest and arrogance, shamelessly manipulated happy-go-lucky slaves and bewildered freedmen. In this widely accepted and remarkably popular version of Civil War memory, the political process of remembering was accomplished by first forgetting: discordant political disagreements over states' rights became the only acceptable explanation for what propelled the country into a bloody sectional conflict; slavery and the morality of human bondage, as well as the presence and participation of African-Americans as soldiers or sailors in the Civil War, were not only ignored but obliterated from public memory. This Southern revisionist explanation for what had occurred became the nationally accepted interpretation of the war. A socially and politically expedient white-only image of America's past became the racist filter through which America as a country came to remember the trauma of Civil War. It overwhelmed, but did not entirely eliminate, what Blight has termed the "emancipationist" memory of the war. In this view of the past, held by African-Americans and their supporters in the white community, the malignancy of slavery was acknowledged as the actual cause of the war. The guarantees of emancipation and equal justice were viewed as promises made but now largely forgotten in the post-Reconstruction era of Jim Crow, disenfranchisement, lynch law, and white sectional harmony bought and sold in the market place of black civil liberties.

Historiography is the academic medium in which both scholarly history and public memory is examined, understood, defined, and finally transmitted as learned knowledge from one generation to another. As America matured into a major world power, the prevailing mainstream historiography regarding the Civil War and Reconstruction, at least as it eventually developed in the late nineteenth and early twentieth century, faithfully reflected what Americans considered the only socially acceptable memory of the past. This was essentially race and reunion on strictly Southern terms, and it was exceptional since it coupled historical recollection and cultural mythology with the idea of white racial superiority. As a result, the real causes and consequences of slavery and the Civil War, the major role played by black soldiers and sailors in the conflict, and the still unresolved question of racial equality and African-American civil liberties, were overwhelmingly absent in the prevailing academic historiography. This historical neglect, fostered by an intensive decades-long Southern propaganda campaign, was reflected in a white-only scholarly historiography, as well as popular history, that for years relied on libel and innuendo to either eliminate or marginalize the black Civil War experience.

All this was to fundamentally change beginning in the mid-to-late 1950s with the desegregation of not only American society but American history. As African-American social history was redefined and rediscovered during the Civil Rights movement, so too was the military contribution of black soldiers and sailors in the Civil War. The historical dominance of a white-only racial historiography was redressed with a literal Niagara of historical works dealing with the Civil War. Over the following decades well-researched, scholarly, and critically acclaimed full-length studies by Benjamin Quarles, Dudley T. Cornish, James W. McPherson, Joseph T. Glatthaar, Joseph P. Reidy, Steven J. Ramold, and Ira Berlin – to name a few among many – revolutionized historical interpretation and reclaimed for all Americans the black Civil War experience. In popular culture, Civil War and Reconstruction memory and history, as reflected D. W. Griffith's *Birth of a Nation* and *Gone With the Wind*, had finally been swept aside and replaced by the compelling reality of *Glory*. And this revolution in historical re-discovery continues without interruption, and at an impressive rate, to this day. What had been relegated to the dustbin of history has been restored to its rightful place as a grand and noble achievement.

While full-length historical studies concerning the African-American Civil War military experience continue to enjoy critical and popular acceptance, they have been augmented over the years by a steady stream of equally important and often pioneering articles. These articles, addressing all aspects of the black Civil War military experience, have appeared in various periodicals, generally over the past 50 plus years. Many have appeared in academic journals; others in more popular publications devoted exclusively to the American Civil War. Some run only a few pages in length; others are thoroughly well-researched and extensive scholarly monographs. Until now none have been collected in a one-volume annotated bibliography complete – not only with basic bibliographic information – but with critical and descriptive commentary. This volume thus fills a long standing gap in Civil War bibliography by providing a comprehensive and useful resource guide for teachers, scholars, students, and librarians.

The articles that follow are listed in alphabetical order by author or editor, since this is the easiest way by far too conveniently present such a large collection of material. They address a wide range of subjects concerning the African-American military experience in the Civil War including but not limited to battles and campaigns, the reaction of Union and Confederate soldiers to black troops (either as soldiers in uniform or on the battlefield), the contentious issue of army pay, recruitment, prisoner treatment, racial atrocities, shipboard race relations, racial prejudice, medical treatment, and the often mind-numbing routine of garrison duty. Each article is presented in standard bibliographical format that includes the name of the author, article title, journal name, volume number and issue number, date of publication, and pages on which the article appears. This is followed by an annotation, which can vary in length from several sentences to several paragraphs per citation, depending on the nature of the article cited and its historical significance. If appropriate, supplemental information regarding maps, tables, charts, illustrations, appendixes, and additional bibliographical data is also provided. For the reader's convenience in locating articles, a subject matter index is included. The number in the index corresponds to the number assigned to the article in the bibliography. As an example, the entry for Fort Pillow in the index is followed by a list of numbers. Each number directs the reader to a numbered article found in the annotated bibliography.

This bibliography of articles dealing with the African-American Civil War experience, arranged as it is in alphabetical order by author or editor, is by its very structure not intended to be a linear unfolding of historical events, since it is based not on a logical, orderly recounting of history but on the specific material contained in the annotated articles. As history it can appear as so many disjointed narrative chunks lacking in continuity and organization. One article annotation may discuss the Fort Jackson mutiny, while the subsequent one describes the medical problems of black garrison troops stationed in the lower Mississippi Valley. Collectively, however, these articles provide a comprehensive if not a chronological history. For those seeking a more coherent and full-length history of the black military experience in the Civil War, from early rejection of military service by Federal officials to the last battle of the war fought by black troops at Palmito Range, Texas, on May 13, 1865, a bibliography of published books is included as Chapter 3. Listed are the latest studies dealing with the African-American Civil War military experience, a number of personal reminiscences by white officers who served in black regiments, several African-American regimental histories, and a number of indispensable reference works.

One note of explanation: Most African-American soldiers were former slaves and, at least upon enlistment, illiterate. Illiterate or not, former slave or free-born, all suffered unconcealed discrimination as black men in a white society. Consequently, only a handful of African-Americans were ever commissioned as officers in the Union Army. As a result, many articles cited in this study are more often concerned with the activities of white officers in black regiments than with the African-American soldiers they commanded. Likewise, a few tactical studies are listed and described that only superficially mention the role played by black troops in a particular battle. They are included because subsequent articles more thoroughly describe the encounter.

Also note that the articles collected and annotated in this bibliography concern African-Americans who wore Union blue and served the Federal cause, either on land or afloat. The use of black slaves by the Confederate Army as general laborers, teamsters, cooks, and medical orderlies, and the escalating Southern debate about recruiting and arming black slaves as soldiers, are not part of this study and are not included in the article annotations.

CHAPTER 2

ANNOTATED ARTICLE BIBLIOGRAPHY

1. Abbott, Richard H. "Massachusetts and the Recruitment of Southern Negroes, 1863-1865." *Civil War History*, 14, 3 (September 1968): 197-210.

Abbott's study examines attempts by Massachusetts elected officials and business leaders to fill the state's draft quota by recruiting African-American soldiers from areas in the South under Federal military occupation. Influential Massachusetts businessmen hoped to reduce white draft quotas by obtaining black recruits and, as a result, protect their commercial interests, maintain uninterrupted industrial production, and keep skilled white factory workers at home, at their jobs, and free of the draft. After intensive lobbying efforts, Congress passed legislation authorizing states to send agents into occupied areas of the South to enlist African-Americans as soldiers. Recruits would be credited against the draft quota assigned to the state. A small number of black recruits were raised, of which approximately 25% were credited to Massachusetts. After a series of complaints by Generals Sherman and Grant, the authorizing legislation was repealed by Congress. The article contains 35 notes based on primary and secondary sources, newspaper accounts, and official records.

2. Aliyetti, John E. "Gallantry under Fire." *Civil War Times Illustrated*, 35, 5 (October 1996): 50-55.

A brief but concise tactical study recounting a series of bloody assaults by three brigades (nine regiments) of African-American troops on New Market Heights, Virginia, on September 29, 1864. The three brigades were part of Major General Benjamin F. Butler's Army of the James. After a series of attacks in which the black regiments suffered substantial casualties, Confederate forces withdrew and their entrenchments occupied. Years later Butler admitted he committed the black regiments to a difficult plan of attack in order "to establish confidence in their reliability." Fourteen black soldiers fighting at New Market Heights would be awarded the Medal of Honor. The article is illustrated with several period photographs.

3. Aptheker, Herbert. "Negro Casualties in the Civil War." *Journal of Negro History,* 32, 1 (January 1947): 10-80.
A dated but still the most comprehensive examination of African-American military fatalities suffered during the Civil War, both on land and sea, by a well-known and controversial Marxist historian. According to Aptheker, the mortality rate among white volunteers in the Civil War was 94.3 per thousand, while that of their black fellow soldiers was 35% greater at 157.5 per thousand. In terms of percentages, 15% of white volunteers died of all causes in military service during the Civil War as compared to 20% of black troops, almost all of which were enrolled in the last two years of the war. Among African-American soldiers the single greatest cause of death was sickness and disease, which accounted for more than eight in ten fatalities. As an example, the 5th United States Colored Heavy Artillery suffered the highest total mortality rate for any Union regiment that saw active duty in the war. A total of 829 men were lost in service, which included eight white officers. Of that number 124 men died in battle or were mortally wounded while 697 died as a result of disease, sickness, or accident. The second highest number of fatalities for a Union regiment was experienced by the 65th United States Colored Infantry while performing garrison duty along the lower Mississippi. While the regiment never fired a shot in anger, it lost a shocking 749 black enlisted men and six white officers to disease.

Aptheker attributes the abnormally high African-American mortality rate by disease and sickness to several factors including woefully inadequate medical care, excessive fatigue duty (a task many black regiments found more reminiscent of slave labor than military service), poor training, inferior equipment, and inadequate leadership – though the latter contention would probably be disputed by many contemporary scholars.

Sometimes heavy-handed in its approach, Aptheker's article is informative and well documented with extensive footnotes and several tables. Unfortunately, several conclusions are based more on ideological considerations than on historical evidence. As an example, he cites the July 18, 1863 assault on Fort (Battery) Wagner by the 54th Massachusetts Infantry (Colored) as proof of the callous and indifferent employment of black troops by white commanders. No mention is made of the white regiments involved in the attack that suffered equally grievous casualties.

4. _____. "The Negro in the Union Navy." *Journal of Negro History*, 32, 2 (April 1947): 169-200.
A well-documented account of the role of African-American sailors in the Union Navy during the Civil War. According to the author, blacks had a long tradition of naval service dating back to the American Revolution. Even before the Civil War, naval authorities – unlike their army counterparts – were allowed to recruit up to 5% of their enlisted ranks from the African-American community. This number increased dramatically to meet the manpower shortage prompted by the outbreak of war and an expanding navy. As a consequence, during the period 1861-1865, African-Americans formed a large percentage of the enlisted ranks in the navy.

Aptheker estimates that at least 25% of the 118,000 naval enlistments during the war were filled by black sailors, either American or foreign born. Later scholarship conducted by Joseph Reidy of Howard University and the National Park Service has concluded that the total percentage was probably nearer a still impressive 16%. The overall number will probably never be known, since the navy did not classify men by race. The navy, unlike the army, was not segregated and ships were integrated with black sailors receiving the same pay as white sailors of the same rank. Free blacks were allowed to hold all naval ranks short of the petty officer rating. This policy was later extended to contrabands that were recruited in large numbers, both on the inland waters and at sea. For the latest and most comprehensive scholarship concerning this subject, see *Slaves, Sailors, Citizens: African Americans in the Union Navy* by Steven J. Ramold.

5. Archambault, Alan and Anthony Gero. "United States Colored Troops, Enlisted Men, Infantry, 1864-1865." *Military Collector & Historian*, 47, 2 (Summer 1995): 88-89.

This article consists of a single black-and-white line drawing illustrating the uniforms worn by five African-American soldiers representing five different black Union Army regiments in the years 1864-1865. A short descriptive text and several notes augment the illustration.

6. Archambault, Alan, Anthony Gero, Roger Sturcke, and William Gladstone. "5th and 3rd Regiment and 4th Regiment of Cavalry, United States Colored Troops, 1863-1866." *Military Collector & Historian*, 51, 3 (Fall 1999): 136-137.

Another black-and-white line drawing illustrating the uniforms worn by soldiers in several African-American cavalry regiments in the years 1863-1866. Included in the article is a short descriptive text supplemented by several notes.

7. Arey, Frank. "The First Kansas Colored at Honey Springs." In *All Cut to Pieces and Gone to Hell: The Civil War, Race Relations, and the Battle of Poison Spring,* edited by Mark K. Christ: Little Rock: August House, 2003, 79-97.

The Battle of Honey Springs, fought in Indian Territory on July 17, 1863, was a resounding Union victory. The 1st Kansas Colored Regiment played a conspicuous part in that victory and by doing so sowed the seeds that fed racial animosity and murder nine months later at Poison Spring, Arkansas. The author provides a summary of the battle with particular emphasis on the beating the 29th Texas Cavalry and the 1st Choctaw regiments received in their encounter with the 1st Kansas Colored. Indeed, the 29th even lost its flag, "the most important symbol of regimental pride." Later, when these three regiments met again at Poison Spring, racial animosity, and a desire to avenge the humiliation of Honey Springs, fueled the Confederate massacre of numerous 1st Kansas Colored soldiers.

8. Armstrong, Warren B. "Union Chaplains and the Education of the Freedmen." *Journal of Negro History*, 52, 2 (April 1967): 104-115.

A good study examining the efforts of Union Army chaplains to provide basic education to freedmen, principally in the western Department of the Tennessee. Particular attention is paid to the activities of Chaplain John Eaton, General Superintendent of Freedmen and later colonel, 9th Louisiana Native Guards (afterward the 63rd United States Colored Infantry). Educational activities relating to African-American soldiers, while not prominent in the article, are discussed on a limited basis.

9. Astor, Aaron. "'I Wanted a Gun.' Black Soldiers and White Violence in Civil War and Postwar Kentucky and Missouri." In *The Great Task before Us: Reconstruction as America's Continuing Civil War*, edited by Paul A. Cimbala and Randall Miller. New York: Fordham University Press, 2010, 30-53.

In this clearly written and well-documented study, Astor examines the ongoing violence common to both Missouri and Kentucky in their relationship with African-Americans during and after the Civil War. In both states the Emancipation Proclamation did not apply, in both states conservative Unionists were the majority of the white population, both were border states, both were slave holding states, and in both states Unionists and Confederates (and after the war former Confederates), "made common cause to resist black emancipation, blacks in the military, and ultimately black citizenship." For whites in Missouri and Kentucky, the recruitment and enlistment of African-American soldiers challenged the very "bedrock social principle of the American republic." As a result, particular violence was directed at black soldiers and their families. Armed black soldiers in the Union Army, according to Astor, were considered a deliberate affront to white social and racial ideas as well as to white conceptions of liberty and citizenship. Consequently, during and after the war a reign of terror was directed against African-Americans which restored white dominance at the expense of black civil liberties. Astor's study is well documented with 103 notes, most of which are based on primary source materials.

10. "At Ease." *Civil War Times*, 54, 6 (December 2015): 14-15.
Lieutenant Samuel K. Thompson and several enlisted men of the
54th United States Colored Troops (USCT) are pictured next to a
huge Rodman cannon. This period picture is tinted for effect.

11. Ayers, Edward L., William Thomas III, and Anne Sarah Rubin.
"Black and on the Border." In *Slavery, Resistance, Freedom*,
edited by Gabor Boritt and Scott Hancock, New York: Oxford
University Press, 2007, 70-95.
Based on the award winning *Valley of the Shadow* web site, this is
a well-researched and informative examination of the valley area of
Virginia and Pennsylvania with particular emphasis on Franklin
County, Pennsylvania, a county "that held the fifth-highest number
of black residents of any county in Pennsylvania." Indeed, African-
American enlistments in the 54th and 55th Massachusetts Regiments
"made Franklin County perhaps the greatest contributor to these
early African-American regiments, on a per capita basis, of any
place in the United States." Brief biographical sketches of
individual enlisted men are provided; additional information
concerning friends and family relationships, age upon enlistment,
marital status, occupation, and wartime experiences is also
presented.

12. Bailey, Anne J. "A Texas Cavalry Raid: Reaction to Black
Soldiers and Contraband." *Civil War History*, 35, 2 (June 1989):
138-152.
Bailey's thoughtful analysis describes a late June 1863 Texas
cavalry raid on the west bank of the Mississippi River intended to
relieve Union Army pressure on Vicksburg. Confederate authorities
in the Trans-Mississippi Department knew that a diversionary
action of this nature would do little to help the besieged city;
nevertheless, they concluded that an attempt had to be made if only
to satisfy public opinion. As a result, several Texas cavalry
regiments raided along the western shore of the Mississippi, burning
and destroying U.S. Treasury-run plantations in Louisiana,
capturing contraband for transportation and eventual re-
enslavement in Texas, and encountering and capturing African-

American soldiers at DeSoto Mound (generally referred to as Mound Plantation, Louisiana in Union accounts).

Many of the prisoners were brutally treated; several black soldiers were murdered immediately after capture or on the forced march from Louisiana to Texas. Brutality of this nature, according to Bailey, was not an isolated occurrence. After examining the attitude of Texas cavalrymen serving in the Trans-Mississippi Department she concluded that atrocities committed against blacks, either in uniform or as contraband, "was no different from those committed by Texans in Arkansas in 1862 and what they would continue to do in 1864." According to Bailey, three basic reasons accounted for this behavior. First, the Texas cavalrymen shared a cultural heritage as Southerners that could not accept blacks in any capacity other than that of slaves; secondly, the relative isolation of the Trans-Mississippi Department from the rest of the Confederacy allowed racial atrocities to be overlooked and escape condemnation from the Richmond authorities, and "probably the most decisive, their strong desire to protect their families in Texas from the ravages of war." Overall a well-written and insightful account. The article includes 49 notes.

13. _____. "Was There a Massacre at Poison Spring?" *Military History of the Southwest*, 20, 2 (Fall 1990): 157-168.
Using statistical data, supplemented by eyewitness accounts, the author concludes that African-American soldiers of the 1st Kansas Colored Infantry were murdered by Confederate soldiers in the aftermath of the Battle of Poison Spring, Arkansas on April 18, 1864. The 1st Kansas Colored, a regiment largely composed of runaway slaves from Missouri and Arkansas, was part of a Union Army foraging party that was attacked and eventually overwhelmed by a much larger Confederate force. According to reports submitted after the battle, twice as many black soldiers were killed as wounded, a highly suspicious statistic, especially since the ratio of killed to wounded in Civil War battles normally averaged one to four or five. In addition, the author points out, of the 62 prisoners held by the Confederates after the battle, only four were African-American.

Black prisoners were murdered, argues Bailey, because of racial animosity, a desire to avenge a Southern defeat nine months earlier at Honey Springs, Indian Territory, the inability of Confederate soldiers – particularly those from Texas – to accept black men in uniform as legitimate soldiers, and the knowledge that transgressions against black prisoners would go unreported and unpunished. According to the author, based on the statistical evidence and corroborating Confederate and Union testimony, the aftermath of Poison Spring deserves the designation "massacre."

14. _____. "The USCT in the Confederate Heartland." In *Black Soldiers in Blue: African American Troops in the Civil War Era*, edited by John D. Smith. Chapel Hill: University of North Carolina Press, 2002, 227-248.

Regardless of the Emancipation Proclamation, and numerous directives from Washington, many Union army officers in the West balked at the idea of employing African-American soldiers in combat units. One such officer was Major General William Tecumseh Sherman whose refusal to use black troops bordered on outright insubordination. Buttressed by a powerful brother in Congress, and a string of victories, he was able to relegate black soldiers to garrison or labor duties. He adamantly refused to allow black soldiers to participate in combat. Ironically, Sherman was "responsible for African-American soldiers participating in a major battle in the Western Theatre" – the Battle of Nashville in December 1864. While Sherman was marching to the sea, far to his rear a Confederate attack was launched on Nashville. Major General George H. Thomas, the commander at Nashville, marshaled all available Union military units to repulse the Confederate attack. Included in this force were two brigades of black troops. The participation of these troops, and the pivotal role they played in the Union victory at Nashville, is described by the author. A map and 36 extensive notes are included.

15. Bailey, Kenneth R. "One of the Famous 54th Massachusetts: A Short Biography of General John W. M. Appleton." *West Virginia History,* 31, 3 (April 1970): 161-179.
A good capsule biography of John W. M. Appleton, an officer in the black 54th Massachusetts Volunteer Infantry. The article traces Appleton's early years in Boston, describes his military service in the Civil War, and concludes with his post-war commercial, civic, and National Guard activities in West Virginia. Appleton, a committed abolitionist, served as a recruiting officer, commanding officer of Company A, and later adjutant of the 54th Massachusetts. Severely wounded during the July 18, 1863 assault on Fort Wagner, he resigned his commission nearly a year later because of additional wounds suffered before Charleston. The article is of particular interest for its account of the regiment's preparation and attack on Fort (Battery) Wagner.

16. Baltzell, George F. "The Battle of Olustee (Ocean Pond) Florida." *Florida Historical Society Quarterly,* 9, 4 (1931): 199-223.
Baltzell provides a straightforward, detailed account of the February 20, 1864, Union defeat at Olustee, Florida, complete with a sketch map and organizational and casualty tables. Three African-American regiments took part in this battle, which was characterized by poor Union leadership and faulty tactical deployments. A number of wounded black soldiers fell into Confederate hands after the battle, some of whom were subsequently murdered. The author, however, makes no mention of these killings.

17. Barnhart, Donald L. Jr. "Texas Two-Step at Palmito Ranch." *America's Civil War*, 28, 2 (May 2015): 38-41.
Fought a month after Lee's surrender at Appomattox Court House, Palmito Ranch, Texas, was the last battle of the war and, ironically, a Confederate victory. Three Union regiments took part in this full-scale Northern fiasco, including the 62nd United States Colored Infantry. The battle is succinctly described and vividly illustrated with four outstanding full color maps.

18. Barnickel, Linda. "'No Federal Prisoners among Them:' The Execution of Black Union Soldiers at Jackson, Louisiana." *North & South*, 12, 1 (February 2010): 59-62.

The wartime massacre of African-American soldiers near Jackson, Louisiana in the summer of 1863 is explored by the author. After careful consideration, and after reviewing wartime and post-war evidence, she concluded – Southern denials not withstanding – that a massacre did take place. Interestingly, in Confederate correspondence concerning the affair, the murder of close to 30 black soldiers was justified since the prisoners were shot "while attempting to escape." Troubling too is the reference in Confederate correspondence to black prisoners not as Federal soldiers or captured Union soldiers but as "negroes in arms." This denial of prisoner status to captured African-American soldiers was a semantic ruse: "negroes in arms" provided the justification under Southern law for executing black prisoners as slaves guilty of servile insurrection.

19. Bauer, Craig and Todd Mefford. "Eyewitness Report on the Battle of Fort Butler, Donalsonville, La., June 27-28, 1863, and a Review of African-American Participation in the Fight." *Louisiana History: The Journal of the Louisiana Historical Association*, 4, 2 (Spring 2004): 201-208.

Several Confederate attempts were made during the war to relieve the Union siege of Vicksburg, Mississippi. One such attempt was the assault on Fort Butler, Louisiana, on June 27-28, 1863. It was a decisive Union victory. However, the "historical debate concerning the battle centers on the possibility that upwards of two hundred black Union troops assisted in the fort's defense." If this was the case, it would mark the first time that a black unit defeated a numerically superior Confederate force in battle. Unfortunately, the assumption is only conjectural, since no *contemporary* documentation exists to support that conclusion. Two Union naval gunboats contributed to the Union victory by firing numerous volleys into the ranks of the attacking Confederates. Both vessels had African-American sailors as crew members. The article contains an after-action report and 15 notes.

For more information regarding the affair at Fort Butler, and the debate concerning African-American participation, see the annotated article in this volume by Donald S. Frazier.

20. Beard, Rick. "$10 a Month." *Civil War Times* 53, 1 (February 2014): 48-55.

According to Secretary of War Edwin Stanton, African-American soldiers who enlisted under the provisions of the Second Confiscation Act and the Militia Act were "entitled to and receive the same pay and rations as are allowed by law to volunteers in the service." Unfortunately, the War Department's solicitor interpreted the Militia Act of 1862 to mean "persons of African descent, who under this law shall be employed, shall receive ten dollars per month and one ration, three dollars of which monthly pay may be in clothing." According to his ruling, black soldiers were to be paid considerably less than their white counterparts. African-American resentment concerning unequal pay, the hardships suffered by their dependent family members, and Lincoln's reticence regarding the discriminatory pay crisis are all explored. According to Beard, the president's position was based solely on party and sectional political considerations.

21. Bearss, Edwin C. "Asboth's Expedition up the Alabama and Florida Railroad." *Florida Historical Quarterly,* 39, 2 (October 1960): 159-167.

A concise study, by one of the recognized deans of Civil War history, describing the July 1864 Union sortie under General Asboth from Fort Barrancas, south of Pensacola on the Florida Panhandle, to the Alabama and Florida Railroad toward Mobile. Included in the Federal force were two African-American formations: the 82nd U.S. Colored Infantry and six companies of the 86th U.S. Colored Infantry. Of limited interest since the expedition was devoid of any military significance.

22. _____. "Marmaduke Attacks Pine Bluff." *Arkansas Historical Quarterly*, 23, 4 (Winter 1964): 291-313.

A tactical account of the abortive October 25, 1863 attack on Pine Bluff, Arkansas by Confederate forces under the command of Brigadier General John S. Marmaduke. African-Americans from a nearby contraband camp played an important role in the Union defense by erecting barricades, building breastworks, and providing the hard-pressed defenders with much-needed water. African-America civilians accounted for nearly a third of the Union casualties. Bearss' article is augmented by numerous footnotes and several maps.

23. _____. "The Trans-Mississippi Confederate Attempt to Relieve Vicksburg." *McNeese Review*, Part I, 15 (1964): 46-70; Part II, 16 (1965): 46-67.

Attempts by Trans-Mississippi Confederate forces to relieve Union pressure on besieged Vicksburg are discussed in this comprehensive and well-researched study. The Battle of Milliken's Bend is briefly touched upon in Part I and described in greater detail in Part II. During the battle the 9th Louisiana Regiment (African Descent) "sustained the greatest number of casualties suffered in a single day by any Union unit during the Vicksburg campaign – 165 killed, wounded, and missing." Total Union Army casualties of 101 killed, 285 wounded, and 266 missing were concentrated among the newly recruited and ill-trained black regiments. The article is extensively documented.

24. _____. "Sergeant-Major Hawkins and the Black Heroes of New Market." *The Henrico County Historical Society Magazine,* 5, 1 (Fall 1981): 5-26.

This is an all-too-brief biography of Thomas R. Hawkins, Sergeant-Major, 6th U.S. Colored Infantry. For conspicuous gallantry in saving the regimental flag at Chaffin's Farm on September 29, 1864, Hawkins was awarded the Medal of Honor. The medal was awarded on February 8, 1870; less than a month later, Hawkins died of consumption. The article is illustrated and contains two maps.

25. _____. "The Battle of Brice's Cross Roads." *Blue & Gray*, 16, 6 (August 1999): 6-10, 12-21, 44-53.

Edwin C. Bearss, former Chief Historian of the National Park Service, has written a thorough description of the June 10, 1864, Union Army defeat and rout at Brice's Cross Roads, Mississippi, by a numerically inferior Confederate force under the command of Nathan Bedford Forrest. One of the Union infantry brigades, commanded by Colonel Edward Bouton, consisted of the 55th and 59th United States Colored Infantry and Company F, 2nd U.S. Colored Artillery. Though only committed during the last phase of the battle, the black soldiers nevertheless fought a successful rear guard action that permitted the bulk of the disorganized Federal force to escape total destruction. Unfortunately, these rear guard actions are not described in the same meticulous detail as most of the battle narrative. Approximately 49% of the Union Army soldiers killed at Brice's Cross Roads (110 out of 223) were African-Americans. The article is accompanied by a number of period photographs and five superb battlefield maps.

26. Belz, Herman. "Law, Politics and Race in the Struggle for Equal Pay during the Civil War." *Civil War History,* 22, 3 (September 1976): 197-213.

This essay is a straightforward analysis of the often legally complex Congressional efforts to equalize pay between white and black soldiers. African-American soldiers originally recruited in South Carolina and Massachusetts enlisted with the understanding that their pay would be the same as white soldiers. However, the Solicitor General of the War Department, when asked for a legal decision regarding this issue, ruled that black soldiers, according to the provisions of the Militia Act of 1862, were to be considered as laborers and could be paid no more than $10.00 per month, of which $3.00 a month would be deducted for clothing. In short, African-American soldiers were to be paid significantly less than their white counterparts. Much of the article discusses the efforts by congressional legislators to equalize pay and provide for retroactive pay for free blacks who had enlisted in African-American military formations. The Military Appropriations Act of June 1864 "did not entirely resolve the equal pay problem, for it denied back pay to colored troops who were slaves at the start of the war." This problem was essentially rectified with the passage of the Enrollment Act of March 1865. The article contains 67 notes.

27. Bennett, Captain Kevin. "The Jacksonville Mutiny." *Military Law Review*, 134 (Fall 1991): 157-172.
See the annotation immediately following. Both articles are by the same author and are essentially the same; they differ only in minor editorial revisions.

28. Bennett, B. Kevin. "The Jacksonville Mutiny." *Civil War History*, 38, 1 (March 1992): 39-50.
Bennett begins his article with a brief description of the execution of six soldiers of the 3rd United States Colored Troops (USCT) at Fort Clinch, Fernandina, Florida on December 1, 1865, months after the cessation of hostilities between Confederate and Union forces. Organized at Philadelphia in July 1863, the 3rd USCT was comprised of freedmen and escaped slaves and campaigned in and around Charleston, South Carolina before being transferred to Jacksonville, Florida, in February 1864. After the end of hostilities, the regiment remained in Florida on occupation duty awaiting discharge. A new commanding officer who "was something of a martinet," combined with simmering discontent among the enlisted men regarding what they considered excessive disciplinary measures, the boredom of occupation duty, drunkenness among the troops, and fear of uncontrolled black behavior among the white officers exploded into violence on Sunday, October 29, 1865, only days before the regiment was scheduled to be mustered out. A violent confrontation occurred between officers and men took place regarding the punishment of a prisoner, a number of shots were exchanged between officers and men, and several officers were physically attacked. After order was restored 15 soldiers were arrested and 14 were subsequently charged with mutiny under the Articles of War.

The punishment for mutiny in time of war – but not in peace – was execution by firing squad. Unfortunately for the accused prisoners, Florida was still considered by the Federal Government to be in a state of armed rebellion, which meant that a military court could condemn the accused to death while also limiting the number of appellate reviews. Ultimately six of the accused were sentenced to execution by firing squad. The author believes that a number of mitigating circumstances should have been taken into account before passing sentence, though he admits "it seems likely that the findings of guilty on the charges of mutiny were supported by the evidence." However, as Bennett points out, 80% of the Union soldiers executed for mutiny during the Civil War were African-Americans, clearly suggesting a prevailing pattern of racial bias.

In the Jacksonville incident, those prisoners spared execution by the military court were sentenced to long prison terms. Upon procedural review, these sentences were vacated in late 1866. Those prisoners that survived captivity were subsequently released and dishonorably discharged. For supporting documentation, the author relied heavily on military service records and court martial transcripts.

29. Bennett, Lerone, Jr. "The Negro in the Civil War." *Ebony*, 17, 8 (June 1962): 132-137.

Bennett's essay is a good general overview of African-American participation in the Civil War. The article includes several illustrations and an informative timeline.

30. _____. "The Shootout at Chaffin's Farm." *Ebony*, 3, 12 (October 1975): 32-42.

Well-written and dramatic, this is a good account of the attack on New Market Heights, Virginia, and subsequent fighting at Chaffin's Farm and Fort Harrison, by nine regiments of African-American soldiers. The exploits of several individual black soldiers, primarily but not exclusively noncommissioned officers, are given special emphasis.

31. _____. "Black, Blue and Gray: The Other Civil War."
Ebony, 46, 4 (February 1991): 96-98, 100, 103, 105.
The contribution of African-Americans as soldiers, sailors, spies, and laborers in the Union war effort is examined. The author concluded that African-Americans were "the indispensable elements in a war that could not have been won without their help."

32. _____. "The Shootout at Chaffin's Farm." *Ebony*, 52, 1 (November 1996): 38-40, 42, 178.
A reprint with some changes of the original article published in October 1975.

33. Bennett, Michael J. "'Frictions:' Shipboard Relations between White and Contraband Sailors." *Civil War History*, 47, 2 (June 2001): 118-145.
Utilizing documentation from a variety of primary and secondary sources, Bennett has written a thought-provoking analysis concerning the negative psychological impact that contraband sailors had on the self-esteem of many of their white shipmates. While the navy had for years recruited at least 5% of its crews from free northern blacks, the enlistment of contrabands in large numbers to meet manpower shortages caused by war challenged existing naval traditions, threatened the perceived status of white sailors, and strained shipboard race relations. Sailors, either in the merchant service or in the navy, traditionally occupied the bottom rung of society or were considered only marginally better than chattel slaves, a not very envious distinction acutely felt by many sailors. According to the author, white sailors originally felt pity for contraband who sought refuge on Union navy vessels, either on ships patrolling the inland rivers or vessels assigned to blockading duties. Part of this reaction can be attributed to "sailor generosity" and part to the realization that contrabands could perform many of the menial and often dirty tasks required to run a naval warship.

The enlistment of contraband slaves as sailors, by order of the Secretary of the Navy, was not initially considered a serious challenge to the status of white sailors, since contrabands could receive no rating other than "boy," the lowest naval enlisted category. However, once naval regulations were changed and contrabands were allowed to rise above the boy rating, and once technical skill and experience counted more than color, many white sailors felt their position in the shipboard hierarchy challenged by those they considered socially and racially inferior. Furthermore, attempts by the navy to enforce shipboard segregation by race proved impractical; as a result "whites began routinely sharing duties with blacks in gun crews, daily chores, and labor details."

For many white sailors, equal treatment challenged their individual self-esteem and stirred profound feelings of apprehension and racial hatred. This was often manifested in what the author terms violent "frictions" between sailors of both races. Friction could involve overt racial hostility, abusive language, minor physical confrontations, and in some cases criminal violence. Many white sailors sought through these incidents to reassert what they considered acceptable boundaries beyond which contraband were not allowed to cross. Ultimately, the author admits, for former slaves their shipboard assimilation "was not simple, unchallenged or bloodless."

Surprisingly, the author makes no mention of the shipboard relationship between free blacks – generally recruited for naval service in northern port cities – and white sailors.

The article is based on numerous primary and secondary accounts and includes over 100 footnotes.

34. Berfield, Karen. "Fair Treatment of Blacks in the Ranks - Julian Bryant: Martyr for Equality." *Civil War Times Illustrated*, 22, 2 (April 1983): 36-41.
A succinct but useful biography of Julian Bryant, scion of a well-connected Illinois family and nephew of William Cullen Bryant, noted editor of the New York *Evening Post*. Julian Bryant fought at the bloody engagement at Milliken's Bend as a major in the newly organized 1st Mississippi Infantry, African Descent (later re-designated as the 51st United States Colored Troops), and

subsequently served as commander of the 46th United States Colored Troops. Bryant, through his uncle's newspaper, helped focus public and government attention on the often excessive employment of black soldiers on fatigue duties. He drowned while on occupation duty in Texas several weeks after the end of the war. The article contains seven of Bryant's Civil War drawings.

35. Berg, Gordon. "Embattled Courage at New Market Heights." *America's Civil War*, 19, 1 (March 2006): 26-33

The author provides a good, basic summary of the successful assault by mostly untested black troops of the 3rd Division, XVIII Corps, Army of the James, on the formidable Confederate defenses along New Market Heights, Virginia on April 12, 1864. The Army of the James was commanded by Major General Benjamin Butler, an early proponent of recruiting and arming African-Americans as soldiers. Butler hoped that his carefully planned attack would eventually result in the capture of Richmond, capital of the Confederacy. Geography in the form of too much open ground bisected by marshlands and wooded ravines worked against the attackers. During the 80 minute ordeal losses were high among the white officers and the command of many companies passed to African-American noncommissioned officers. Interestingly, after the battle, Butler's attempts to have several black sergeants promoted to the commissioned ranks were rejected by the War Department. However, the battle was important, according to black correspondent Thomas Morris Chester, because it "wiped out effectively the imputation against the fighting qualities of colored troops."

Fourteen black soldiers were awarded the Medal of Honor for bravery during the battle. Ironically the awards were bestowed on April 6, 1865, days before Lee's surrender of the Army of Northern Virginia at Appomattox Court House. The article also contains an interesting description and illustration of Butler's Badge of Honor, a medal struck in silver and paid for by Butler to award several hundred African-American soldiers for bravery at New Market Heights.

36. Bergeron, Arthur W., Jr. "The Battle of Olustee." In *Black Soldiers in Blue: African American Troops in the Civil War Era*, edited by John David Smith. Chapel Hill: University of North Carolina Press, 2002, 136-149.

For much of the Civil War Florida was a little noticed backwater far removed from any significant military or political activity. That changed in early 1864 and ended disastrously for the Union at the Battle of Olustee, fought on February 20, 1864. Three African-American regiments took part in the battle: the 54th Massachusetts, the 1st North Carolina Colored Infantry (later re-designated the 35th United States Colored Troops), and the 8th U.S. Colored Infantry. A concise, well-written, and well- researched article; the battle is meticulously described with particular emphasis on the role played by the three African-American regiments in the battle. According to the author, "no wholesale massacre of blacks occurred" after the battle.

37. Bernstein, Steven. "Blood for Salt." *America's Civil War*, 29, 2 (May 2016): 48-55.

Union attempts to starve the South by cutting off its supply of salt are described. In the 19th century the United States used more salt than any other country and the South used more than any other region in the United States. Bernstein's article examines the Federal government's attempts to disrupt the manufacture of salt throughout the Confederacy. The Union attack on the salt works at Saltville, Virginia, which were considered the most productive in the South, is described in detail. The October 1864 engagement between Union and Confederate forces is examined and the slaughter of black soldiers after the battle is addressed. The Union command at Saltville contained at least 600 men from the newly recruited 5th U.S. Colored Cavalry (USCC) and several men from the 6th USCC. When Union forces retreated a number of wounded black soldiers were left behind. What happened to these soldiers afterwards is still a matter of controversy. As Bernstein, indicates, some scholars have estimated that as many as 100 or more African-American soldiers left on the battlefield or in nearby hospitals were murdered; other historians, however, dispute this figure and estimate that no more than seven African-Americans were slaughtered. A recent study of previously unknown and unexamined documents, including the report of the surgeon of the 5th USCC, indicates that the true number falls between both extremes. Studies now indicate that that least 45 to 50 black soldiers "were never accounted for after the battle and are presumed to have been murdered by Confederate renegades." In December 1864, Union forces, at the second battle of Saltville, destroyed much of the region's salt making capability.

38. Berry, Mary F. "Negro Troops in Blue and Gray: The Louisiana Native Guards 1861-1863." *Louisiana History*, 8, 2 (Spring 1967): 165-190.

During the Civil War, African-Americans of the Louisiana Native Guards had the unique distinction of serving both sides. The First Native Guards Regiment, Louisiana Militia, was authorized by the Confederate Governor of Louisiana, Thomas O. Moore, on May 12, 1861 and consisted of free men of color. Based in New Orleans, many of the regiment's officers were skilled tradesmen, several were quite prosperous, and a few even owned slaves. During its militia service the regiment performed only routine company drill; it was never officially mustered as a regular Confederate army unit and it was never issued arms. When New Orleans fell to Federal forces in April 1862, the regiment disbanded but its members remained in the city.

Benjamin Butler, commanding officer at Union occupied New Orleans, desperately needed more troops to defend the city. Since reinforcements were unavailable from the North, he decided, for military and political reasons, to raise additional soldiers from among the city's black inhabitants. Within a short time three regiments of Louisiana Native Guard Infantry were recruited. The officers of the 1st and 2nd Regiment were black and included men and officers with prior Confederate militia service; officers of the 3rd were both black and white. All three regimental commanders were white.

Subsequent service saw two of the regiments participating in the siege of Port Hudson. Under General Nathaniel Banks, Butler's replacement as commander of the Department of the Gulf, black officers in all three regiments, as a matter of government policy, were purged and replaced by whites.

39. Bigelow, Martha M. "The Significance of Milliken's Bend in the Civil War." *Journal of Negro History*, 45, 3 (July 1960): 156-163.
According to the author, the June 7, 1863, battle at Milliken's Bend, Louisiana, marked "a significant point in the Federal government's evolutionary policy in regard to the Negro freedman." And it definitively answered the question: will the black man fight? Fight they did: the black regiments at Milliken's Bend suffered 652 killed, wounded, and missing out of a total of 1,061 men in the regiments that composed the African Brigade.

40. Bilby, Joseph G. "Uncommon Soldiers." *Military Images*, 14, 6 (May-June 1993): 10-11.
A biography and period photograph of Timothy Shaw of New Jersey, as well as a capsule history of the 43rd Regiment, U. S. Colored Infantry, is provided. Shaw, an African-American, enlisted in the regiment for one year during the closing days of the Civil War and served as part of the army of occupation in Texas. Upon joining the army, Shaw received an $800.00 Camden County, New Jersey, bonus and a third of his Federal bonus of $100.00.

41. Binder, Frederick M. "Pennsylvania Negro Regiments in the Civil War." *Journal of Negro History,* 37, 4 (October 1952): 383-417.
Much of this article discusses the citizen-directed and civilian-funded Philadelphia Supervisory Committee for Recruiting Colored Regiments. The committee, in an 18 month period beginning in late June 1863, succeeded in recruiting 8,612 officers and men for service in 11 regiments of African-American infantry. The majority of recruits were raised from among the black population of Philadelphia and were credited to the state quota assigned by the War Department, though a number of men were enlisted from neighboring New Jersey, Delaware, and Maryland.

Of special interest is the Committee's establishment of the Free Military School for Applicants for Commands of Colored Troops. This privately funded school offered a concentrated course on military tactics, drill, army regulations, and general knowledge for white officer candidates seeking commissions in newly raised black regiments. The training was highly effective and enabled most graduates to successfully pass the War Department officer exam. The majority of African-American regiments raised in Pennsylvania served in Grant's Virginia campaign.

42. Bingham, Millicent Todd. "Key West in the Summer of 1864." *Florida Historical Quarterly*, 43, 3 (January 1965): 262-265.
This short account contains excerpts from three letters by an officer of the 2nd U.S. Colored Troops describing the yellow fever epidemic at Key West, Florida, during the summer of 1864.

43. Birrer, Christopher. "The Fifty-Fourth Massachusetts: A Revolutionary Symbol of the Black Struggle for Equality." *Journal of America's Military Past*, 31, 1 (Spring/Summer 2005): 5-35.
Ostensible a history of the 54th Massachusetts Infantry, but more an interpretive assessment of the symbolic meaning of the regiment and its impact on white perceptions regarding African-Americans, both as soldiers and fellow countrymen.

44. Black, Andrew K. "In the Service of the United States: Comparative Mortality among African-Americans and White Troops in the Union Army." *Journal of Negro History*, 79, 4 (Fall 1994): 317-333.
A well-researched and thoroughly documented study that explores the disparity in the death rate between black and white Union troops in the Civil War. According to the author's research, "white troops were twice as likely to die for reasons of ill health as in battle, while black troops were almost ten times more likely to do so."

Black concludes the higher African-American mortality rate was driven by several factors, including the location where the soldiers served, excessive and strenuous fatigue details (which adversely affected overall health), and poor medical care. Accepted medical knowledge of the time considered African-American troops more immune to certain illnesses than white troops and, as a result, they were "routinely stationed in locations considered unhealthy by whites." Records indicate that approximately 70% of all United States Colored Troops served in the Mississippi Valley, the most disease ridden area of the country.

Interestingly, the data used in the study is based on the 1888 report by the Surgeon General, which was published in segregated white and black volumes. The article, which contains a number of informative tables, should be used in conjunction with the Herbert Aptheker study dealing with the same subject.

45. _____. "The Black Soldier and the Civil War." *New Crisis*, 106, 1 (January/February 1999): 32.
This one-page synopsis of the black Civil War military experience is too brief to be of much value.

46. Blackburn, George M., editor. "The Negro Viewed by a Michigan Civil War Soldier: Letters of John C. Buchanan." *Michigan History*, 47, 1 (March 1963): 75-84.
This article contains excerpts from several letters written by John C. Buchanan, an officer in the 8th Michigan Infantry, regarding African-Americans, slavery, and the idea of black men as soldiers. A firm opponent of slavery, Buchanan was originally opposed to enrolling African-Americans in the Union Army. After months of service, his attitude changed. By June, 1863, he concluded "I would as soon they (African-Americans) shoot *Mr. Reb* as to do it myself."

47. Blassingame, John W. "The Recruitment of Negro Troops in Maryland." *Maryland Historical Magazine*, 58, 1 (March 1963): 20-29.
Throughout the war, attempts by the Lincoln administration to recruit Maryland African-Americans, either slave or free, were initially opposed by small independent, non-slave owning farmers as well as slaveholders. Small farmers, according to the author, were dependent on free blacks to harvest their crops. Many feared

that the loss of free black labor would force them to hire slaves at ruinous rates. Slave owners were equally vigorous in their opposition to losing their slaves to the army without compensation. As a result, on October 1, 1863 Lincoln temporarily ordered the suspension of African-American recruitment throughout the state. Later in the month the regulations contained in War Department General Orders 329 were implemented. These regulations outlined procedures for the recruitment of free blacks and slaves in Missouri, Tennessee, and Maryland. They also provided for the establishment of recruiting offices throughout Maryland and a sliding scale of compensation for Maryland slave owners who allowed their slaves to enlist. Slaves theoretically could only be impressed, without the owner's consent and without compensation, if county quotas were not filled within a 30 day period.

Objections to recruiting African-Americans as soldiers eventually "vanished because poor whites saw the enlistment of the Negro as their salvation from the draft, while a large number of slaveholders saw the enlistment of slaves, with compensation, as a way to get something out of 'property' that would have soon been expropriated."

48. _____. "Negro Chaplains in the Civil War." *Negro History Bulletin,* 27, 1 (October 1963): 23-24.
This is a short account of the activities of a number of black chaplains assigned to African-American army units, including Henry M. Turner of the 1st U.S. Colored Troops (who would later achieve national prominence as a bishop of the A.M.E. Church and chancellor of Morris Brown College), and Samuel Harrison of the 54th Massachusetts Volunteer Infantry (Colored). Upon accepting his appointment, Harrison demanded the same pay as white chaplains. As a result of political pressure, Attorney General Edward Bates directed, on April 23, 1864, that Harrison be paid the same as his white counterparts serving in white regiments.

49. _____. "The Recruitment of Negro Troops in Missouri during the Civil War." *Missouri Historical Society Review,* 58, 3 (April 1964): 326-338.

Blassingame's article provides an excellent description of the travails experienced by the Federal Government in its efforts to recruit Missouri slaves as solders. Missouri had the largest white population of any slave state, possessed a relatively small number of slaveholders, and had moved, in June 1863, to introduce gradual slave emancipation throughout the state. Many Missouri radicals firmly believed that "No traitor is too good to be killed by a Negro, nor has any traitor a right to insist on being killed by a white man." However, stubborn resistance to the recruiting of slaves by slaveholders, coupled with conservative provost marshals, successfully hindered army recruiting efforts. It was, as the author remarks, a "startling contrast between popular desire and official performance." As a consequence, Missouri only furnished slightly more than 8,000 African-Americans soldiers in five regiments to the Union war effort. However, the majority of black soldiers "recruited in Kansas, Illinois, and Iowa were runaway Missouri slaves."

50. _____. "The Freedom Fighters." *Negro History Bulletin*, 28, 5 (February 1965): 105-106.

A short article concerning 16 African-American soldiers who were awarded the Medal of Honor in the Civil War. Of these 16, 11 were free, the average age was 24, and the majority of the awards were given for conspicuous gallantry during the engagements at Chapin's Farm and New Market Heights on September 27, 1864. No mention is made of the black sailors who were also awarded the Medal of Honor.

51. _____. "The Union Army as an Educational Institution for Negroes, 1861-1865." *Journal of Negro Education,* 34, 2 (Spring 1965): 152-159.

During the Civil War, Union military authorities in the South faced the problem of dealing with large numbers of indigent and illiterate contrabands who had made their way into Federal lines. General

Grant was one of the first to address this problem when he appointed John Eaton as Superintendent of Negro Affairs in the Department of Tennessee. Eaton was ordered to provide assistance and the rudiments of educational instruction to contrabands. Ironically, one of the most systematic provisions for educating freedmen was instituted in Louisiana by Major General Nathaniel P. Banks, who, as commander of the Department of the Gulf, had ruthlessly drummed out of service African-American commissioned officers serving in the Louisiana Native Guards.

The majority of African-American regiments were recruited in the South from among the slave population, and most were illiterate. Many white officers serving in black regiments thought it their moral duty to educate their troops and, as a result, numerous schools were established at the company and regimental level to impart the rudiments of education and teach African-American soldiers how to read and write. The most extensive military educational system for black soldiers, according to Blassingame, was inaugurated due to the untiring efforts of Benjamin F. Butler, newly appointed commander of the Army of the James in 1863. Butler ordered schools established in each African-American regiment and ordered officers, assisted by chaplains, to set aside a two hour period every weekday for instruction, military conditions permitting.

The educational efforts implemented by the army, and the freedmen's desire to learn, helped to reduce the widespread illiteracy found among the former slaves. In addition, the author maintains, "the educational ventures of the Union Army were important because they were the forerunners of the Freedmen's Bureau."

52. _____. "The Selection of Officers and Non-Commissioned Officers of Negro Troops in the Union Army, 1863-1865." *Negro History Bulletin*, 30, 1 (January 1967): 8-11.
This work offers a brief but excellent account of the selection procedures utilized by military authorities and government officials to select, nominate, and appoint white officers – and white officers

only – to command positions in black military units. Several methods were employed. In the regiments raised by the Bureau of Colored Troops, the bulk of officers were selected after passing rigorous exams given by the War Department's Board of Examiners. Candidates were tested regarding military tactics, drill, morality, and general knowledge, and those who failed the exam were not eligible for re-examination. In the Washington area, the failure rate was so high that Brigadier General Silas Casey, president of the local examination board, prevailed upon the civilian- run and privately funded Philadelphia Supervisory Committee to open a school to prepare white soldiers for the War Department exam. As a result, the Free Military School was opened on Christmas Day, 1863. The school offered a concentrated one month program that included classroom instruction and practice in drilling and commanding black troops that were in training at nearby Camp William Penn. Graduates were quite successful and only a few subsequently failed the War Department exam.

In the African-American regiments raised by Adjutant General Lorenzo Thomas in the Mississippi Valley, officers were appointed for service in black regiments. Appointments were generally based on the recommendation of a superior officer (or officers) and the ability of the candidate to pass an examination given by a division board. The governors of two states, Connecticut and Massachusetts, reserved the right to appoint officers to state raised black military units carrying state designations, as for example the 54th or 55th Massachusetts Infantry (Colored) and the 29th Connecticut Infantry (Colored).

The author also discusses the refusal by military authorities to commission African-Americans as officers. Only a handful were promoted from the ranks or received direct commissions from civilian life. Most black officers had served with the Louisiana Native Guards, and most of them were subsequently dismissed or drummed out of the service by Nathaniel Banks, commander of the Department of the Gulf.

53. _____. "The Recruitment of Colored Troops in
Kentucky, Maryland, and Missouri, 1863-1865." *Historian,* 29,
4 (August 1967): 533-545.

One of the thorniest problems faced by the Lincoln administration,
from 1861 to late 1863, was how to successfully conduct the war
without antagonizing Union support in the border states of
Missouri, Kentucky, and Maryland. All three were slave states
pivotal in Union strategic considerations. All three states – since
they were not in rebellion and had remained in the Union – were
exempt from the provisions of the Emancipation Proclamation. In
order not to offend loyalist sentiment in these states, the
administration policy was to describe the war as an effort to
preserve the integrity of the Union, and not as a war to destroy the
institution of slavery. Slavery in the border states would not be
touched, and slaves in these states would not be recruited as
soldiers. However, according to Blassingame, two factors changed
the border state equation: the Emancipation Proclamation and the
pressing need for additional Union military manpower.

While the Proclamation may not have freed any slaves in the border
states, it "sowed the seeds of doubt about the permanence of slavery,
and the recruitment of Negro troops became the mechanism that
destroyed slavery in the border states." Slaves were a great
untapped manpower pool, and repeated Union efforts through
bounties and conscription failed to fill the white ranks of the Union
Army. As a consequence, Lincoln "maneuvered, implored, and
coerced border state officials into allowing the recruitment" of
African-American slaves as soldiers.

In all three states, abuses occurred among recruiting agents. Some
agents were directly ordered to forcefully "take and enlist" all slaves
who had left their masters but had not joined the army. In addition,
recruiters encountered a major problem regarding the legality of
slavery. If a slave enlisted and was found physically unfit, he could
be, at least theoretically, returned to his master. To overcome this
problem, in both Maryland and Kentucky, and probably to
encourage the idea that enlistment meant immediate emancipation,

African-Americans who failed to pass the physical examination for military duty were enrolled in labor and garrison regiments.

Recruiting slaves as solders proved the most difficult in Kentucky, where the idea of tampering with the institution of slavery faced stubborn opposition. Kentucky slaveholders were staunch defenders of slavery and obstinate in their opposition to the recruitment of slaves. Slaves attempting to enlist were often beaten, clubbed, whipped, and in some cases killed. Seven Union Army recruiting agents, between November 1863 and February 1865, were murdered.

Nevertheless, the three states combined contributed approximately 41,500 African-Americans to the Union war effort with the largest number, 24,438, recruited in Kentucky.

54. Blight, David W. "The Meaning or the Fight: Frederick Douglass and the Memory of the Fifth-Fourth Massachusetts." *The Massachusetts Review*, 36, 1 (Spring 1995): 141-153.
A provocative essay by David W. Blight, a well-known and highly regarded writer on black studies, in which he discusses Douglass' moral and political views regarding African-Americans and the Civil War, and the meaning for American society of the 54th Massachusetts Infantry. Blight's thoughtful study artfully examines how the significance of the 54th has been interpreted in public memory, in American culture and history, on the screen, and in the famous Boston bronze relief by St. Gaudens.

55. Blumberg, Arnold. "Bloody Fiasco at the Crater." *Military Heritage*, 9, 1 (August 2007): 42-49, 70.
A popularly written account of what is considered the most mismanaged Union Army assault of the Civil War – the ill-starred July 30, 1864, Battle of the Crater outside Petersburg, Virginia, a battle described by U.S. Grant as "a stupendous failure." The author provides a basic tactical account of the Union plan and assault and the Confederate response and counter-attack. Even though approximately 38% of the total Union casualties were suffered by eight regiments of African-Americans, no mention is made of the

widespread murder of captive black soldiers. The article contains two maps and several illustrations.

56. Bodnia, George, editor. "Fort Pillow 'Massacre: Observations of a Minnesotan." *Minnesota History*, 43, 5 (Spring 1973): 186-190.

This article contains a reprint of a letter written by Charles Robinson, a civilian at Fort Pillow, regarding the events of April 12, 1864. Robinson, who was evidently employed as a photographer at the post, provides a vivid eyewitness account of the carnage at Fort Pillow written only days after the Confederate assault. Published in its entirety, the letter offers gruesome testimony to what occurred and leaves little doubt that a massacre took place. Interestingly, Robinson, while describing the murder of surrendered Union soldiers, never mentions race or color. The article is edited with an introduction by George Bodnia.

57. Bohannon, Brian C. "Fort Wagner and the 54th Massachusetts Volunteer Infantry." *America's Civil War*, 4, 3 (September 1991): 30-39.

This retelling of the assault on Fort Wagner, South Carolina, is well-written, easy to understand, and suitable for the general reading public as well as the specialized Civil War audience. Illustrated and written with dramatic flair, it is, nonetheless, a historically accurate account of the entire Fort Wagner engagement. Though the actions of the 54th Massachusetts are stressed, the participation of white regiments in the battle is also described. This is an excellent overview of the ill-fated Federal assault.

58. Bohannon, Keith S. "It was fit and Proper That he be Buried with Them." *Civil War Times*, 55, 1 (February 2016): 26-33.

Three rare Confederate accounts of the defense of Fort Wagner are reprinted. Two of the documents directly deal with the burial of Colonel Shaw. One letter, dating from June 1904, from Captain John Ferrell Lewis, former captain in the 32nd Georgia, describes Shaw's burial. He was found, according to Lewis, surrounded by the bodies of two black sergeants and two black corporals. The head of the Confederate burial detail remarked "Yes, you have been over these negroes; I will now put the negroes over you." With that Shaw's body was unceremoniously dumped into a mass grave. Another Confederate account was published in the *Boston Herald* on September 1, 1911. In it the former colonel of the 32nd Georgia remarked that the bodies of slain Federal officers would be returned after the battle "except that of Col. Shaw. We were pretty bitter then as to the commanders of negro troops." Four years after the Boston article the officer explained, in a private letter, his rationale for burying Shaw in a mass grave: "I thought having selected these [African-Americans soldiers] as his chosen comrades in life, it was fit and proper that he be buried with them." The article is illustrated and includes a period sketch map of Morris Island and its defenses.

59. Bordewich, Fergus M. "What Price Glory." *Smithsonian*, 36, 4 (July 2005): 44-53.
A description of the assault by the 54th Massachusetts on Fort Wagner interweaved with efforts by modern-day conservationists to save Morris Island from development. The article also discusses the Confederate dilemma regarding captured black soldiers and includes several color and black-and-white illustrations.

60. Boyd, Mark F. "The Federal Campaign of 1864 in East Florida." *Florida Historical Quarterly,* 29, 1 (July 1950): 3-37.
The Federal campaign in East Florida, which culminated in the Union debacle at Olustee on February 20, 1864, is examined in considerable detail in Boyd's article. Seven African-American regiments participated in the expedition. Some of these units fought at Olustee and suffered substantial casualties; others performed garrison duties further to the east at Jacksonville. After a series of fits and starts, Florida remained what it was: a sideshow in the war. A dated but still a good overall study of the Federal missteps in the ill-starred East Florida campaign.

61. _____. "The Joint Operations of the Federal Army and Navy near St. Marks, March, 1865." *Florida Historical Quarterly*, 24, 2 (October 1950): 96-124.
An excruciatingly meticulous account of the abortive Union Army foray into the Florida Panhandle and the Federal defeat at Natural

Bridge on March 6, 1865. Two of the three Union regiments engaged were African-American, the 2nd and 99th United States Colored Infantry; together, both regiments accounted for 90% of all Federal casualties. Of limited value except for students of the Civil War in Florida, "the smallest tadpole in the cesspool of secession."

62. _____. "The Battle of Marianna." *Florida Historical Quarterly*, 29, 4 (April 1951): 225-242.
An account of a late September 1864, sortie of Union military units from Fort Barrancas, located on Pensacola Bay, and their subsequent engagement with Home Guard and regular Confederate forces at the Florida Panhandle town of Marianna. Included in the Federal raid were several companies of mounted infantry from the 82nd and 86th U.S. Colored Infantry. According to later civilian accounts, the African-American troops were "unruly."

63. Bragg, William Harris. "'Victory at Honey Hill: 'A Mere Flicker of Light.'" *Civil War Times Illustrated*, 22, 9 (January 1984): 12-19.
A very good and fairly detailed description of the November 30, 1864, engagement at Honey Hill, South Carolina, between Federal forces and mostly Georgia State Troops and militia, supported by several small regular Confederate units. In an attempt to isolate Savannah and prevent Confederate reinforcements and supplies from reaching the city from either of the Carolinas, Major General William T. Sherman ordered that the Charleston & Savannah Railroad be severed. A Union expedition of some 5,500 men, which included seven regiments of African-American troops, sailed from Hilton Head, landed at Boyd's Neck, South Carolina, and attempted to march inland ten miles and cut the rail line near the small town of Grahamville. Surprise was lost when the fleet was becalmed by fog; confusion further reigned after the landing when several regiments became lost. The entire Union effort was badly managed and thoroughly bungled. In a hotly contested action, the Union suffered 746 casualties to approximately 50 for the Georgia State Troops and militia. One black soldier described Confederate musketry at Honey Hill as "something fearful." It was, as the author concludes, "another sorry chapter in the undistinguished history of

the Department of the South." The battle was essentially senseless, since several months later Savannah fell to Sherman's advancing forces.

64. Braun, Lundy. "Spirometry, Measurement, and Race in the Nineteenth Century." *Journal of the History of Medicine and Allied Sciences*, 60. 2 (April 2005: 135-169.
Spirometry measures lung functions and volume and is used in the diagnosis of pulmonary disease. Developed in Europe, it was imported to America and used by the U.S. Sanitary Commission to compare the mean differences in lung capacity between black and white Union Army soldiers. Not surprisingly, the results, however racially questionable, became "deeply entrenched in the popular and scientific imagination of the nineteenth century." This article is more for the student of pathology than African-American Civil War history.

65. Brennan, Pat. "Last Stand in the Heartland: The Fight for Nashville, December 1864." *North & South*, 8, 3 (May 2005): 20-45.
Brennan has written a highly detailed account of the Union victory at Nashville in December 1864. Two brigades of African-American troops took part in the battle and suffered substantial casualties. The article contains a full-page map, numerous photographs, and 69 notes.

66. Brewer, Charles C. "African-American Sailors and the Unvexing of the Mississippi River." *Prologue: Quarterly of the National Archives and Records Administration*, 30, 4 (Winter 1998): 279-286.
Brewer interweaves personal stories of contraband sailors serving on steam gunboats with the activities of the Union Navy's Mississippi Squadron, especially during the Vicksburg campaign. The routine of naval service, including rotating watches, and gun drills are explained. Pension records served as partial basis for the author's description of contraband sailor life, both during and after the war. By the end of 1863, the Mississippi Squadron had an enlisted strength of 5,500 men, 1,049 of whom were former slaves.

The article contains illustrations, a table of naval pay by rating, and extensive original source notes.

67. Bright, Thomas R. "Yankee in Arms: The Civil War as a Personal Experience." *Civil War History*, 19, 3 (September 1973): 197-218.
Bright's article compares the army careers, and the effects of military service and the Civil War, on two white Massachusetts-born soldiers. The first, Arthur Carpenter, became case-hardened by war and eventually received a regular army commission. Promoted to captain after the war, he remained in military service and was "uncomfortable in peacetime America." The second, John Augustus Wilder, an affluent and well-educated member of the Massachusetts Bar, was initially reluctant to disturb his "comfort" and enlist in the army. Instead he worked for the American Missionary Association, and was dispatched to Fortress Monroe to work with his uncle, who was Superintendent of Contrabands. He viewed black contrabands he met as racially inferior beings; nevertheless, he sought and obtained a commission as second lieutenant in the 54th Massachusetts Volunteer Infantry. After performing recruiting duties for the 54th Massachusetts he was mustered as a captain in Company A, 2nd Regiment United States Colored Troops.

Wilder, unlike Carpenter, saw no battles and "was perfectly willing to serve his country but was unwilling to make sacrifices for it." Transferred to Key West with his regiment, he ended his military career as a lieutenant colonel and was named judge advocate general of the Department of Florida immediately after the Confederate surrender. Wilder sought through his army commission not combat or glory but comfort, convenience, and security. More loyal to himself than his country, service at Lancaster–County provided Wilder with peace and contentment – hardly the aggressive characteristics expected of an infantry officer. Wilder had no sympathy for blacks, and years of service in an African-American regiment did not change his attitude or feeling of white superiority. As a lawyer, however, he believed that African-Americans were entitled to equal treatment before the law. He was murdered in the streets of Kansas City in 1870.

68. Brinsfield, John. "The Battle of New Market Heights." *Soldiers*, 51, 2 (February 1996): 50-51.
Brinsfield, a chaplain and colonel in the U.S. Army, has written an account of the battle of New Market Heights, Virginia. Of the 16 African-American soldiers who were awarded the Medal of Honor during the Civil War, 14 received the medal for valor at New Market Heights. Brinsfield describes the attack in a brisk but complete manner. "Of the 3,000 black troops engaged, 1,302 were killed, wounded or missing."

69. Brodnax, David, Sr. "'Will they Fight:' Iowa's African American Regiment in the Civil War." *Annals of Iowa*, 66, 3-4 (Summer-Fall 2007): 266-292.
Based on "an intensive search of archival and local materials," this essay reconstructs the Civil War service of the 1st Iowa Volunteers (African Descent), later re-designated as the 60th United States Colored Infantry. Recruited in Iowa and Missouri, the regiment saw most of its service in and around Helena, Arkansas. As with most African-American regiments, its service consisted mostly of fatigue details, guard duty, drill, and scouting. In common with most regiments, white or black, the 60th lost more men to disease than combat. However, Companies C and F, in conjunction with several other units, did experience combat at Wallace's Ford, Arkansas, on July 26, 1864. During a fighting withdrawal to Helena several critically wounded members of the regiment were left on the field. They were subsequently murdered by Confederate soldiers.

Before mustering out, black enlisted men of the regiment held a convention requesting the right to vote. By public referendum in 1868, and with a margin of 57% for and 43% against, Iowa granted the franchise to the state's black population.

Well researched and well written, this article is a valuable addition to the growing library of African-American regimental histories.

70. Broadwater, Robert P. "The Black and Mixed-Race Troops of the Louisiana Native Guards offered to Serve both South and North." *America's Civil War*, 17, 1 (March 2004): 18, 20, 70, 72.

Most of this article focuses on the May 27, 1863 assault by black and mixed-race troops of the Louisiana Guards against the Confederate entrenchments at Port Hudson. As Broadwater points out, the Louisiana Guard regiments were the first African-American troops to be officially mustered into Federal service, and their use in combat occurred two months before the more famous July assault of the 54th Massachusetts on Fort Wagner.

71. Brooksher, William R. "Betwixt Wind and Water." *Civil War Times Illustrated*, 32, 5 (November-December 1993): 64-68, 70, 82-83, 85, 87.

Fort Pillow, a Union occupied Tennessee fort located on the east bank of the Mississippi River, some 40 to 50 miles upriver from Memphis, was the scene of the Civil War's worst racial atrocity. Controversy surrounding the battle continues to this day, and many of the articles cited in this bibliography deal with the battle and its immediate and long-term consequences. William R. Brooksher, a retired Air Force brigadier general, recounts the April 12, 1864 battle in this useful account. The Confederate forces were commanded by the legendary "Wizard of the Saddle," Major General Nathan Bedford Forrest, probably the best cavalry commander of the war. The Union garrison consisted of Battery F, 4th U.S. Colored Light Artillery, soldiers from the 11th U.S. Colored Troops, and white soldiers of the Unionists 13th Tennessee Cavalry. Before the battle, was over a shocking 42% of the African-American and 21% of the white troops were killed or mortally wounded, leading to charges that Forrest had intentionally ordered a massacre. (Most modern historians of the battle calculate a much larger black and white mortality rate.)

The author maintains that hostility to the white Tennessee Union troops, and deep-seated racial hatred for the black soldiers, did lead to unrestrained excesses on the part of the Confederate assaulting force, and Forrest and his officers were slow in re-reasserting control over their troops. However, according to the author, "the body of available evidence will not... conclusively support the charge of intentional atrocity." The debate – excessive force or intentional massacre – will probably never be settled. The article contains several illustrations and a map.

72. Brown, D. Alexander. "The Battle of Brice's Cross Roads." *Civil War Times Illustrated*, 7, 1 (April 1968): 4-9, 44-48.
The Battle of Brice's Cross Roads, fought on June 10, 1864, saw a numerically inferior Confederate force lead by Nathan Bedford Forrest decisively defeat a much larger, better equipped, but poorly lead Union Army. Brown's tactical study is a workmanlike account of the battle; unfortunately, little attention is paid to the black regiments that prevented the Union rout from becoming worse than it was.

73. Bryant, William Cullen II, editor. "A Yankee Soldier Looks at the Negro." *Civil War History*, 7, 2 (June 1961): 133-148.
This is an edited collection of letters written by a well-educated private in a Massachusetts regiment serving in Louisiana from January to July 1863. The letters contain a number of interesting observations regarding African-Americans as soldiers.

74. Burkhardt, George S. "No Quarter! Black Flag Warfare 1863-1865." *North & South,* 10, 1 (May 2007): 12-29.
According to Burkhardt's powerful and unsettling article, "Confederate soldiers regularly massacred black Federals in every theater" during the Civil War. In addition, the author maintains that these massacres were "not discrete, isolated, and unrelated" events but were encouraged by default since Confederate military authorities, and Richmond government officials, never punished the guilty. The idea of black soldiers, in uniform and as armed enemies, according to Burkhardt, infuriated white Southerners. Armed black men were viewed as a threat to the entire social structure of the agrarian South and were in violation of the "iron taboo." According to this idea, any black slave who physically attacked a white man was considered in "servile insurrection" and deserved immediate

execution. White Southerners, more than whites in any other area of the country, lived in a homogenous society. They shared a common heritage, a common culture, and a common predilection toward physical violence. Armed black men challenged prevailing Southern ideas of status, manhood, honor, family, and, most importantly, white supremacy; consequently, black soldiers captured on the battlefield commonly faced at best Confederate mistreatment if not immediate execution.

Using a number of both Southern and Northern eyewitness accounts, Burkhardt presents a litany of large-scale atrocities committed by Confederates beginning at Milliken's Bend, Louisiana, in June 1863, and continuing to the last major massacre at Saltville, Virginia, on October 2, 1864. Interestingly, the author estimates far more black prisoners were murdered after surrendering at the Battle of the Crater on July 30, 1864, than at the more publicized Fort Pillow incident.

The author also contends that white racial violence spurred an inevitable black reaction. Charles Francis Adams, Jr., commander of the 5th Massachusetts Cavalry (Colored), remarked that because of Fort Pillow and other atrocities "the rebels dread the darkies more than the white troops; for they know that…[they] cannot expect quarter." At Fort Blakely during the Mobile campaign, according to observers, African-American soldiers chanted "Fort Pillow, Fort Pillow" when they went into battle and later slaughtered at least 50 white soldiers attempting to surrender. If Burkhardt is correct in his assertions, the execution of mostly African-American prisoners by Confederate troops was, sadly, far more widespread than previously assumed. The article contains several illustrations and extensive endnote documentation.

75. Butts, Heather M. "Alexander Thomas Augusta – Physician, Teacher and Human Rights Activist." *Journal of the National Medical Association,* 97, 1 (January 2005): 106-109.
By any measure, Alexander Thomas Augusta was a remarkable man. Born free in Norfolk, Virginia, in 1825, he was educated in secret, studied medicine while working as a barber, later moved to

Canada, and graduated with a medical degree – with full honors – from the Medical College of the University of Toronto. Returning to the United States, he was the first African-American commissioned as a regimental surgeon and ultimately the first black officer to be interred in Arlington National Cemetery. Augusta's experiences in the Union Army (he was one of only eight black doctors holding commissions), his fight for pay commensurate with his rank, and his post-war medical practice are all briskly related. Augusta was "a model to all Americans" and a man "who demonstrated the talent, courage, and character to overcome racial barriers." The article contains 35 notes, many of which are quite detailed.

76. Carle, Glenn L. "The First Kansas Colored." *American Heritage,* 43, 1 (February/March 1992): 78-91.
In this article Carle, a Foreign Service officer, presents an overview of the 1st Kansas Colored Volunteers. The author points out that Kansas, under the direction of Senator James H. Land, began recruiting black troops early in June 1862 when it was "against the law, and the public and Army were on the whole strongly hostile to it." The initial reluctance of many runaway slaves to volunteer is also described. Indeed, "some of the 1st Kansas Colored's initial missions in the fall of 1862 were raids to "liberate slaves and bring them into the Army by bayonet point." Of particular interest is the conduct of Colonel James M. Williams, commander of the 1st Kansas Colored, who executed a Confederate prisoner in retaliation for the murder of several black soldiers held captive by Rebel troops. The author recounts the July 2, 1863, Battle of Cabin Creek in Indian Territory. The near annihilation of the regiment at the April 18, 1864, Battle of Poison Springs, Arkansas, is only lightly touched upon.

77. Campbell, John (?). "Is This Lt. John Campbell's Letter?" *Annals of Iowa*, 39, 7 (Winter 1969): 542-545.
Dated only two days after the battle of Milliken's Bend, Louisiana, this letter, which was found in the files of the *Des Moines Daily State Register*, contains numerous details, both factual and erroneous, concerning untested African-American troops and the

role they played in the defense of Milliken's Bend. The author –
who may or may not be Lieutenant Campbell – was evidently a
member of the 5th Iowa Infantry.

78. Carter, Dan T. "The Anatomy of Fear: The Christmas Day
    Insurrection Scare of 1865." *The Journal of Southern History*,
    42, 3 (August 1976): 345-364.

Carter explores the panic that gripped wide areas of the South in
late 1865, months after the war's conclusion over a possible
uprising of the freedmen. Of interest to student of African-
American soldiers in the Civil War because one of the elements in
that unreasoning - but palpable fear that gripped the South - was
white hostility towards black soldiers serving as Federal occupation
troops.

79. Castel, Albert. "The Fort Pillow Massacre: A Fresh
    Examination of the Evidence." *Civil War History*, 4, 1 (March
    1958): 37-50.

According to the author neither side in the Fort Pillow controversy
is "altogether wrong or altogether right." This article examines the
battle and divides it into three categories for study: the capture of
the fort, the massacre, and the atrocities. After a thorough review of
the evidence, Castel concluded that the Confederate forces, after
having captured the fort and because of "race hatred, personal
animosity, and battle fury … proceeded to kill a large number of the
garrison after they had ceased resisting or were incapable of
resisting." The article contains 50 notes based on primary and
secondary sources.

80. _____. "Enlistment and Conscription in Civil War
    Kansas." *Kansas Historical Quarterly*, 27, 3 (Autumn 1961):
    313-319.

An abbreviated but still very good overview of Kansas regiments
recruited during the Civil War, either through enlistment or the
1864 conscription quota. Two black regiments were recruited in the
state, mostly from among runaway Missouri and Arkansas slaves.
To avoid the draft, according to the author, a black protégé of a

leading abolitionist "engaged in the business of furnishing his fellows as substitutes."

81. _____. "Civil War Kansas and the Negro." *Journal of Negro History,* 51, 2 (April 1966): 125-138.
In this interesting study, Castel, a renowned scholar of the Civil War, points out that the pre-war Kansas population contained only a small number of radical abolitionists and, while most of the population was anti-slavery, they were also anti-black, and in this regard differed little from their Midwestern neighbors. During the war, the black population of the state increased dramatically from a total of 816 in 1860 to almost 13,000 five years later, a rapid increase fueled by the influx of runaway Missouri and Arkansas slaves. Many former black slaves found employment on the state's farms, as a critical labor shortage had resulted because of heavy white enlistments in the Union army.

As the war dragged on, more military manpower was required, and a growing number of Kansas residents felt that an African-American "could just as well become food for powder as a white man." The ever-opportunistic Senator Jim Lane spearheaded African-American enlistments throughout the state, though there was at first much local opposition. Indeed, many blacks were reluctant to join the army because of a fear of rampant prejudice and concern for the welfare of their families at home. Eventually two regiments were formed, though in some cases recruits were kidnapped in order to fill the ranks.

82. _____. "Fort Pillow: Victory or Massacre." *American History Illustrated*, 9, 1 (April 1974): 4-10, 46-48.
The massacre of African-American and a number of white Tennessee Union troops at Fort Pillow, on April 12, 1864, remains to this day the most well-known, most controversial, and most publicized racial atrocity of the Civil War. In this article Castel again revisits the evidence to determine if a massacre took place by first describing the battle then examining the historical data. His concludes, as he did in his previous article, that "there can be little doubt that in a great many instances. Union soldiers, mostly Negro,

were shot after they surrendered." Furthermore, Confederate denials of a massacre made years later by biographers sympathetic to Forrest ring hollow and lack credibility. Castel's closing remarks echo his earlier 1958 findings: Forrest did not order a massacre, that it was not deliberately planned, and that the slaughter was perpetrated out of a frenzy "of race hatred, personal and political animosity, and battle fury." The article contains several illustrations as well as a map.

83. _____. "'Captain We Will Meet You on the Other Shore:' The Story of Some Black Union Soldiers From Michigan." *Georgia Historical Quarterly,* 87, 2 (Summer 2003): 275-296.
The reminiscences of Morris S. Hall, a young Michigan-born officer of the 44th United States Colored Troops, are recounted in this article. Included in his recollections are accounts of the fighting and surrender at Dalton, the Nashville campaign, and the pursuit of Hood after the Nashville victory. Hall and his regiment were mustered out in April 1866. Albert Castel provides an introduction to the various sections. Included in the article are maps, 23 notes, and several illustrations.

84. Chicoine, Stephen. "The Oldest Soldier." *American Legacy: Celebrating African-American History and Culture,* 10, 1 (Spring 2004): 47-48, 50, 52, 54.
Chicoine's article is a moving tribute to Henry Mack, born a slave in Fayette, Alabama, "around" 1836. He and his mother escaped in the early1860s to Helena, Arkansas, where he enlisted in the 4th Arkansas Infantry Regiment (African Descent), later re-designated the 57th USCT. Mack and his regiment served mainly on guard and garrison duty in Arkansas. Following his discharge at Fort Leavenworth, Kansas, on December 1866, Mack moved several times before finally settling in Minneapolis, Minnesota. He was active for decades in the Grand Army of the Republic (GAR) and even participated in the national reunion of Civil War veterans at Gettysburg in 1938. Henry Mack was Minnesota's last surviving Civil War soldier when he passed away on April 8, 1944.

85. Christ, Mark K. "Who Wrote the Poison Spring Letter?" In *All Cut to Pieces and Gone to Hell: The Civil War, Race Relations, and the Battle of Poison Spring,* edited by Mark K. Christ: Little Rock: August House, 2003, 99-105.

The almost complete text of a letter discussing the murder of black soldiers at the Battle of Poison Spring on April 18, 1864 is reproduced. The letter "provides an eyewitness account from a Southern soldier who was present on the field at the time the atrocities took place."

86. _____. 'They will be armed': Lorenzo Thomas Recruits Black Troops in Helena, April 6, 1863." *Arkansas Historical Quarterly,* 72, 4 (Winter 2013): 366-383.

In 1863, Brigadier General Lorenzo Thomas was directed by the Lincoln administration to visit the Mississippi Valley and organize contrabands as soldiers. When Thomas visited Helena, Arkansas, he addressed several thousand white soldiers and publically extoled the advantages of black military recruitment. Thomas's fervent appeal "took the appearance of a tent revival" and was received "with rapturous applause." Included in the article is a copy of the address that Thomas delivered several days later made in Louisiana. It is "almost certainly" the same as that delivered in Helena. The speech is printed in its entirety. Also included are two rather long letters from two enlisted men concerning the enlistment of African-Americans as soldiers. One later became an officer in the 2nd Arkansas Infantry Regiment (African Decent).

87. Cimprich, John. "The Fort Pillow Massacre: Assessing the Evidence." In *Black Soldiers in Blue: African American Troops in the Civil War Era,* edited by John David Smith. Chapel Hill: University of North Carolina Press, 2002, 150-168.

Conflicting and inconsistent accounts continue to this day regarding what occurred at Fort Pillow, Tennessee, on April 12, 1864. Historically two competing interpretations regarding the massacre have evolved: one Federal, one Confederate. According to Northern accounts an indiscriminate slaughter of African-American soldiers took place. The continually changing Southern response, anchored in the myth of the Lost Cause, argued that black soldiers continued to fight or attempted to escape rather than surrender. As a result, many were shot down. However, as the author points out, early Confederate admissions of a massacre changed over the years as part of a defensive reaction to Federal criticism. Reviewing and carefully analyzing all the available evidence, Cimprich concludes, as have most modern historians, that a massacre of black soldiers did take place. The article contains 40 notes, two period illustrations, and a map of Fort Pillow as it appeared on the day of the battle.

88. _____. "Fort Pillow during the Civil War." *North & South*, 9, 6 (December 2006): 60-70.

In this article John Cimprich, a professor at Thomas Moore College and a well-known scholar of the Fort Pillow massacre, traces the history of the fort, from its original construction and subsequent occupation by Confederate and Union forces to the April 12, 1864 massacre. Cimprich maintains the massacre – and he leaves little doubt that it was a massacre – highlights and ties together several important Civil War themes, among them "the importance of military experience, the hardships of soldier life, the breakdown of traditional rules of war, the conflict between masters and slaves, and the struggle within Southern white society between Unionists and Secessionists." Cimprich recounts the day's horrid particulars and points out an often overlooked detail: most Confederate soldiers serving under Forrest carried at least two fully loaded revolvers, besides a rifle or a carbine. According to the author "the large number of revolvers carried by Confederates enabled them to conduct a mass killing efficiently." Cimprich does not believe, however, that Forrest ordered a massacre; indeed, when Forrest became aware of what was happening, he acted energetically to stop the bloodletting. The article contains a number of period illustrations and 39 notes.

89. Cimprich, John, and Robert C. Mainfort, Jr. "Fort Pillow Revisited: New Evidence about an Old Controversy." *Civil War History*, 28, 4 (December 1982): 293-306.

Using six mostly unpublished documents, the authors conclude that a massacre did take place at Fort Pillow. Of the six documents, two are letters (one by Achilles V. Clark is described in this bibliography), three are newspaper accounts filed by Southern correspondents with Forrest's army, and the last is an after-action report by an officer of the 6th United States Colored Heavy Artillery Regiment. "Confederate writers," according to the authors, "freely admitted that a massacre took place." It was only after the accusation of massacre was raised by Northern newspapers and political leaders that the Southern versions of the incident began to change.

90. _____. "Dr. Fetch's Report on the Fort Pillow Massacre." *Tennessee Historical Quarterly*, 44, 1 (Spring 1985): 27-39.

Dr. Charles Fitch's official report is probably the single most damning documentary confirmation of the massacre that occurred at Fort Pillow on that April day in 1864. Only recently appointed as Post Surgeon, Dr. Fitch had been in attendance at the fort for only ten days before the Confederate attack. His official report, which was written less than three weeks after the attack, lay buried in the government archives until discovered in the early 1980s. It was not part of the documentation collected by the congressional committee investigating the massacre; indeed, Dr. Fitch did not testify before or cooperate with the investigating committee. Nevertheless, his report leaves little doubt that a massacre occurred at Fort Pillow, especially when he describes the indiscriminate shooting and murder of prisoners. He defends the actions of Confederate General James Chalmers and his attempts to limit the carnage.

91. _____. "The Fort Pillow Massacre: A Statistical Note."
Journal of American History, 76, 3 (December 1989): 830-837.
Cimprich and Mainfort used compiled service records in the National Archives to arrive at what they consider a more precise estimate of the number of Union soldiers, black and white, that were killed at Fort Pillow on April 12, 1864. According to the authors, the 600 man garrison was roughly divided between black and white troops. Their research "indicates that of the 585 to 605 men present on April 12, 1864, between 277 and 297 Federals, 47-49 percent of the garrison was killed or morally wounded." Moreover, they concluded that over 64% of the black troops and 31% of the white troops died or were mortally wounded. The evidence, they maintain, "unequivocally demonstrates that a massacre occurred." This well-documented study contains 20 detailed footnotes and three statistical tables.

92. "Civil War Plot." *Canada's History*, 91, 5 (October/November 2011): 13.
The discovery of a forgotten African-American soldier's grave in a Hamilton, Ontario cemetery is described. The unmarked grave was that of Nelson Stevens. Born a slave in Virginia, he arrived as a free man in Canada. In 1865 he returned to the United States and enlisted in Company B, 25th U.S. Colored Troops.

93. Clark, Achilles U. "A Letter of Account: Sergeant Clark Tells of Fort Pillow Massacre." *Civil War Times Illustrated,* 24, 4 (June 1985): 24-25.
Achilles V. Clark was a sergeant in the 20th Tennessee Cavalry and participated in the Confederate assault on Fort Pillow on April 12, 1864. Two days after the battle, he wrote a letter to his two sisters describing what had occurred. According to Clark's account, his fellow soldiers "gave little quarter" to the Union troops, either black or white, and the place was "a great slaughter pen." Clark claims that he and several others attempted to stop the butchery but were personally ordered, by General Forrest, to shoot the Union soldiers "down like dogs." No other documentation exists, either Union or

Confederate, to support Clark's claim regarding the actions of General Forrest.

94. Clark, Charles Branch. "Recruitment of Union Troops in Maryland, 1861-1865." *Maryland Historical Magazine*, 53, 2 (June 1958): 153-176.

The sharp political divisions in Maryland society, a slave-holding border state, were reflected in the state's chronic inability to meet its Federal quota allotments. Maryland, according to Clark, only fulfilled its troop quota requirements in one year, 1864. Of the 46,638 men who responded to various Federal calls, 6,404 were African-American. The article contains a short discussion of white opposition to black recruiting. In addition, the author also briefly describes the bounty system devised for slaves (and their owners) who volunteered for service in the Union Army.

95. Clifford, James. "Christian Fleetwood." *On Point: The Journal of Army History,* 13, 3 (Winter 2007-2008): 21-24.

Clifford provides a concise biography of Sergeant Major Christian Fleetwood, 4th United States Colored Troops, and Medal of Honor winner at Chaffin's Farm, Virginia, on September 29, 1864. Fleetwood's postwar achievements are also described in some detail. Interestingly, Fleetwood received his Medal of Honor while recuperating from typhoid as a patient at the U.S. General Hospital for Colored Troops in Wilmington, North Carolina. The medal was delivered in the mail.

96. Cochran, Darrell. "They Didn't Falter." *Soldiers*, 47, 2 (February 1992): 34-36.

This is a short history of the 54th Massachusetts Infantry from its muster to the assault on Fort Wagner on the night of July 18, 1863. There is also an insert biography of William H. Carney, Jr., the first African-American to win the Medal of Honor.

97. Coddington, Ronald S. "Black Men in Blue." *The Civil War Monitor*, 1, 2 (Winter 2011): 36-43.
This is a collection of seven period photographs of African-American soldiers. A brief biography for each soldier – including one commissioned black officer – is provided in a sidebar accompanying each photograph.

98. Coles, David J. "They Fought Like Devils: Black Troops in Florida during the Civil War." In *Florida's Heritage of Diversity: Essays in Honor of Samuel Proctor,* edited by Mark I. Greenberg, William Warren Rogers, and Canter Brown, Jr. Tallahassee: Sentry Press, 1997, 29-41.
Much of this essay describes the role of black regiments in the battle of Olustee, Florida, on February 20, 1864. Other Florida engagements in which black troops participated are only briefly acknowledged.

99. _____. "Shooting Niggers Sir." In *Black Flag over Dixie:* In *Racial Atrocities and Reprisals in the Civil War,* edited by Gregory J. W. Urwin. Carbondale: Southern Illinois University Press, 2004, 65-88.
The author examines the mistreatment of black soldiers that fell into Confederate hands after the Battle of Olustee, Florida on February 20, 1864. Three black regiments took part in the battle and suffered one-third of the Union Army casualties. The political and military background leading up to the battle is described as well as the battle itself. Based on primary source material, Coles concluded that "at least some black troops were killed by vengeful foes after the battle's close."

100. Comtois, Pierre. "Frontier Battle of Honey Springs." *America's Civil War*, 10, 4 (November 1997): 54-60.
This short tactical study examines the battle of Honey Springs, the largest and most important military engagement of the Civil War to take place in Indian Territory. Fought on July 17, 1863, the battle pitted mostly Confederate regiments of Choctaws, Cherokees, and Creeks, and some Texas units, against Union forces which included

Indian Home Guard regiments. The lopsided Federal victory owed as much to the inferior gunpowder used by the Confederate forces as to tactical skill. Among the Union regiments participating in the battle was the 1ˢᵗ Kansas Colored Infantry. The article contains a number of illustrations and a detailed map.

101. "Congress Erupts over Arming Freed Slaves." *America's Civil War*, 25, 3 (July 2012): 19.
Whitelaw Reid's newspaper account describes the uproar in the U.S. House of Representatives over General David Hunter's letter about arming freed slaves in South Carolina. Robert Mallory of Kentucky, a Union backer but slavery proponent, described the idea of arming blacks as monstrous, inhuman, barbaric and "contrary to the practice of civilized nations." It was, as Reid observed, as if a "bombshell" had been dropped in the chamber.

102. Conner, Mathew. "Minstrel-Soldiers: The Construction of African-American Identity in the Union Army." *Prospects,* 26 (2001): 109-136.
According to the author the study of American culture and "its ideal of the citizen-solder offers a new way of understanding the black experience in the Civil War." Unfortunately, most of Connor's intellectual analysis is overly concerned with racism inherent in the linguistic construction of Thomas Wentworth Higginson's *Army Life in a Black Regiment.* More of a nuanced cultural and intellectual study than a straight historical accounting.

103. Coopersmith, Andrew S. "Battlelines and Headlines: The Debate over 'Negro Soldiers.'" *North & South,* 9, 4 (September 2006): 72-82
On the eve of the Civil War, over 3,700 newspapers were published in the United States. This article describes the pivotal role newspapers played in the debate over arming African-Americans in the conflict, either agitating for or against their employment. Newspapers were closely identified with political parties and, as to be expected, most Southern papers were Democratic-inclined. Collectively these papers viewed blacks as lazy, ignorant, and inherently savage but lacking the courage to fight a white man's

war. While northern Republican newspapers were not above outright racist statements, they generally believed that blacks had the capacity to serve as soldiers. This was particularly true after Fort Wagner and similar battles in which African-Americans participated. Ironically a number of Southern papers, albeit a very tiny minority, argued late in the war that the time had come to enlist slaves to fight for the Confederacy in exchange for their freedom. Abundantly illustrated, the article contains 20 notes based on period newspapers – from both North and South.

104.   Cornish, Dudley Taylor. "Kansas Negro Regiments in the Civil War." *Kansas Historical Quarterly*, 20, 6 (May 1953): 417-429.

Cornish has written a well-documented and lucid account of two black regiments – the 1st and 2nd Kansas Colored Infantry – that were raised under Kansas state sponsorship during the Civil War. The recruitment of black soldiers in Kansas became essential early in the war since the number of white troops required to patrol the borderlands proved inadequate. As a consequence, Kansas Senator Jim Lane, on his own initiative, unofficially began raising a black regiment as early as August 1862. Lane justified his recruitment efforts under the provisions of the Second Confiscation Act of July 1862 though he conveniently ignored War Department objections that enlisting a black regiment, at that time, was illegal. As a result, and until the Emancipation Proclamation became official, black soldiers were technically enlisted as laborers. A number of runaway Missouri and Arkansas slaves willingly enlisted, but to bring the regiment to full strength a number of African-Americans were forcibly impressed. On January 13, 1863, the 1st Kansas Colored Volunteer Regiment was officially mustered into the Union Army and became the fourth black regiment, after the three regiments enrolled by Ben Butler in New Orleans, to enter Federal service.

Cornish traces the fortunes of the 1st Kansas Colored from Honey Springs to its near total destruction 15 months later at Poison Springs, Arkansas, where the regiment had 117 killed and 65 wounded. The 2nd Kansas Colored, which was raised by the middle of October 1863, took part in the same campaign and was bloodied at Jenkins' Ferry on April 30, 1864. Both regiments spent the remainder of the war escorting refugee trains, guarding supply convoys, performing fatigue duties, and pursuing Confederate guerilla bands from Little Rock to Fort Smith. The 1st Kansas Colored Volunteer Infantry (later re-designated the 79th (New) U.S. Colored Infantry) had 156 men killed in action during the Civil War, the highest number for any Kansas regiment.

105. _____. "The Union Army as a School for Negroes." *Journal of Negro History*, 37, 4 (October 1952): 368-382.
Most black soldiers serving in the Union Army were recruited in Southern states where it was against the law to teach a slave to read and write. As a consequence, many if not most enlisted men serving in regiments of United States Colored Troops were illiterate. And while no general program for the education of black soldiers was attempted by the Bureau of Colored Troops, there were extensive efforts, conducted principally but not exclusively at the company level, to provide black soldiers with the rudiments of education. In this article, Cornish provides an overview of the educational efforts carried out by military officers and civilian teachers to raise black soldiers "from the darkness of ignorance."

106. _____. "To Be Recognized as Men: The Practical Utility of History." *Military Review,* 58, 2 (February 1978): 40-55.
Adapted from a lecture given at the United States Army Command and General Staff College at Fort Leavenworth, Kansas, in February1977, Cornish's survey article traces the role of African-American soldiers in the Civil War from initial rejection to acceptance through necessity, recruiting, officer selection, battles, and ultimate significance.

107. "Corps d'Afrique." *Military Images*, 22, 5 (March/April 2001): 22.

At its peak, the Union Army's Corps Afrique in Louisiana contained five regiments of black engineers, four of which were mustered in New Orleans. This article documents the lineage and unit designation changes for all five regiments from organization to discharge. It also contains period photographs of two white engineer officers.

108. Costa, Dora L. "Pensions and Retirement among Black Union Army Veterans." *Journal of Economic History*, 70, 3 (September 2010): 567-592.

Utilizing statistical tables and figures, the author examines the effects of income transfers in the form of pension payments to black Civil War veterans. Prior to 1890, pension payments were based on service-connected disabilities. However, the 1890 pension expansion act guaranteed universal pensions for Union veterans, regardless of race or disability. The only eligibility requirement was military service during the war. As a result, black veterans became eligible for income transfer in the form of pension payments. This had a positive effect "on the retirement rates and living arrangements of African-American Civil War veterans." The article contains 44 extensively detailed notes, a number of scholarly references, two figures, and six tables,

109. Costa, Dora L. and Matthew E. Kahn. "Forging a New Identity: The Costs and Benefits of Diversity in Civil War Combat Units for Black Slaves and Freemen." *The Journal of Economic History,* 66, 4 (December 2006): 936-962.

Written by two economists, this intriguing statistical analysis examines the costs and benefits of diversity in African-American Civil War combat units. Diversity factors considered by the authors include age, place of birth, free or slave status on enlistment (three quarters of black men who served in the Union Army were former slaves), the social consequences of free blacks and slaves serving in the same or in separate regiments, year of enlistment, officer leadership, and where and when the regiment served. Data was collected and analyzed based on the service and pension records of 5,673 African-American Union Army soldiers who served in 51 infantry companies; 72% of the soldiers in the sample data sets were from border and Southern states, 29% were free men.

Based upon their analysis, the authors found that regiments recruited early in the war from among slaves were more likely to have commanders with abolitionist sympathies; former slaves were more loyal to their company than free blacks and, when compared to regiments with differing age, slave and free status, were less likely to desert or be arrested for military infractions. However, former slaves were more likely to be able to read and write if they served in a company with "a large fraction" of free men, the longer they served in the army the more likely they were to be literate, and the more diverse the company the more the former slave learned of the broader world beyond the plantation. Upon enlisting in the army, 32% of the men in the statistical sample discarded their slave name and adopted a new name – and with it a new identity.

After systematically reviewing the collected data, the authors concluded that "in the short run, the combat unit benefited from homogeneity . . . but, in the long run, men's human capital and information was best improved by serving in heterogeneous companies." The article includes six tables, 58 notes, and a bibliography.

110.   Coulter, E. Merton. "Robert Gould Shaw and the Burning of Darien, Georgia." *Civil War History,* 5, 4 (December 1959): 363-373.

Darien was an old coastal Georgia colonial town of some charm and beauty that was burnt to the ground by invading Union forces on June 11, 1863. According to historian E. Merton Coulter, the destruction of Darien was "one of the most wanton acts of vandalism during the Civil War." The Federal forces were under the direction of Colonel James Montgomery, commanding officer of the black 2nd South Carolina Regiment. Montgomery was an ardent abolitionist and former Kansas jayhawker who had learned "hard war" on the Kansas-Missouri border. Included in his brigade was the newly formed African-American 54th Massachusetts Infantry commanded by Colonel Robert Gould Shaw. Shaw was appalled by the looting and destruction he witnessed, especially since the town was defenseless and of no military significance. He feared that conduct of this nature would be "injurious to the reputation of black troops and of those connected with them." Ironically, Shaw was originally blamed for instigating the "barbarous tragedy." Following the war, Shaw's mother and Shaw family members helped rebuild St. Andrews Episcopal Church in Darien. The church had been burnt to the ground during the brief Federal occupation and its restoration, his mother felt, was something Colonel Shaw would have approved.

111.   Cowdrey, Albert E. "Slave into Soldier: The Enlistment by the North of Runaway Slaves." *History Today*, 20, 10 (October 1970): 704-715.

Most of Cowdrey's account is concerned with the events leading up to the issuing of the Final Emancipation Proclamation on January 1, 1863. The author points out that "Americans who hated slavery also hated the man who happened to be enslaved." As a consequence, Lincoln waited for public opinion to "ripen" before publicly issuing his revolutionary but pragmatic document. Short term results for the Union cause, were not impressive: "In the north the desertion rate remained high, volunteer enlistments low, and the Republicans lost the fall elections." In the long run, black soldiers proved invaluable to winning the war. According to Lincoln, they were "the great available and yet unavailable force for restoring the Union." A few pages are devoted to the establishment of the 1st South Carolina Volunteer Regiment, commanded by Boston abolitionist Thomas Wentworth Higginson. Higginson became commander of the first *slave* regiment officially mustered into Union Army service.

112.   Cozzens, Peter and Michael Haynes. "Smokescreen at Honey Hill." *Civil War Times Illustrated*, 38, 7 (February 2000): 32-38.

The authors have written an excellent general account of the battle of Honey Hill, South Carolina, fought in the late autumn of 1864. Repeated blundering by Federal army and navy commanders is recounted, as well as the spirited defense provided by several brigades of Georgia militia. African-American regiments participating in the affair included the 54th and 55th Massachusetts and the 32nd and 35th United States Colored Infantry. Federal casualties for the November 30, 1864, engagement totaled well over 700; Confederate losses included four killed and 40 wounded.

113.   Craighead, Sandra G., compiler. "Index of Maryland and West Virginia Civil War Colored Troopers and Their 'Loyal Slaveowners.'" *Journal of the Afro-American Historical and Genealogical Society*, 15, 1 (Spring 1996): 40-50.
Under the Adjutant Generals Office, General Order 329, loyal slaveholders could be compensated for their slaves who voluntarily enlisted in the Union Army. As a result, the Federal government received thousands of claims between 1863 and 1866 for compensation at the rate of $300.00 per slave. Compensation claims became part of the soldier's Compiled Service Record. This article contains an alphabetical list of black soldiers who enlisted and their "loyal" Maryland and West Virginia owners. Interestingly, most of the slaves did not share a common surname with their owner; some individuals are listed by both surname and an alias.

114.   Cunningham, Roger D. "Douglas's Battery at Fort Leavenworth: The Issue of Black Officers during the Civil War." *Kansas History*, 23, 4 (Winter 2000-2001): 200-217.
If the idea of recruiting African-Americans as soldiers was revolutionary, the prospect of commissioning black men as officers was not only revolutionary but anathema. White society considered African-Americans as intellectual inferiors no better than children and quite incapable of assuming command or leadership positions. As a consequence, they were, with few exceptions, denied the opportunity to become commissioned officers in the Union Army. One black unit, however, "enjoyed the unique distinction of being the only Federal unit to serve entirely under the leadership of black officers." That unit, the little known Independent Battery, U.S. Colored Light Artillery, otherwise known as Douglas's Battery, is the subject of this remarkable account by Roger D. Cunningham. Cunningham, a West Point graduate and retired army officer, traces

the unit's history from original formation, muster in December 1864 at Fort Leavenworth, Kansas, and final discharge in July 1865. Biographical information regarding the unit's black officers is also presented.

The article is illustrated with drawings, contemporary photographs, and numerous footnotes. Of particular interest is a table listing the distribution by unit of all 108 African-Americans who served as officers in the Union Army.

115. _____. "Welcoming 'Pa' on the Kaw: Kansas's 'Colored' Militia' and the 1864 Price Raid." *Kansas History*, 25, 2 (Summer 2002): 86-101.

In this straightforward account, the author describes the mobilization of African-American Kansas militiamen called to active service in the fall of 1864. Confederate Major General Sterling Price, from his base in northeastern Arkansas, had launched a mounted raid deep into Missouri that threatened Kansas. On October 8, 1864, Kansas Governor Thomas Carney called the state militia to arms. A state law mandated a white-only militia and barred African-American from enrolling. However, Major General Samuel R. Curtis, commander of the Union Department of Kansas, desperately needed troops to oppose an expected Confederate attack. As a result, he quickly issued General Orders No. 55 that declared martial law in the state. In addition, his emergency edict ordered all men between 18 and 65, white or black, to arm themselves and report for immediate military service. Over 1,000 black men (most were former Missouri and Arkansas slaves) volunteered and served in a number of improvised Kansas militia companies, many serving under African-American officers. Cunningham provides summary biographical information on some of these officers. As time passed, the service of black militiamen during the Price raid, in another glaring case of historical amnesia, was "ignored, misidentified, or forgotten."

116. _____. "Defending Fort Scott, Kansas, from 'Old Pap' Price." *Journal of America's Military Past*, Volume 36, Issue 2 (Spring/Summer 2011): 32-38.

Fort Scott, Kansas, on the border with Missouri, was, by 1864, a major Union Army quartermaster, supply, training, and recruiting depot. When Confederate Major General Sterling "Old Pap" Price invaded Missouri in 1864 there was widespread fear that he would attack Fort Scott and rampage through Kansas. As a result, the Kansas militia was mustered which included not only whites but 14 companies of African-Americans. At Fort Scott, First Lieutenant William D. Matthews, an African-American, was charged with defending the post with a number of black citizen-soldiers trained and organized by him. No attack occurred and Price, after a number of costly defeats, retreated to Arkansas. Interestingly, Matthews was one of only three commissioned African-American artillery officers in the Civil War.

117. Davidson, Roger A., Jr. "'They Have Never Been Known to Falter:' The First United States Colored Infantry in Virginia and North Carolina." *Civil War Regiments: A Journal of the American Civil War*, 6 (Number 1): 1-26.

Because of white mistrust, most African-American regiments saw service not in combat but rather as garrison troops or as labor units. Indeed, 35 black regiments suffered approximately three-quarters of the combat losses experienced by African-Americans during the war. One such regiment was the 1st U.S. Colored Infantry which was originally formed in Washington, DC. During the war the 1st "participated in 13 battles in two major campaigns." In this summary of unit history the author outlines the regiment's campaigns from Virginia (including the siege of Petersburg) to North Carolina. Later service as an occupation force in North Carolina is also described. During the Civil War, the regiment lost 185 officers and enlisted men killed in combat or died of disease. Scores more were discharged because of wounds or disabilities. Personal vignettes are used extensively by the author to flesh out the unit's organizational history.

118.   Davies, Wallace E. "The Problem of Race Segregation in the Grand Army of the Republic." *Journal of Southern History*, 13, 3 (August 1947): 354-372.

This article documents a series of episodes within the Grand Army of the Republic, a politically influential Union veteran's organization established after the end of the Civil War, and the refusal of local departments – principally in the Deep South – to admit African-American veterans on the basis of equality. Officially Grand Army leadership recognized full membership status for black Union Army veterans; however, when the "national organization tried to uphold the blacks, it found it could enforce its decisions only at the expense of disrupting its Southern departments." As a result, many members preferred to "expand the white membership rather than insist on equality of status." Though dated, the article remains one of the few to address the travails of black Civil War veterans in the era of Jim Crow and segregation.

119.   Davis, George L. "Pittsburgh Negro Troops in the Civil War." *Western Pennsylvania Historical Magazine*, 36, 2 (June 1953): 101-113.

Most of this article is about Pittsburgh area African-Americans who served in the 54th and 55th Massachusetts Infantry, though some detail is provided concerning other black units raised in the state - including Company I, 12th Pennsylvania Volunteers. In total, Pennsylvania contributed 8,612 African-Americans to the Union war effort.

120.   Davis, Robert Scott, Jr. "A Soldier's Story: The Records of Hubbard Pryor, Forty-fourth United States Colored Troops." *Prologue, Quarterly of the National Archives and Record Administrations* 31, 4 (Winter 1999): 267-68, 270.

Hubbard Pryor was a runaway slave from Polk County, Georgia, who achieved immortality as the subject of two well-known and widely circulated Civil War photographs. As recounted by Robert Scott Davis, the article's author, an officer of the Colored Bureau of the Adjutant General's Office had two photographs taken of Pryor. In the first he appears in the rags of a runaway slave; in the second Pryor is fully uniformed and armed as a private in Company

A, 44th United States Colored Troops. Both photographs were attached to an official report and used to illustrate the Union Army's success in turning slaves into soldiers. In the remainder of the article Davis traces Pryor's military service and subsequent career, while also providing a summary of the recruitment and service of African-American soldiers in the western theater.

121. _____. "White and Black in Blue: The Recruitment of Federal Units in Civil War North Georgia." *Georgia Historical Quarterly*, 85, 3 (Fall 2001): 347-374.
Of limited value for students of the black Civil War military experience, since most of the article concentrates on the recruitment of whites from Georgia by the Union Army. The author does, however, describe regimental recruiting activities among Georgia African-Americans by Major George Luther Stearns. Stearns was a pre-war supporter of John Brown and was instrumental in the recruitment of the 54th and 55th Massachusetts Infantry. Officially, 3,486 African-Americans from Georgia served in the Union Army.

122. _____. "'Near Andersonville': An Historical Note on Civil War Legend and Reality." *Journal of African American History*, 92, 1 (Winter 2007): 96-105.
Only a few paragraphs of this "special report" are concerned with the treatment of African-American Union Army prisoners at Camp Sumter in southwest Georgia, otherwise known as Andersonville, the most notorious of the war's prisoner-of-war camps. According to the author, black prisoners were placed "on special work details that brought them extra physical labor and punishment, but allowed them better rations and thus a better chance of survival." Two divergent white prisoner views regarding black treatment in the camp are recounted. One doubtful claim maintained that blacks, while forced into slavery, lived better than their white fellow prisoners. The other, by a white Andersonville survivor, paints a grim picture of black prisoners suffering relentless cruelty at the hands of their Confederate captors. Only one African-American prisoner, Robert Holmes of the 106th U.S. Colored Troops, successfully escaped from Andersonville.

123.   Davis, William C. "The Massacre at Saltville." *Civil War Times Illustrated*, 9, 10 (February 1971): 4-11, 43-48.

Davis, a prolific writer and renowned Civil War historian, has produced a concise study of the long-neglected October 2, 1864 battle at Saltville. Located in a remote corner of southwestern Virginia, the tiny village was named for the vital substance that it produced (salt was necessary for the preservation of meat). The attacking Union force of 3,600 men included approximately 600 members of the 5th U.S. Colored Cavalry. After a resolute and unexpectedly stout defense, Federal forces were forced to retreat leaving behind many of their wounded. The next morning, Saltville became the scene of exceptionally brutal acts of violence as Confederate soldiers began scouring the battlefield for wounded black soldiers. Any they found were summarily shot. The murders continued throughout the morning and even included massacring wounded African-American soldiers temporarily housed in a makeshift field hospital. One shocked Confederate soldier described Tennessee troops as "shooting every wounded negro they could find." A number of unwounded prisoners held in Confederate captivity, both black soldiers and white, were also murdered. Davis estimates that as many as 100 African-American soldiers were slaughtered. Today the massacre, like the battle, is virtually forgotten.

124.   DeBlack, Thomas A. "An Overview of the Camden Expedition." In *All Cut to Pieces and Gone to Hell: The Civil War, Race Relations, and the Battle of Poison Spring,* edited by Mark K. Christ: Little Rock: August House, 2003, 11-30.

An overview of the Union Army's Camden Expedition that took place in central and southern Arkansas between March and May 1864 is presented. A substantial part of the narrative describes the actions of the 1st and 2nd Kansas Colored Regiments and the Battle of Poison Spring. The article contains 47 notes.

125.	"Deeds of Noble daring." *America's Civil War,* 26, 6 (January 2014): 64-65.
The significant role African-American troops played in the decisive Union victory at Nashville, Tennessee is briefly discussed. Nine regiments of black troops in two brigades were deployed in the battle. One regiment, the 13th USCT, suffered 221 casualties. The article contains an excerpt from the report of Colonel Charles R. Thompson, the white commander of one of the black brigades, in which he praises the performance of the unit's troops. A Confederate view is voiced by a soldier from the 1st Georgia describing combat with African-American soldiers. We trapped them in a cross-fire and "took no prisoners" he wrote. The article also contains a photograph of Sergeant George Singleton, Company C, 17th USCT.

126.	Dhalle, Kathy. "The Battle of Honey Hill." *Bits of Blue and Gray,* (February 2002): www.bitsofblueandgray.com/Feb2002/htm.
The author presents a fairly detailed account of the Union defeat at Honey Hill, South Carolina, on November 30, 1864. A number of African-American regiments took part in the abortive Union attack, including the 26th, 35th, 102nd USCT and the 54th and 55th Massachusetts. The tactical maneuvers described in the article would be easier to understand if a battle map had been included.

127.	Dingledine, Don. "The Whole Drama of the War: The African American Soldier in Civil War Literature." *PMLA: Publication of the Modern Language Association of America,* 115, 5 (October 2000): 1113-1117.
This is a literary critique of Thomas Wentworth Higginson's *Army Life in a Black Regiment* and the image of African-American soldiers in selected post-Civil War literature.

128.   Dirck, Brian R. "By the Hand of God: James Montgomery and Redemptive Violence." *Kansas History*, 27, 1&2 (Spring-Simmer 2004): 100-115.

This is an excellent character study of James Montgomery, zealous abolitionist, Kansas jayhawker, and later commanding officer of the 2nd South Carolina Colored Infantry.

Montgomery, according to the author, "blended rigidity of moral purpose with an eagerness to destroy property and kill people." The article contains several illustrations and 59 notes.

129.   Dodge, George W. "The Burial of United States Colored Troops at Arlington National Cemetery." *Arlington Historical Magazine*, 11, 1 (October 1997): 43-54.

Two African-American Civil War soldiers who received the Medal of Honor, Sergeant James H. Harris of the 38th U.S. Colored Troops and Sergeant Milton M. Harris of the 5th U.S. Colored Troops, and one sailor, William H. Brown, of the USS *Brooklyn*, are buried at Arlington National Cemetery, the "nation's most renowned military cemetery." Not only does this article provide biographies of all three medal holders, but it also presents personal information on a number of both ordinary and prominent black Civil War soldiers interred at the cemetery, including Major (later brevet Lieutenant Colonel) Alexander Augusta, a Canadian-trained surgeon who overcame racial barriers to become "the highest ranking black officer in the Civil War era."

130.   Douglas, Joseph A. "The Ironic Role of African Americans in the Elmira, New York Civil War Prison Camp." *Afro-Americans in New York Life and History*, 26, 1 (January 1999): 7-24.

One of the most notorious Union Civil War prisoner-of-war camps was located at Elmira, New York. Established in 1864, and dubbed "Hellmira" by its Confederate inmates, conditions at the camps were so chaotic, and the mortality rate so high, the camp was later described as the Andersonville of the North. Ironically, African-American soldiers, specifically the 20th USCT, were stationed for some time at the prison. Their mission was twofold: bring order out of chaos in the camp and control unruly white regiments known for poor discipline and a penchant for desertion. Black troops were employed because they were the only troops considered "entirely reliable and trustworthy." In addition, African-American soldiers "were responsible for much of the decent treatment that deceased Confederates received." Civilian John Jones, an escaped slave, was responsible with providing decent burial for deceased Confederate prisoners. Smith's record keeping was so precise that years later they became the basis for the establishment of Woodlawn National Cemetery, Elmira, New York.

131. Dunkelman, Mark H. "A Bold Break for Freedom." *American History*, 34, 5 (December 1999): 22-28.
The extraordinary story of Robert Smalls is recounted in this brief biographical portrait. Smalls, a South Carolina slave and pilot, "abducted" the Confederate supply ship *Planter* in Charleston Harbor and sailed to freedom with his family and several close friends. Smalls' subsequent role as a ship's pilot for the Federal Navy, his political career as a Republican South Carolina congressman, and later government official, are also described. A good overview as well as an interesting narrative sketch of a remarkable man.

132. _____. "Through White Eyes: The 154th New York Volunteers and African-Americans in the Civil War." *Journal of Negro History*, 85 3 (Summer 2000): 96-111.
In this well-researched study, Mark H. Dunkelman, drawing extensively on primary source materials, analyzes the racial attitudes of soldiers of the battle-hardened 154th New York Volunteer Infantry regarding African-Americans, both as human beings and later as fellow soldiers. The 154th New York, one of the most documented of all Union Civil War regiments, was raised upstate among "those generally of Anglo-Saxon stock with a thin sprinkling of European immigrants." Most had never encountered African-Americans in any number until they crossed the Mason-Dixon Line. Their initial reaction was mixed: some despised those they met and considered them racially inferior; others were sympathetic, and still others were moved by the horrors of slavery

to embrace abolitionism. By 1864 the regimental attitude regarding African-Americans changed for the better, especially since so many former slaves accompanied the 154th as cooks, teamsters, laborers, and officer servants.

According to the author, the recruitment of blacks as soldiers was "universally lauded by members" of the regiment and black soldiers were viewed as valuable and trusted allies in the fight against the Confederacy. Most generally approved of the drill and appearance of African-American troops they encountered.

Overall, the article provides excellent eyewitness accounts of changing white perceptions regarding slavery, African-Americans, and the role of black soldiers in the Civil War. Interestingly, three privates who served in the 154th were of mixed black and white heritage.

133.   Duren, Charles M. "The Occupation of Jacksonville, February 1864 and the Battle of Olustee. Letters of Lt. C. M. Duren, 54th Massachusetts Regiment." *Florida Historical Quarterly,* 32, 4 (April 1954): 262-287.

Written by Lt. C. M. Duren, a white officer in Company D of the 54th Massachusetts Infantry, the letters span the period from February 9 to April 19, 1864. In his letters, Duren makes some interesting observations concerning commissions for black enlisted men, equal pay between white and black soldiers, the demands of occupation duty, the fate of African-American soldiers captured at the Battle of Olustee, and his company's high literacy rate. The young lieutenant thought his regiment "the best colored regiment in the service" but he had little use for army chaplains.

134.   Dyer, Brainerd. "The Treatment of Colored Union Troops by the Confederates, 1861-1865." *Journal of Negro History,* 20, 3 (July 1935): 273-286.

As a response to the problem presented by black prisoners of war, and white officers serving in African-American regiments, the Confederate government developed a number of official and often confusing policies. Some of these policies, which are addressed in this article, were based on proclamations issued by President Davis, others on acts of the Confederate Congress, and still others on correspondence between Richmond authorities and state government and local military officials. Early in the war, the Confederate government had declared that "all negro slaves captured in arms be at once delivered over to the ...respective States in which they belong to be dealt with according to the laws of said State." This policy was affirmed by the Confederate Congress which subsequently declared that the same policy applied to free blacks as well as slaves. Theoretically, upon return to state jurisdiction, black prisoners taken in arms, free or slave, could be executed for inciting servile insurrection. Generally, what eventually evolved, according Dyer, was a system in which slaves captured in arms were returned to their masters, if possible; free blacks, and slaves with no master, were handed over to Confederate authorities for confinement. They were not to be recognized as prisoners of war. Late in 1864 this policy changed. General Lee, after consultation with Confederate Secretary of War James A. Seddon, informed General Grant that "all negroes in the military or naval service of the United States taken by us who are not identified as the property of citizens...are regarded as prisoners of war."

Confederate policy regarding white officers, at least on the surface, was equally drastic. According to a proclamation by President Davis, which was later reiterated by a joint resolution of the Confederate Congress, white officers serving in African-American regiments could be executed upon capture. As far as can be determined, this policy, as a government directive, was never officially enforced. The author asserts (and many modern scholars would strongly disagree) that black soldiers, upon capture, were generally not murdered and usually treated like white prisoners, though he admits in the heat of battle black soldiers were sometimes given no quarter.

135. Edrington, William E. "True Glory." *Blue & Gray Magazine*, 7, 4 (April 1990): 45.
Reprints an October 12, 1863 letter by William E. Edrington, Company K, 54th Massachusetts Infantry, recounting the disastrous assault on Fort Wagner.

136. Ehlers, Mark. "Seeing the Elephant: Milliken's Bend, Louisiana." *War & Society,* 25, 1 (May 2006): 21-34.
"Seeing the elephant" was Civil War soldier slang for the experience of combat. For the newly liberated bondsmen of the African Brigade, the elephant was met head-on at Milliken's Bend, Louisiana, on June 7, 1863. In this fine account, author Mark Ehlers presents a dramatic portrayal of this often overlooked and poorly documented heavyweight slugfest between newly recruited, ill-trained, and poorly armed former slaves and attacking Texas troops. The author describes the background of the four black regiments "collectively known as the African Brigade," the camp at Milliken's Bend and its location on the west bank of the Mississippi River, the ferocious Confederate attack and the equally fierce and determined African-American defense, Confederate and Union casualties, and the battle's significance on the larger national scene. Not only a highly recommended study, but the best capsule descriptions of one of the war's most savage encounters. The article contains 39 notes and two very good maps.

137. Ellison, Mary. "African-American Music and Muskets in Civil War New Orleans." *Louisiana History*, 35, 3 (Summer 1994): 285-319.
An insightful analysis exploring the intensely intricate relationship between New Orleans African-American freedom songs and the ideas of emancipation, freedom, and military service. According to the author, "musicians were prominent among those New Orleans free men of color and slaves who rushed to enlist with the Union army." In addition, "black men . . . . garnered an enviable reputation as soldiers and musicians playing martial music for both black and white regiments." Also discussed are the regiments of Louisiana Native Guards, the problems of race discrimination faced by black

Guard officers appointed by General Benjamin Butler, and the battles of Port Hudson and Milliken's Bend. Based on a wide variety of primary and secondary sources, the article contains numerous excerpts of New Orleans freedom songs, both in English and French.

138. Emberton, Carole. "Only Murder Makes Men:' Reconsidering the Black Military Experience." *Journal of the Civil War Era*, 2, 3 (September 2012) 369-393.

Journal of the Civil War Era, 2, 3 (September 2012) 369-393.

This is a deeply intellectualized essay illustrating the different interpretations of black military service during the Civil War. The author contrasts the optimistic ideas of Frederick Douglass regarding the merits of black service with the darker opinions expressed by W.E.B. DuBois. For Douglass, military service was the "indispensable vehicle for the internal transformation of slaves into free men and citizens." DuBois "sensed some troubling contradictions" regarding the narrative of black military manhood and the supposed long-term benefits of army service. These issues, and how black soldiers were perceived by white America, are explored in depth. Interestingly, the author highlights the often overlooked draconian measures that forced many African-Americans, often at bayonet point, to serve in the Union Army. According to the author, "the brutality and degradation freed people hoped to leave behind" was replicated in the army. Throughout the South, Union Army press gangs, violence, and coercion were pervasive inducements for African-American enlistment. The article contains 39 very comprehensive notes.

139. Everett, Donald E. "Ben Butler and the Louisiana Native Guards 1861-1862." *Journal of Southern History*, 24, 2 (May 1958): 202-217.

Everett provides a well-documented, good overview history of the "free colored men" of the Louisiana Native Guards. The author traces the history of the Native Guards from their inception as unarmed Confederate militia to their recruitment by Major General Benjamin Butler as trained and armed soldiers of the Federal government. The politically well-connected Butler, in desperate need of reinforcements and ever the opportunist, ultimately raised, on his own initiative, three regiments of Native Guards theoretically composed entirely of free men. As the author points out, Butler's definition of free as in "free colored men" was quite expansive. Ironically, all three African-American regiments did not receive official approval during Butler's tenure of commander of the Department of the Gulf. Official recognition occurred during the administration of his successor, Nathanial P. Banks, who "had little use for the Negro as a soldier."

140.   Fagg, Jane. "Independence County Black Soldiers: The 113th United States Colored Infantry." *The Independence County Chronicle*, 29, 3-4 (April – July 1988): 2-9.
This is a compilation of Independence County, Arkansas, African-American soldiers who served in the 113th U.S. Colored Infantry. Information noted includes name, age, rank, company designation, date and place of enlistment and, if available, mustering out date. Included in the article is a biography of two black soldiers who served in the regiment.

141.   Fannin, John F. "The Jacksonville Mutiny of 1865." *Florida Historical Quarterly*, 88, 3 (Winter 2010): 368-396.
This article describes the mutiny that convulsed the 3rd USCT at Jacksonville, Florida in March 1865. The 3rd was raised from free men and former slaves in Philadelphia and had seen limited combat; most of its service was spent in routine occupational duty in Jacksonville. Days before mustering out, a volatile combination of nascent racial tensions between white officers and black enlisted men, sagging regimental morale, the mind-numbing tedium of garrison duty, and an objection to harsh army discipline, all led to an explosion of violence by a number of enlisted men. The mutiny that occurred is described in detail, as are the subsequent courts martials and military executions that followed. The article contains 64 notes based on both primary and secondary sources.

142.   Fellman, Michael. "A White Man's War." *Civil War Times*, 48, 6 (December 2009): 48-53.

William T. Sherman's "adamant refusal to field African-American troops," and his disobedience to direct orders from President Lincoln to use black troops, is discussed. According to Fellman, Sherman's vehement resistance to the employment of black troops bordered on outright insubordination; however, Lincoln chose to overlook this insubordination because of Sherman's successful campaign in Georgia. At one point Sherman even went so far as to order the arrest of "recruitment officers who tried to enlist black laborers as soldiers." The article is illustrated with seven color and black and white photographs.

143.   Ferry, Richard J. "The Battle of Olustee (or Ocean Pond), February 20, 1864." *Blue & Gray Magazine,* 3, 4 (March 1986): 6-16, 44-61.

Fought among the pine-barrens and scrub brush of northern Florida, the Battle of Olustee on February 20, 1864 was the largest military engagement fought in the state. This thoroughly comprehensive study examines the battle, discusses the events which lead to Union defeat, and addresses several of the controversies surrounding the battle, including the treatment of wounded and captured African-Americans. Amply illustrated with period and modern photographs and drawings, the study contains numerous and extensive quotes from personal diaries and general orders. Several maps make following the tactical deployments easy to follow. Also included is a tour guide of the present battlefield.

144.   Finch, Jackie Sheckler. "Camp Nelson: Union Army Depot and USCT Recruiting Center in Kentucky." *Blue & Gray*, 22, 6 (Winter 2006): 29-30.

A two-page account, with several illustrations, of Camp Nelson, Kentucky, the third- largest training depot for United States Colored Troops during the Civil War. Today extant sections of the camp are preserved as part of Camp Nelson Heritage Park and are open to the public. During the summer of 1864, Brigadier General Speed Fry, the camp's commander, caused a political crisis by expelling the

80

families of black recruits and openly co-operating with slave owners for the return of slave "property." The article also contains a mini biography of Sergeant Elijah Marrs, 12th U.S. Colored Heavy Artillery.

145.   Fincher, Jack. "The Hard Fight was Getting into the Fight at All." *Smithsonian*, 21, 7 (October 1990): 46-61.
It was to be, at least in the beginning, a white man's war; and the most difficult problem for African-Americans, according to Jack Fincher, "was in getting a chance to fight." Early black efforts to form home guard units or volunteer for military service were everywhere rebuffed. Appalling body counts, a scarcity of white volunteers, a desperate need for more soldiers, relentless pressure from abolitionists, and changing presidential political considerations would ultimately result in the recruitment of African-Americans as soldiers in the Union Army. Except for some minor errors of fact — Godfrey Weitzel during his Louisiana service was a brigadier general and not a lieutenant — Fincher's article chronicles changing Union attitudes regarding recruiting and arming black soldiers while also providing a very readable survey of African-American military participation in the war.

146.   Finkelman, Paul. "The Union Army's Fighting 54th." *American Visions*, 4, 6 (December 1989): 20-26.
A popular account of the most famous African-American Civil War regiment, the 54th Massachusetts Infantry. The 54th was, according to the author, a truly "national regiment" since blacks from all over the North served in its ranks. The difficulties blacks faced in their attempts to volunteer for service, white prejudice against enlisting them as soldiers, and the unsuccessful assault of the 54th on Fort Wagner are described.

147.   Fischer, Le Roy H. "Indian Territory's Gettysburg: The Battle of Honey Springs." *Oklahoma Today*, 21, 1(Winter 1970/71): 15-18.
The Battle of Honey Springs – "The Gettysburg of the Trans-Mississippi West" – was a resounding Union victory. Fought on July 17, 1863 it was the climatic Civil War battle fought in Indian

Territory. The events leading up to the battle and the battle itself are described. Much of the Union victory can be credited to the African-American 1st Kansas Colored Infantry, a regiment composed largely of runaway slaves. According to the author, the battle "was one of the first engagements of the Civil War in which Negroes proved their qualities as fighting men." The article contains a battle map and several period photographs.

148.   Fisher, Mike. "The First Kansas Colored - Massacre at Poison Springs." *Kansas History*, 2, 2 (Summer 1979): 121-128.

Drawing on the Official Records, the author has written a comprehensive tactical account of the Union defeat at the Battle of Poison Springs, Arkansas, on April 18, 1864. Of all the Union regiments in the battle, the 1st Kansas Colored Regiment suffered the heaviest losses. Many wounded African-American soldiers who "fell into the hands of the enemy . . . were murdered." The article provides a good overview of the battle and contains several photographs and 69 notes.

149.   _____. "Remember Poison Spring." *Missouri Historical Review*, 74, 3 (April 1980): 323-342.

Fisher's article examines in great detail the April 30, 1864, Battle of Jenkins' Ferry, the last battle of the abortive Federal Camden expedition in southern Arkansas. The author describes the deployment of Federal forces, Confederate and Union troop movements and counter-moves during the encounter, and the significant role played by the 2nd Kansas Colored Volunteers during the fighting. Less than two weeks before, at Poison Spring, Arkansas, African-Americans prisoners from the 1st Kansas Colored Volunteers had been murdered by their Confederate captors. During the Jenkins' Ferry battle, Colonel Samuel Crawford, commander of the 2nd Kansas Colored, sent a Confederate prisoner back to his lines with a simple message: as long as Confederates fought under the black flag of no quarter, the 2nd Kansas Colored Regiment would do likewise and "Remember Poison Spring." A good, comprehensive history of a little-known western encounter in an often overlooked theater of the Civil War.

Unfortunately, the author's estimates of total Union and Confederate casualties are too large by half. The article contains period illustrations, two maps, and 70 notes based on post-war histories and the Official Records.

150. Fitzgerald, Michael. "Another Kind of Glory: Black Participation and Its Consequences in the Campaign for Confederate Mobile." *Alabama Review*, 54, 4 (October 2001): 243-275.

The 1865 Union Army campaign for Mobile, Alabama, and the April 9 assault and capture of Fort Blakely on Mobile Bay, marked the last *major* infantry action of the Civil War. Foremost in the storming of Confederate-held Fort Blakely were several regiments of African-American troops. Indeed, Federal forces during the Mobile campaign contained the largest concentration of African-American soldiers in the western theater, approximately 5,500 effectives in nine infantry regiments in addition to supporting units. This carefully researched and well-documented study by historian Michael W. Fitzgerald provides an overview of the campaign, examines the part played by African-Americans in the Fort Blakely attack, addresses allegations that black soldiers murdered Confederate prisoners after the battle, and, most importantly, describes white racial perceptions as hostilities ended and the routine of occupation began.

The assault by African-American units on the best defended portion of Fort Blakely is presented as a straightforward, concise narrative. The question of prisoner slaughter, the assertion Confederate prisoners were murdered after surrendering by out-of-control black soldiers, is examined. After carefully weighting the available evidence, Fitzgerald concluded that atrocities attributed to black soldiers were exaggerated but that "the evidence does suggest that some of the soldiers were reluctant to take prisoners." However, according to the author, the true consequences of the battle occurred after victory was secure. While white Union soldiers admired war-time black bravery in combat, admiration for bravery did not transfer to acceptance or even tolerance in peacetime. The result of victory was the triumph of racial intolerance and animosity toward black soldiers and civilians, not only, as expected, by white Southerners, but also by white Union soldiers. Fitzgerald concluded "... that heroic service for the Union could accomplish only so much in challenging racial assumptions of white troops, and once peace returned the memories of the USCI's exploits faded." Concentrating on one local campaign and its aftermath, Fitzgerald presents an excellent, thoroughly documented study of the black military experience from battle to the racial pitfalls of peacetime America. The article contains 110 notes based on official reports, personal letters, memoirs, as well as numerous primary and secondary sources.

151.   Fleetwood, Christian A. "'... to Benefit My Race': A Black Medal of Honor Winner's Bitter Account of Army Treatment." *Civil War Times Illustrated*, 16, 4 (July 1977): 18-19.
In this letter written to his former employer shortly after the cessation of hostilities, Christian A. Fleetwood, Sergeant Major, 4th U.S. Colored Troops, bitterly condemns government policy regarding the granting of commissions to deserving black soldiers. Fleetwood was one of 13 African-American soldiers awarded the Medal of Honor for gallantry at the Battle of Chaffin's Farm, Virginia, in September 1864.

152.   Fleche, Andre. "'Shoulder to Shoulder as Comrades Tried:' Black and White Union Veterans and Civil War Memory." *Civil War History*, 51, 2 (2005): 175-201.
Fleche has written a fascinating and well-researched study challenging accepted historical perceptions that the post-war legacy of African-American veterans was "mostly negative." According to the author, many white members of the Grand Army of the Republic (GAR), the largest and most powerful of all Union Army veterans' organizations, defended in principle and in reality the concept of equality for black veterans. "Whatever the private racial prejudices of many white war veterans, the majority continued to join their African- American fellow-in-arms in honoring and celebrating . . . their shared experience of war." Many white Civil War veterans accepted the idea that wartime service resulted in a valid claim to the rights of citizenship, and many viewed African-Americans as

exemplary soldiers who deserved recognition for their service. Though all-white and all-black GAR posts existed, "integrated posts were more common than generally assumed." Segregation was not a GAR policy and for years the organization's leadership rejected demands for segregated posts in the South.

In addition, the GAR, through its newspaper, the *National Tribune,* which had a peak weekly circulation of 150,000, kept the memory of African-American Civil War service alive in an increasingly racist America with scores of articles laudatory in their praise of black soldiers. Indeed, the *National Tribune* "published more than forty articles during the first decades of the twentieth century portraying the service of the USCT in a positive light."

Based on his research, the author concludes that "black and white Union veterans formulated a joint vision of the war at odds with the more reconciliationist, segregationist, and racist trends found in postwar society as a whole."

153.   Fletcher, Marvin E. "The Negro Volunteer in Reconstruction, 1865-1866." *Military Affairs,* 32, 3 (1968): 124-131.

Most studies of the African-American military experience in the Civil War end abruptly with the cessation of hostilities. Often forgotten is the post-war service of African-Americans as occupation troops in the South. This article describes that duty and the increasingly bitter racial conflicts that arose between black soldiers and white civilians, as well as between black and white soldiers. Contrary to Southern assertions, according to Fletcher, black soldiers were initially used as occupation troops not to humiliate or embarrass the South, but simply because they were the only soldiers available in large numbers. Unlike their white counterparts, many black soldiers, because of their recruitment late in the war, still had another year of service remaining on their enlistment. Even as late as June 1866, over a year after the end of the war, 14,656 African-American soldiers still remained in the army, most performing garrison duty in the South. Fletcher argues that racial friction was inevitable since white Southerners wanted to keep freedmen in a servile relationship and "Southerners resented the fact their former slaves now had an important role in the army." The article contains 18 notes based on primary and secondary sources.

154.   Flint, Allen. "Black Responses to Colonel Shaw." *Phylon: The Atlanta University Journal of Race and Culture*, 45, 3 (3rd Quarter 1984): 210-219.

This is a literary review of four poems written by African-American poets concerning Colonel Robert Shaw and the celebrated 54th Massachusetts Volunteer Infantry. One of the poems is attributed to an anonymous soldier serving in the 54th.

155.   Foster, E. C. "Battle of Milliken's Bend." *Crisis,* 81, 9 (November 1974): 295-300.

A somewhat misleading title, since the June 7, 1863 battle at Milliken's Bend, Louisiana is only superficially described. Most of the article traces, in broad strokes, Federal efforts to recruit African-Americans as soldiers.

156.   Foster, Gaines M. "The Fort Pillow Massacre: An Essay Review." *Louisiana History*, 48, 2 (Spring 2007): 227-230.

This review essay compares two books dealing with the Fort Pillow massacre. The first, *Fort Pillow, a Civil War Massacre, and Public Memory* is by a noted scholar of the episode, John Cimprich; the second, *River Run Red: the Fort Pillow Massacre* is by journalist Andrew Ward. The reviewer maintains that Cimprich's book is "more focused" but that Ward's book, which is much longer, offers a "more vivid and dramatic account." Both writers extensively utilized contemporary records, though Ward also used more post-war documentation to support his claims. Both men agree that "Confederate troops massacred . . .many African American troops." They disagree, however, on the role played by Forrest. Ward persuasively argues that Forrest "played a central role" in what occurred, while Cimprich is more restrained and maintains there is no conclusive evidence pointing to Forrest's complicity in the massacre.

157.   Francis, Edward, Marshall Myers and Chris Propes, editor. "'I Don't Fear Nothing in the Shape of Man:' The Civil War and Texas Border Letters of Edward Francis, United States Colored Troops." *Register of the Kentucky Historical Society,* 101, 4 (Autumn 2003): 457-478.

This is a collection of 11 letters written by former Kentucky slave Edward Francis to his wife. Three letters from his wife are also reprinted. Edward Francis served in the 114th USCT from 1864 to 1866. The letters contain little if any mention of the regiment's Civil War experiences or of post-war duty in Texas.

158.   Frazier, Donald. "'The Battles of Texas will be fought in Louisiana': The Assault of Fort Butler, June 28, 1863." *Southwestern Historical Quarterly,* 104, 3 (January 2001): 332-362.

The June 27-28, 1864, Confederate assault on Fort Butler, located at the juncture of the Mississippi River and Bayou Lafourche, Louisiana, is noteworthy not only because it was such a decisive Confederate defeat but also because "there is ample evidence of black participants in the defense." Indeed, as Frazier points out, most "most Confederate reports indicate the presence of armed African American combatants." And "nearly all Confederate accounts of the battle corroborate the idea that blacks played an important role in the successful defense of Fort Butler." Nevertheless, absolutely no Union accounts - and there only a few - mention the presence of African-American soldiers in the fort. In addition, no after-action report was written since the commanding officer at Fort Butler, the officer responsible for writing the report, was murdered two days after the battle. Consequently, no official account was ever written or submitted to the War Department.

Still, the author is confident that armed blacks did participate in the battle. Several extenuating factors could explain why no mention was made of African-American troops as part of the defending garrison. The African-Americans in the fort could have been recruits waiting to be mustered into the Corps d'Afrique and thus had no official organizational status; or, as the author suggests, the presence of black troops in any garrison anywhere was no longer considered a novelty and subsequently was not commented upon. In the absence of any corroborating documentation, the truth will never be known. The article contains 64 notes; many of which are based on primary sources.

159.   Freeman, Elsie, Wynell Burroughs Schamel and Jean West. "The Fight for Equal Rights: A Recruiting Poster for Black Soldiers in the Civil War." *Social Education*, 56, 2 (February 1992): 118-120.

The Teaching with Documents section of this magazine includes a reprint of an 1863 recruiting poster addressed "To Colored Men!" A synopsis of the black Civil War military experience, possible teaching activities related to the recruiting poster, and suggestions for further research are presented.

160.   Freemon, Frank R. "The Health of the American Slave Examined by Means of Union Army Medical Statistics." *Journal of the National Medical Association*, 77, 1 (January 1985): 49-52.

In an effort to determine the health of pre-war slaves, Freemon, a medical doctor, examined the medical records of black and white Civil War soldiers. Analyzing data based on monthly regimental surgeon reports published years after the war, Freemon determine that black soldiers experienced a higher mortality rate from typhoid fever than white soldiers "but had a similar rate for smallpox, measles, and tuberculosis." African-Americans had higher incidences of measles, mumps, smallpox, pneumonia and an incredibly high mortality rate from malaria. The author attributes this much greater mortality to black garrisons stationed in the malaria wastelands throughout the South. No determination was reached regarding the health of pre-war slaves. The article contains notes and a statistical table.

161.   Friedrich, Otto. "We Will Not do Duty any Longer for Seven Dollars per Month." *American Heritage*, 39, 1 (February 1988): 64-73.

The issue of equal pay was one of many contentious issues facing African-American soldiers during the Civil War. Initially, the War

Department promised African-Americans who volunteered for military service the same pay as white soldiers. However, the Militia Act of July 1862, which authorized the employment of blacks as soldiers, stipulated that African-Americans would be paid $10.00 per month *minus* a clothing deduction of $3.00, considerably less than white soldiers who were paid $13.00 per month *plus* an additional clothing allotment of $3.50 per month. All black soldiers, regardless of rank - from private to sergeant major - would be paid the same. The decision to award lower pay to black soldiers was approved by the War Department's solicitor and supported by President Lincoln who viewed it as "a necessary condition to smooth the way to their employment . . . as soldiers." According to Sergeant Walker, of 3rd South Carolina Infantry (later 21st U.S. Colored Troops), a government promise regarding equal pay was a government promise broken and dishonored. As a result, in August 1863, he refused to "do duty any longer for seven dollars per month." Charged with mutinous conduct, Walker was tried, found guilty, and executed by firing squad at Jacksonville, Florida, on February 29, 1864. Three months after Walker's execution, Congress agreed to grant equal pay to black soldiers who were free men upon enlistment. One month before Lee's surrender, Congress awarded equal pay to all African-American soldiers retroactive to January 1, 1864, a full year after publication of the Emancipation Proclamation.

Friedrich's article, which contains several extracts from Walker's court-martial proceedings, also provides a useful overview regarding the fight for equal pay and the feeling of government betrayal it engendered among African-American soldiers.

162.   Frisby, Derek W. "Remember Fort Pillow." In *Black Flag over Dixie: Racial Atrocities and Reprisals in the Civil War*, edited by Gregory J. W. Urwin. Carbondale: Southern Illinois University Press, 2004, 104-131.

The investigation of the massacre at Fort Pillow by the congressional Joint Committee on the Conduct of the War is examined. The committee, dominated by Radical Republicans under the leadership Senator Benjamin F. Wade of Ohio, took advantage of the massacre to rally Northern public opinion in support of their goal of hard war. Hard war meant dehumanizing their Southern opponents and radically transforming the economic and social structure of Southern society. Politics not facts dominated the committee's collection of evidence, much of which was based on hearsay or third party accounts. While the truth was ugly enough – a massacre did occur – shaping the perception of the truth was, for the Radical Republicans, more important. Approximately 60,000 copies of the committee's report were rushed in to print much of which, according to the author, reads "like a literary composition."

163.   Fuller, James, editor. "The Letters of Louden S. Langley." *Vermont History*, 67, 3&4 (Summer/Fall 1999): 85-91.
Louden S. Langley was a free African-American from Vermont who enlisted in the 54th Massachusetts Infantry. This is a collection of four letters by Langley; only one was written during his wartime service and that was addressed to *The Weekly Anglo-African*, "the second most-read black newspaper in the Untied States." In this January 30, 1864 letter Langley bitterly condemns the Federal government for its discriminatory pay policy toward African-American soldiers. Langley ended his service as a Sergeant Major in the 33rd U. S. Colored Infantry.

164.   Gallagher, Gary W. "The Union Army brought Emancipation to Thousands." *Civil War Times*, 49, 5 (October 2010): 22-25.
The author argues that the Union Army was a "critical agent of change" in the process of emancipation by its historic enlistment of African-Americans as soldiers.

165.   "Gallantry in Action." *American Heritage*, 60, 2 (Summer 2010): Special Section PA 7.
This one-page article contains information about several African-Americans who won the Medal of Honor during the Civil War.

166.   Gallman, J. Mathew. "'In Your Hands that Musket Means
        Liberty.' African American Soldiers and the Battle of Olustee."
        In *Wars Within a War: Controversy and Conflict over the
        American Civil War*. Edited by Gary W. Gallagher and Joan
        Wright. Chapel Hill: North Carolina Press, 2009, 87-108.

Among the Union troops that fought at the battle of Olustee, Florida
on February 20, 1864, were three African-American regiments: the
54th Massachusetts, the 1st North Carolina (later re-designated the
35th USCT), and the 8th USCT. While all three regiments had much
in common they were in many ways dissimilar. They came late to
the war because of restrictive government policies; all three
provided needed manpower for a faltering Union recruiting effort;
all were black regiments commanded by white officers, and all three
experienced unequal treatment and rampant racial discrimination.
In addition, they faced execution or enslavement if captured by the
enemy. And, finally, all three represented a revolution in Northern
notions concerning the arming of black soldiers. But there the
similarities end.

The 54th Massachusetts was a veteran regiment that represented "the
best and brightest of the sons of northern black elites." Most enlisted
men were born free and were recruited in the North. As a fighting
regiment it had been bloodied before Fort Wagner and in
subsequent fighting in and around Charleston harbor. And almost
all of its replacements came from the New England states.

By contrast, the 1st North Carolina was newly recruited regiment
from eastern Virginia, North Carolina, and South Carolina. Its
enlisted men were freedman making the transition from slavery to
army service; as soldiers they were comparatively "green" having
seen only limited siege operations in and around Charleston.

The men of the 8th USCT were different. They had, in Civil War
parlance, "never seen the elephant," and Olustee would be their first
battle. They were recruited among the black working class of
Philadelphia and eastern Pennsylvania. They were free men who
knew that wages for African-American men in Philadelphia were

much higher than they could ever earn in the military. They were acutely aware of unequal pay in the army, the lack of a paid bonus for black volunteers, the refusal to commission African-American as officers, and the prejudice and discrimination that permeated the Union Army. Yet they eventually volunteered for service "despite all the good reasons not to." The question posed by Gallman is simply this: why did they enlist knowing what awaited them? To answer this question the author explores several possible explanations including patriotic editorials, the rousing rhetoric of black and white civic leaders, family pressure, appeals to manhood, and a desire to advance African-Americans to full citizenship. So the 8th USCT joined its brother regiments at Olustee. At Olustee they demonstrated they could be killed but had not yet learned how to kill. By the end of the war the 8th had learned its trade. It was listed as one of the Union Army's 300 fighting regiments.

167. _____. "Snapshots: Images of Men in the United States Colored Troops." *American Nineteenth Century History*, 13, 2 (June 2012): 127-151.

In this insightful essay, Professor Gallman addresses what he considers two intertwined but different cultural developments that emerged during the Civil War. The first was photographic technology and the second the revolutionary idea of recruiting and arming African-Americans as soldiers. Though unrelated, these two developments foretold a democratization process in American life, however incomplete. The author addresses both developments and their implications in considerable length. Photography, and in particular the ubiquitous 2½ by 3½ inches *cartes de viste,* made access to photographic portraiture both common and affordable. Printed and then glued to an index card, *cartes de viste* photographs allowed "African Americans of even fairly limited means … the opportunity" to have their portrait taken. During the war large numbers of black soldiers sat for their *cartes de viste.* "It is reasonable to conclude," Gallman asserts, "that a large percentage of Northern free black men who enlisted sat for a portrait." This was a crucial cultural change in the status of African-American men. Black soldiers posed for their photographs "dressed in their new uniforms, often carrying a weapon." The *cartes de viste* of African-

American soldiers went a "long way towards erasing evidence of a previous condition of servitude." That development coupled with the relationship of black soldiers to the Federal military "suggested wondrous possibilities." The article contains 53 notes, extensive references, and the *cartes de viste* of several black soldiers from the 108th USCT.

168. _____. "Thoughts on Private Booth." *Military Images,* 34, 1 (Winter 2016): 16.

According to the author, the article's photograph of Private Booth, 5th Massachusetts Cavalry, represents three powerful Civil War symbols. The first is that of a black man armed and now serving in the Union Army, the second is the democratization of portrait photography characterized by the ubiquitous *cartes de vistie,* and, thirdly, is the idea that mounted black soldiers "presented a marked challenge to the very core of white Southern manhood." Booth's *cartes de visite* speaks to the twin ideas of democracy and equality. For more 5th Massachusetts Cavalry *cartes de vistie,* see the entry by James Paradis entitled" Men of Nerve."

169. Galvin, John T. "The Hallowells: Fighting Quakers." *Proceedings of the Massachusetts Historical Society,* 75 (January – December 1963): 27-38.

Galvin's study is a biography of the two Hallowell brothers who served as commanding officers of the two black infantry regiments from Massachusetts – the 54th and 55th Massachusetts Volunteers Infantry. Often identified with the Brahmans of Boston, the Hallowells were "fighting Quakers" originally from Pennsylvania. The article contains 37 notes based on letters, primary and secondary sources, and newspaper accounts.

170. Gannon, Barbara A. "Sites of Memory: Sites of Glory: African-American Grand Army of the Republic Posts in Pennsylvania." In *Pennsylvania's Civil War,* edited by William Blair and William Pencak, University Park: The Pennsylvania State University Press, 2001, 165-302.

The Grand Army of the Republic (GAR) was a nationwide fraternal organization of Union veterans founded shortly after the war. In an era when all aspects of African-American life were under siege, the GAR stood as a rare beacon of white and black fraternity. "The GAR consciously maintained a race-blind admissions policy." The only qualification for membership was honorable Civil War service. While most GAR posts in Pennsylvania were either all-white or all-black-a few were integrated. Some activities between the races were shared, as for example joint Memorial Day celebrations, camp meetings, GAR reunions, and parades.

According to Gannon, all-black GAR posts preserved the memory of African-American service and sacrifice during the war. "Black Pennsylvanians consciously created African-American posts to thwart the efforts of those who would forget the black experience in the Civil War." They reminded the nation that the "black struggle for freedom constituted the central drama of the Civil War." The author also discusses the key role played by African-American women as auxiliaries to the black GAR posts.

171.   Garrison, Webb. "Striking Back: Corps d'Afrique, December 9, 1863." In *Mutiny in the Civil War*. Webb Garrison, Shippensburg, PA: White Mane Books, 2001, 75-83.

This article recounts the December 9, 1863, mutiny of the 4th Regiment, Corps d'Afrique at Fort Jackson, Louisiana.

172.   Gart, Jeanne Brooks. "Life after Glory: A Glimpse into Past Lives through Pension Records." *Journal of the Afro-American Historical and Genealogical Society*, 12, 1&2 (Spring/Summer 1991): 33-42.

Excerpts from the pension applications of several veterans of Company C, 54th Massachusetts Volunteer Infantry - and in many cases their post-war dependents - are presented without modification by the author, who is a certified genealogist. The pension applications, many of which are quite touching, illuminate the post-war travails of many black veterans.

173.   Gates, Henry Louis, Jr. "From Civil War to Civil Rights."
American Heritage, 60, 2 (Summer 2010): Special Section PA
12-PA 13.
The career of J. R. Clifford, the first black man admitted to the West
Virginia bar, newspaper publisher and editor, one of the co-
founders of the Niagara Movement, and civil rights crusader is
recalled. Clifford's service in Company F, 13th United States
Colored Heavy Artillery is also described.

174.   Gero, Anthony F. and Roger Sturcke. "33rd United States
Colored Troops, 1st Regiment South Carolina Volunteer
Infantry 1862-1866." *Military Collector & Historian*, 29, 3
(Fall 1977): 122-123.
A single black-and-white line drawing is used by the authors to
illustrate the uniforms worn by African-American soldiers serving
in the 1st Regiment South Carolina Volunteers (later 33rd U.S.
Colored Troops), 1862-1865. The article includes a brief descriptive
text supplemented by several notes.

175.   Gero, Anthony, Roger Sturcke and Barry E. Thompson.
"Independent Battery, United States Colored Light Artillery
(Douglas's Battery), 1864-1865." *Military Collector &
Historian*, 35, 2 (Summer 1983): 81-82.
This article contains a single black-and-white plate that illustrates
the uniforms worn by Douglas's battery in the closing days of the
Civil War, the only black unit in Federal service in which all the
officers were African-Americans. Included is a short discussion of
an unidentified photograph of a black light artillery battery found in
the archives of the Kansas Historical Society. After review, the
authors determined the photograph is actually that of Douglas's
light battery.
NOTE:
The illustration of Page 82 is misidentified. The correct caption
for the illustration is found on Page 80, Plate 542.

176.	Gero, Anthony. "Description of the Drum Corps, 7ᵗʰ United States Colored Troops, 25ᵗʰ Army Corps, March 1865." *Military Collector & Historian*, 55, 1 (Spring 2003): 26.
This is a description, not an illustration, of the uniform worn by the drum corps of the 7ᵗʰ United States Colored Troops. Included in the article is an excerpt from an unidentified African-American publication describing the uniform and an announcement that the actual uniform illustration will appear in a subsequent issue.

177.	_____. "Musicians and Drummers, African-American Volunteers, 1863-1867." *Military Collector & Historian*, 55, 4 (Winter 2003/2004): 252-253.
Containing a short descriptive text and ten notes, this article illustrates in a single plate various uniforms worn by African-American musicians and drummers in a number of black military units during the period 1863-1867.

178.	Giambrone, Jeff T. "Defense of the Mississippi Valley." *North & South* 7, 6 (October 2004): 50-65.
Giambrone's excellent study examines overall Union efforts to defend the Mississippi Valley after the fall and occupation of Vicksburg in July 1863. Not only was Union – held Vicksburg, Mississippi to be garrisoned and fortified for defense, but it was also intended to serve as a staging area for offensive attacks into the enemy-held interior of the state. Initially, most of the garrison soldiers were white; however, the Union command "came to rely more and more on colored solders." By August 1864, out of a garrison of 6,600 Union troops present for duty, only 1,900 were white. Most of this study does not directly concern African-American soldiers, but it does contain a brief description of the 3ʳᵈ U.S. Colored Calvary action in late November 1864 at Canton, Mississippi. The article contains a number of period photographs, several maps, and 78 notes.

179.   Gibbs, C. R. "Blacks in the Union Navy." *Negro History Bulletin*, 36, 6 (October 1973): 137-139.

The author has written an interesting three-page summary of African-American service in the navy before but mostly during the Civil War. Included in the article is an account of four war-time black sailors who were awarded the Medal of Honor.

180.   Giesberg, Judith. "Jacob Plowden." *The Civil War Monitor*, 4, 3 (Fall 2014): 26-27, 70, and 71.

The execution of six black soldiers of Company E, 3rd United States Colored Troops for mutiny at Fort Clinch, Amelia Island, Florida on December 1, 1865 is described. The mutiny, led by Private Jacob Plowden, occurred in October, at Jacksonville. A protest against the physical punishment of a fellow soldier had escalated into a violent encounter with several of the regiment's white officers. As a result, the soldiers involved were subsequently arrested, tried for mutiny under the provisions of Article 7 of the Articles of War, and condemned to death by firing squad. The execution was carried out by 36 members of the 34th USCT. Ironically, at the time of the mutiny, the regiment had only a few days to serve before mustering out.

181.   Gill, Samuel T. "The Pain of Pyrrhic Victory." *Civil War Times Illustrated*, 23, 3 (May 1984): 8-15, 42-43.

This article presents an hour by hour, regiment by regiment, account of the Battle of Jenkins' Ferry, Arkansas, fought on April 30, 1864. Jenkins' Ferry was the last battle in the abortive Federal campaign in Arkansas, a campaign launched in support of the equally unsuccessful Union Red River offensive in Louisiana. Among the Federal regiments participating in the battle was the 2nd Kansas Colored Infantry (later re-designated the 83rd U.S. Colored Infantry). The 2nd Kansas was a newly recruited "green" regiment soldiering under the threat of the "black flag," the unofficial Trans-Mississippi Confederate policy that no African-American soldiers would be taken as prisoners. Only days before at Poison Springs, the 1st Kansas Colored had suffered grievously under the black flag of Confederate retribution. When doubts concerning the 2nd were raised, its colonel flatly declared "I can take that regiment where any live regiment will go." The 2nd fought well and captured several Confederate guns at bayonet point. "Three Confederate prisoners were murdered, in revenge for Poison Springs." The article contains period photographs and two maps.

182.   Gladstone, William. "Private Lewis Martin and His Brief War." *Prologue*, 35, 2 (Summer 2003): 44-49.
The Civil War for Private Lewis Martin, 29th U.S. Colored Troops, consisted of "seeing the elephant" on a hot summer day in July 1864. Martin, who was probably a runaway Arkansas slave, enlisted in Illinois on February 9, 1864; five months later at Petersburg, in his one and only battle, Martin, lost his right arm and part of his left leg in the Battle of the Crater. The 29th U.S. Colored Troops "went into action with 450 soldiers and left the battlefield with 128 soldiers." Martin's military service and subsequent disability applications, as well as a general account of African-American regiments at Petersburg, are described by Gladstone. The article is based principally on Martin's Compiled Military Service Record and pension applications, and contains reproductions of his certificate of disability, disability photograph, regimental muster information, and hospital records and invalid pension declaration. Martin's personal story is that of a black soldier's brief but terrible Civil War.

183.   Glass, Hermina. "Men of Color to Arms." *Atlanta*, 54, 3 (July 2014): 74-75.
A succinct but touching narrative focusing on the brutality of slavery and the part it played in the enlistment of black soldiers in the Union Army.

184.   Glatthaar, Joseph T. "'Glory,' the 54th Massachusetts Infantry and Black Soldiers in the Civil War." *History Teacher*, 24. 4 (August 1991): 475-485.
Joseph T. Glatthaar, author of *Forged in Battle: The Civil War Alliance of Black Soldiers and White Officers*, comments in this article on the movie "Glory." He points out what is accurate in the movie and what is not, and by doing so provides a good capsule

history of the 54th Massachusetts and the difficulties black soldiers faced. Despite several shortcomings, Glatthaar found the movie "depicts many of the personal experiences of service in the United States Colored Troops extremely well."

185. _____. "Black Glory: The African-American Role in Union Victory." *In Why the Confederacy Lost*, edited by Gabor S. Boritt. New York: Oxford University Press, 1992, 133-162.

"Blacks were at the very heart of the Civil War" and the enlistment of black soldiers, writes Joseph T Glatthaar "made the difference between a Union victory and stalemate or defeat." As the number of white volunteers sharply declined, African-Americans became the largest untapped reservoir of Union military manpower. How that manpower was acquired, how it was used, and how it helped guarantee Union victory is explored. The essay also notes the profound influence African-American civilians had on the war as teamsters, laborers, and cooks for the Union Army, or as unwilling slaves on Southern plantations.

186. _____. "The Civil War through the Eyes of a Sixteen-Year-Old Black Officer: The Letters of Lieutenant John H. Crowder of the 1st Louisiana Native Guards." *Louisiana History*, 35, 2 (Spring 1994): 201-216.

Letters from African-American Civil War soldiers are rare; rarer still are letters from a black officer. This article reprints a collection of 11 letters written by Lieutenant John H. Crowder, Company K, 1st Louisiana Native Guards, mainly to his mother. The letters, dated between late 1862 and May 1863, deal mainly with personal problems, including untrue but injurious rumors, plans for the future, pay and financial pressures, friction with fellow black officers, and administrative pressure to resign his commission because of race. Sixteen-year old Crowder, who lied about his age to obtain his commission, was quite emphatic about resigning: "I do not intend to resign, nor will I resign…as long as there is a button to hold to I will hold to it." Crowder was killed on May 27, 1863, during the assault on Port Hudson. His mother used his collected letters in her application for a dependent pension from the Federal government. The pension, in the amount of $100. per year, was awarded in 1874. The article includes 11 notes including a number of pension affidavits.

187.   Gold, David. "Frustrated Glory: John Francis Appleton and Black Soldiers in the Civil War." *Maine Historical Society Quarterly,* 31, 2 (Summer 1991): 174-204.
John Francis Appleton was born into an anti-slavery Unitarian family in Bangor, Maine, in 1838. His father was a socially prominent member of society and a justice of the Maine Supreme Court. He was destined to follow his father in the legal profession, but war and a "love of the Union and a hatred of slavery intervened." Commissioned as a captain in Company H, 12th Maine Volunteers, he fought bravely at Port Hudson, Louisiana. Commissioned as a colonel in the 9th Regiment Corps d'Afrique and assigned the added responsibilities as brigade commander, Appleton vainly lobbied for a combat assignment for his soldiers. Unfortunately, his service was representative of the experience of many white officers serving in black regiments. The potential for military glory was replaced by the tedium of garrison duty and rear area service as a noncombatant labor force. Frustrated with army authorities, denied a chance to demonstrate the military abilities of his brigade, and broken in health, he resigned his commission on July 29, 1864. The article contains 47 notes, many based on Appleton's personal correspondence.

188.   Gourdin, John R. "Name Changing Since the Civil War: A Case Study of Three USCT Regiments from South Carolina." *Journal of the African-American Historical and Genealogical Society,* 21, 1 (Silver Anniversary Edition, 2002): 49-56.
An interesting study by an African-American genealogist of name-changing patterns of black veterans after the Civil War. The author examined approximately 400 pension application records of the 103rd, 104th, and 128th United States Colored Infantry regiments. All three regiments consisted of former slaves; all three were recruited in the Charleston, South Carolina, area. According to the author in later years one-third of the veterans changed their names when applying for a pension. Gourdin maintains a small number of name

changes can be attributed to earlier administrative errors; others can be attributed to slaves giving fictitious names upon enlistment. However, after careful analysis, the author concluded " . . . the most prevalent pattern of name changes is that when slaves escaped the plantation to enlist in the army, they took or were given the surnames of their most recent former owners and after the war, they took the surnames of their fathers."

189.   Grant, Susan-Mary. "Pride and Prejudice in the American Civil War." *History Today*, 48, 9 (September 1998): 41-48.

The author examines the experiences of African-American soldiers during the war and reviews efforts to spur black enlistments by Benjamin Butler, Jim Lane of Kansas, and Major General David Hunter in South Carolina. The difficulties black troops encountered are summarized including poor equipment, excessive fatigue duty, ineffective medical attention, and unequal pay. Combat operations are also addressed in limited form. However, when the Civil War was over, Grant maintains, black military participation in the conflict was deliberately forgotten. Indeed, during the era of Jim Crow, the American public purposely "chose to ignore the sacrifice of black regiments" and effectively erased their contributions from the national memory.

190.   _____. "Fighting for Freedom: African-American Soldiers in the Civil War." In *The American Civil War: Explorations and Considerations,* edited by Susan-Mary Grant and Brian Holden Reid. Harlow, England: Pearson Education Limited, 2000, 191-213.

Grant surveys the early and clumsy efforts to recruit African-Americans as soldiers and describes the deliberately prejudicial policies faced by black troops. Issues such as inferior equipment, abysmal medical services, excessive fatigues duties, and discriminatory government policies regarding bonus payments and unequal pay are addressed. The author points out that blacks expected full racial equality when Union victory was secured; white America never accepted such a notion. As a result, in the era of sectional reconciliation, the sacrifice of African-Americans soldiers was all but forgotten.

191.   Grear, Charles D. "The One-and-a-Half Million Dollar Raid." *North & South*, 11, 6 (December 2009): 24-31.
The bulk of this article describes the Confederate victory at Second Cabin Creek in September 1864. However, prior to Cabin Creek, a detachment of Kansas troops collecting prairie hay was overwhelmed and routed at their camp at Flat Rock, Indian Territory on September 16, 1864. The Union Army detachment consisted of men from the 1st Kansas Colored and 2nd Kansas Cavalry. When the camp was stormed after hours of fighting, Confederate soldiers killed "all the colored soldiers they could find." According to the author, only four black soldiers escaped. A Texas cavalryman remarked that "The water was red with the blood of the dead negroes." The article is illustrated with a map and 50 notes.

192.   Grimsley, Mark. "Race in the Civil War." *North & South*, 4, 3 (March 2001): 36-46, 52-55.
In this well-written and provocative article, the author describes Civil War racial attitudes of white society to marginalized people of color – both black and red Americans. The all-encompassing racism practiced by white society, the author concludes, was either "hard" or "soft" in its application. The soft version saw African-Americans as a docile people content in their lowly status in society; the hard version "viewed the negro as inherently depraved and savage if removed from white control." As a consequence, for white Southerners the arming of black men was seen as an invitation to slave insurrection and race warfare. Lincoln, however, realized that slavery was the root cause of the rebellion and that Africans-Americans represented an untapped pool of military strength. For Lincoln, the recruitment of black soldiers served a dual purpose: it added to Union military strength while at the same time it attacked the institution of slavery. In addition, as far as the hard version of race relations was concerned, it "was a way of harnessing the potential for violence and placing it under military control."

The author maintains that the killing of black prisoners by Confederate soldiers was largely spontaneous; however, no direct order was required to induce a massacre of captured African-American soldiers. Armed black men were considered by most Confederate soldiers to be in servile insurrection and a potent threat to the social structure of the white South. Conversely, the murder of Confederate prisoners by black soldiers seems to have been limited in scope and, when it occurred, of short duration.

The article also addressees the participation of 20,000 Native Americans who fought in the Civil War some for the Confederacy and some for the Union. As a group they were viewed as savages and not fit for white society. Unlike black Americans, they were worse off after the war than before.

Overall, this is a thoughtful analysis filled with valuable insights regarding the racial attitudes of Civil War American society, black military recruitment and service, and shifting government policy regarding the black and red man by both North and South. The article includes a number of illustrations and 37 notes.

193.   Grzyb, Frank L. "The Black Soldiers of the 14th Rhode Island Heavy Artillery Toiled for the Cause of Freedom." *America's Civil War*, 14, 1 (March 2001): 16-19.

During the Civil War most African-American regiments were raised under the direct supervision of Federal authorities. A mere handful were organized by state governments and given state designations that they retained throughout their military service, as for example the 54th and 55th Massachusetts and the 29th Connecticut Infantry. Most black regiments raised by state governments were taken into Federal service and given new unit designations. Such was the case of the 14th Rhode Island Heavy Artillery (ultimately re-designated the 11th U.S. Colored Heavy Artillery), the subject of this matter-of-fact regimental history. Though raised in Rhode Island in August 1863, most of its men were recruited from New York, New Jersey, and Connecticut, and as far away as Canada; only one company was composed of Rhode Islanders. The author maintains that the 14th mirrored the experience of most African-American army units: an experience dominated by excessive work details, little chance for combat, rear area boredom, and the drudgery of garrison life in the

Union occupied South, often in inhospitable climates with little or no relief from the daily tedium. As with most African-American units, the 14th suffered an appallingly high mortality rate. During its service in the Department of the Gulf - mainly in southern Louisiana - the 14th lost three men captured by Confederate forces (and subsequently murdered), and approximately 300 hundred men to disease and illness.

The 14th Rhode Island served as did most African-American regiments during the Civil War: without glory or fanfare, but faithfully and with honor.

194.   Haller, John Seymour. "Civil War Anthropometry: The Making of a Racial Ideology." *Civil War History*, 16, 4 (1970): 309-324.
During the Civil War the United States Sanitary Commission, a semi-official civilian organization, and the War Department's Provost Marshal General's Bureau, conducted extensive physical measurements of black and white soldiers. Data collected compared the physical dimensions of white and black soldiers. The collected anthropometric measurements, buttressed by post-war autopsies and medical studies, became the main support for scientific theories of black physical and mental inferiority. Indeed, "institutionalized attitudes of racial inferiority focused upon the war anthropometry as the basis for their belief." Ironically, "the war which freed the slave also helped to justify racial attitudes of nineteenth century society."

195.   Hamlin, Cyrus. "Father Knows Best." *Civil War Times Illustrated*, 37, 1 (March 1998): 22, 65-67.
This is a collection of four letters sent by Cyrus Hamlin, Colonel, 8th Corps d'Afrique (later 80th U.S. Colored Troops) to his father, Hannibal Hamlin, Lincoln's first term vice-president. Hamlin's letters, three of which originated in Louisiana, discuss officer promotion, the recruitment and organization of African-American regiments, and the pride he felt in the performance of black soldiers.

196.   Hammond, Thomas M. "William H. Carney's Grit at Fort
   Wagner Earned Him the Distinction of Being the First Black
   Soldier to Receive the Medal of Honor." *America's Civil War*,
   20, 1 (March 2007): 69-70.
William H. Carney was the first African-American to earn the
Medal of Honor. During the abortive July 18, 1863 Union assault
on Fort Wagner, Carney, though wounded four times, saved the
National colors. "Boys, the old flag never touched the ground" he
reportedly exclaimed after returning to Union lines. Carney's medal
was awarded on May 23, 1900, 37 years after the assault.
Nevertheless, he is considered the first black soldier to win the
award since his actions preceded those of other African-American
Medal of Honor recipients. The article also describes Carney's post-
war career.

197.   Hancock, Marvin J. "The Second Battle of Cabin Creek,
   1864." *The Chronicles of Oklahoma*, 39, 4 (Winter 1961): 414-
   426.
Fought in Indian Territory on September 19, 1864, the Confederate
victory at Second Cabin Creek is of limited interest only because
two African-American regiments – the 1st Kansas Colored and the
79th USCT – took part in the intial skirmishing and later follow-up.
Union reports written after the battle stated that the 1st Kansas
Colored suffered "indiscriminate slaughtering . . . by the Texans."

198.   Hannon, Helen. "African Americans in the Navy during the
   Civil War: Interview with Steven J. Ramold and William B.
   Gould IV." *Journal of African American History,* 89, 4 (Fall
   2004): 358-361.
Book-length historical studies of black Civil War sailors are few in
number. Two of the best are Steven J. Ramold's *Slaves, Sailors,
Citizens: African Americans in the Union Navy* and *Diary of a
Contraband: The Civil War Passage of a Black Sailor* by William
B. Gould, IV. This article consists of an interview with both authors
regarding their research and conclusions. Interestingly, both men
were impressed by the surprising difference in experience between
African-American sailors as opposed to African-American soldiers.
As Gould points, out black "... sailors were not segregated, they did

not receive differing rates of pay, they all lived in the same quarters" as white sailors. Ramold concluded that the Federal Navy "as a 19th century institution was notable because there wasn't anything in its official polices that was racist."

199.   Hansen, Chadwick. "The 54th Massachusetts Volunteer Black Infantry as a Subject for American Artists." *Massachusetts Review*, 16, 4 (Autumn 1975): 745-759.

The 54th Massachusetts Volunteers, the Shaw memorial on Boston Commons, and musical compositions and poetry inspired by both the regiment and Augustus-Saint-Gaudens' famous bas-relief sculpture are discussed.

200.   Hardwick, Kevin T. "'Your Old Father Abe Lincoln is Dead and Damned:' Black Soldiers and the Memphis Race Riot of 1866." *Journal of Social History*, 27, 1 (Autumn 1993): 109-128.

The race riots that exploded in Memphis, Tennessee, in the early days of May 1866 are described in this carefully researched and comprehensive account. Spearheaded by the city's predominately Irish police force, 46 African-Americans were killed, scores injured, several black women raped, black schools were destroyed, and 91 black houses burnt to the ground. The riot began the day after the last black regiment in Memphis was mustered out of Federal service. It lasted for several days before martial law was finally declared. Former black soldiers and their families were initially targeted by the white mob.

During the war Memphis became a destination for runaway slaves and a center for the recruitment of black soldiers. A number of black regiments garrisoned in the city during and after the war and many of their dependents lived in nearby encampments. Black soldiers were prominent in the Memphis African-American community and the uniform they wore carried the prestige and authority, as well as the protection, of the Union Army. Black soldiers, and particularly black noncommissioned officers, were leaders in the community and, together with Memphis freedmen, "challenged the traditional norms of black behavior and demeanor." They demanded equal rights and refused to accept the antebellum status quo and, as soldiers, they were armed and trained. These demands were regarded by white Southerners as both an economic threat and a danger to the established social order. Simmering racial conflict in the weeks before the riot resulted in numerous clashes between the police and black soldiers. However, when mustering out black soldiers lost the protection of the uniform and they "became vulnerable to white repression." With no armed black troops remaining in the city, white mobs began attacking African-American individuals and institutions. The outcome was preordained: white Southern society had violently reasserted its social control over the black population of post-emancipation Memphis. This highly recommended and well-written article contains 49 notes many of which are based on primary source material.

201.   Heller, Charles E. "Between Two Fires: The 54th Massachusetts." *Civil War Times Illustrated,* 11, 1 (April 1972): 32-41.

Though a popular treatment, this is still an excellent account of the 54th Massachusetts Infantry in capsule form. The history of the regiment is traced from its organization, through its battles on James and Morris Island, through Olustee, and finally concluding with Potter's Raid in the waning days of the war. Issues of pay disparity and racial prejudice are also addressed. Interestingly, when the 54th paraded through Boston before embarking for the Charleston area, "over one hundred policemen waited in hiding along the parade route in case of violence." The article contains a reprint of a September 28, 1863 letter from Corporal James Henry Gooding of the 54th Massachusetts to President Lincoln protesting unequal pay. Gooding perished while a Confederate prisoner at Andersonville.

202.   _____. "George Luther Stearns." *Civil War Times Illustrated,* 13, 4 (July 1974): 20-28.

George Luther Stearns was a wealthy Massachusetts industrialist, friend of John Brown, committed abolitionist, and, as a recruiter, instrumental in the successful enlistment and formation of the 54th and 55th Massachusetts Volunteer Infantry. He was appointed by

Secretary of War Edwin M. Stanton as "Assistant Adjutant General with the rank of major." Major Stearns successfully organized black regiments in Philadelphia and Nashville. In Nashville, in just three months, he recruited six regiments of African-Americans. Dedicated to civil rights, he campaigned tirelessly for equal pay, black enlistment bonuses, and fair treatment of black soldiers. Following the war, he used his influence and wealth to crusade for equal rights and African-American suffrage. This useful biography of Stearns before, during, and after the war contains several period drawings and photographs.

203. Henig, Gerald S. "The Unstoppable Mr. Smalls." *America's Civil War*, 20, 1 (March 2007): 40-49.
This is an excellent biography of the incredible, and unstoppable, Robert Smalls. Born a slave in 1839, he eventually became a "wheelman" on a Confederate ship in Charleston harbor. The term wheelman was "another name for pilot – a title not permitted to Smalls because he was black." Smalls escaped captivity with his family on the Confederate ship *Planter*. His subsequent service as a Union pilot, his participation of a number of naval engagements, and his later political career is described. The article contains a number of photographs, drawings, and a map of Charleston Harbor.

204. _____. "William Tillman: The Union's First Black Hero." *North & South*, 10, 2 (July 2007): 80-85.
Historically, privateers were privately owned vessels authorized by a government to seize enemy ships during wartime. The captured vessel would be brought to a friendly port and the vessel, along with its contents, sold for profit. In the early months of the Civil War the Confederate government, in the absence of a credible naval force, issued letters of marque permitting privateering and unwittingly provided the North with its first black hero. On Sunday, July 7, 1861 the schooner *S. J. Waring,* sailing out of New York, was seized by the Confederate armed privateer *Jefferson Davis*. A prize crew was put aboard and the *S. J. Waring* set course for Charleston. Among the crewmen on the *S. J. Waring* was William Tillman, a free black originally from Delaware but a resident of Rhode Island. He was told by his captors, free or not, he would be sold into slavery along

with the ship and its cargo. Working basically alone, Tillman killed three of the prize crew and seized control of the vessel and on Sunday, July 21 arrived back at New York. Overnight Tillman "was lionized as a great hero" and his bravery applauded throughout the Union. Ultimately, and with much difficulty, he was awarded a cash prize by the ship's underwriters. He then disappeared from history. Well documented, this is a vivid account of a forgotten chapter in Civil War naval history.

205. _____. "The First Black Battlefield Reporter." *Civil War Times*, 46, 10 (January 2008): 40-45.

Thomas Morris Chester was not an African-American soldier, but he was a correspondent for the *Philadelphia Press* and the first black battlefield reporter. Most of his dispatches were concerned with the Petersburg campaign and black and white soldiers of the Army of the James. Several full-color illustrations are included in this thumbnail biography.

206. Hewitt, Lawrence Lee. "An Ironic Route to Glory: Louisiana's Native Guards at Port Hudson." In *Black Soldiers in Blue: African American Troops in the Civil War Era*, edited by John David Smith. Chapel Hill: University of North Carolina Press, 2002, 78-106.

On May 27, 1863, almost two months before the more celebrated assault on Fort Wagner by the 54th Massachusetts, two regiments of black soldiers took part in the Union attack on Port Hudson, Louisiana. This definitive combat study describes the role of the African-American 1st and 3rd Louisiana Native Guards, as well as white units, in the attack. Though both regiments were unable to storm the Confederate entrenchments, their assault "almost singularly convinced Northern whites to accept the enlistment" of black soldiers. The study contains several period drawings, a map of the May 27 attack, and 40 notes.

207.   Hicken, Victor. "The Record of Illinois' Negro Soldiers in the Civil War." *Journal of the Illinois State Historical Society Journal,* 56, 3 (Autumn 1963): 529-551.
During the Civil War the state of Illinois officially provided 1,811 African-American soldiers to the Union Army, though many light-skinned African-Americans probably "had volunteered and served as soldiers in white regiments from the first days of the war." By far the largest single contingent of black soldiers from Illinois served in the 29th U.S. Colored Infantry, a regiment that proved difficult to organize. Obstacles to recruiting included a thriving labor market, a market in which black laborers were paid considerably more than they would receive as ordinary soldiers, low enlistment bounties, racial discrimination, "and the outright antipathy of many people of Illinois." Nevertheless, the regiment was organized company by company and officially mustered into Federal service at Washington, DC on April 24, 1864. As a regiment it saw hard service during the Petersburg campaign, particularly at the ill-fated Battle of the Crater. After the war, it performed garrison duty on the Texas-Mexican border at Brownsville until mustered out in November 1865. Regimental losses during the war "totaled about 158, most of which came in the Petersburg affair." This more than adequate regimental history is documented with 38 notes based on official records and documents, personal reminiscences, newspaper accounts, and secondary sources.

208.   Hill, Steven W. "Effects of Canister Shot in the Civil War: Skull of a Soldier of the 54th Massachusetts Volunteers." *Military Medicine*, 179, 10 (October 2014): 1172-1172.
The skull of a soldier from the 54th Massachusetts Infantry, found on Morris Island in 1876, is illustrated. The wound was caused by a single iron canister ball fired from a Confederate 12-lb field howitzer. The skull was on display during an exhibit of Civil War medicine at the National Museum of Health and Medicine.

209.   Hirneisen, Laura. "Peace, Union, Glory: Berks County
   African Americans in the Civil War." *Historical Society of
   Berks County,* www.berkshistory.org/articles.
The military service of several Berks County, Pennsylvania
African-Americans are profiled.

210.   Hoar, Jay S. "Black Glory: Our Afro-American Civil War
   Old Soldiery." *Gettysburg Magazine,* 2 (January 1, 1990): 123-
   155.
Biographies of the last surviving African-Americans veterans of the
Civil War are related in abbreviated form. Most served in the United
States Colored Troops though a few were body servants to
Confederate officers.

211.   Hollandsworth, James G. "The Execution of White Officers
   from Black Units by Confederate Forces during the Civil War."
   Louisiana History, 35, 5 (Fall 1994): 475-489.
On May 1, 1863, the Confederate Congress passed a resolution
stipulating that white officers in African-American regiments "who
commanded, armed, trained, organized, or prepared black men for
military service" were guilty of instigating servile insurrection and,
if captured, could be executed or "otherwise punished." The author,
in this exceptionally well-researched and meticulous study,
attempted to discover how real was the threat of execution and,
more importantly, how many white officers, after capture, were
executed. He concluded that the number of white officers officially
executed was not great, partly because of the threat of Federal
retaliation. There was, however, "another way in which the spirit of
the decree could be followed without fear of retaliation.
Confederate troops could avoid taking prisoners in the first place."
As a result, at the battles of Milliken's Bend, Poison Springs, Fort
Pillow, and the Crater "white officers were less likely to survive
than the black troops they commanded." Hollandsworth concluded
that the Confederate government did not carry out its threats of
execution nor was the policy ever officially sanctioned; evidence
suggests, however, that some Confederate soldiers carried out the

spirit if not the letter of the law by shooting white officers "trying to escape." The article contains two tables and 21 notes.

212.   Hoptak, John David. "A Forgotten Hero of the Civil War."
        Pennsylvania Heritage, 36, 2 (Spring 2010): 6-13.
Nick Biddle was not a soldier but he may well have been the first casualty of the Civil War. Delaware-born Biddle was a runaway slave who settled in Pennsylvania. Though not an enlisted soldier, he served since 1840 as an orderly in the Washington Artillery, a local Pottstown, Pennsylvania militia organization. Dressed in his uniform, Biddle accompanied the Washington Artillery when it was rushed to the defense of Washington in the opening days of the war. During transit through Baltimore the Pennsylvanians were attacked by a Secessionist mob and Biddle was severely injured when struck on the head with a brick. "It was the sight of Biddle in uniform that especially infuriated the mob." Now almost forgotten by history, Nick Biddle may have shed the first blood in the Civil War. The article is heavily illustrated and contains a *carte de visite* of Biddle in his uniform.

213.   Holzer, Harold. "A Spirit and Power Far Beyond its Letter."
        American Heritage, 60, 2 (Summer 2010): Special Section PA 8-PA 9.
Lincoln's Emancipation Proclamation and its effects upon the nation, as well as on Frederick Douglass, is discussed. According to Douglass, the Emancipation Proclamation placed "the North on the side of justice and civilization."

214.   _____. "'Ethiopia' on Broadway." *Civil War Times*, 52, 5 (October 2013): 44-49.
Eight months after the infamous New York Draft Riot, a riot that saw the brutalization and murder of countless African-Americans, residents of the city turned out to celebrate the send-off of the first black regiment recruited in the state. Holzer has provided a fascinating account of that day in March 1864 when over 100,000 New Yorkers assembled in the city's Union Square to observe the occasion. The regiment's organization was largely the result of efforts by the city's well-connected and prominent Union League

Republicans and their wives. The idea for the regiment was opposed by the state's Democratic governor who was fearful of alienating the state's Irish-American voters. Nevertheless, well-to-do Republicans championed the regiment's organization to partially atone for the awful events of July 1863. At the conclusion of the parade and departure ceremonies, the regiment boarded the streamer *Ericsson* for garrison duty in Louisiana.

215. Horton, James Oliver. "In the Defense of the Republic: From Camp William Penn to the Grand Review." *American Heritage*, 60, 2 (Summer 2010): Special Section PA 4 to PA 6.
This article recounts the review of African-American soldiers held in Harrisburg, Pennsylvania in November 1865. This review was in response to the earlier Grand Review held in Washington shortly after the close of the war. Over 200,000 white Union troops participated in the Washington review; black soldiers were excluded from participation. The article also highlights the experience of African-American soldiers in the war. Contrary to the author's assertion, there is no definitive evidence that Nathan Bedford Forrest "ordered his soldiers to kill captured blacks" at Fort Pillow.

216. Howard, Victor B. "The Civil War in Kentucky: The Slave Claims His Freedom." *Journal of Negro History*, 67, 3 (Autumn 1982): 246-256.
While most of this study deals with the demise of slavery in Kentucky, the role of the Union Army in not overlooked. For African-Americans, the army played a pivotal role for "the enlisted slave became a free man, a circumstance which in itself weakened the institution of slavery in Kentucky." When black soldiers enlisted they were usually accompanied by their families. In fact, the greatest obstacle in recruiting blacks for military service, according to the author, was concern for the safety of their families, particularly at the hands of vengeful slave masters. One Union Army officer noted that if you "attend to their wifes and families they will immediately rush to arms." As a consequence, numerous African-American dependents flooded into the military training camps for protection and security. Unfortunately, at Camp Nelson,

in November 1864, black military dependents were expelled from the camp and "forced to wander along the highways and through the wood in a destitute condition on the coldest night of the season." The Camp Nelson tragedy resulted in a Federal law granting freedom to the dependents of African-American soldiers. One Union general estimated that "on an average five dependents were freed each time a black soldier enlisted in Kentucky." Howard's study is extensively documented with primary source materials.

217.   Howland, Chris. "Foiled at Fort Wagner." *America's Civil War*, 26, 5 (November 2013): 58-61.

Written for a broad audience, Howland provides a basic description of the Confederate defenses of Fort Wagner and the unsuccessful July 18, 1863, Union attack. Particularly useful are two maps: one provides an overview of the Charleston campaign; the other is a detailed map of the unsuccessful Union assault on Fort Wagner.

218.   _____ "Massacre at Baxter Springs." *America's Civil War,* 28, 4 (September 2015): 42-45.

The Confederate victory at Baxter Spring, Kansas on October 6, 1863 is described. During the battle Missouri bushwhackers under the command of William Clark Quantrill massacred a number of Union soldiers. Union soldiers garrisoned in a nearby fortification, including Company A, 2nd Kansas Colored Infantry, survived the massacre. Confederate casualties were insignificant. The article is accompanied by two superb full-color maps. The first details the July to October 1863 border war and the second presents a graphic depiction of the engagement at Baxter Springs.

219.   Hubbell, John T. "Abraham Lincoln and the Recruitment of Black Soldiers." *Journal of the Abraham Lincoln Association,* 2, 1 (1980): 6-21.

Lincoln's policies regarding emancipation and the employment of African-Americans as soldiers are traced in this article. Initially Lincoln believed that emancipation and black enlistment would cost the administration the support of the border states; however, neither the country nor the president anticipated the war's enormous cost in manpower and treasure. Cruel circumstances dictated that a policy change was necessary; the conflict could no longer be considered strictly a "white man's war." Ever sensitive to shifting political winds, "Lincoln did not openly lead the movement toward the enlistment of blacks." Nevertheless, he did conclude, if the war was to be won, emancipation and the arming of African-Americans was "an indispensable necessity." The key for Lincoln was timing and public opinion; as a result, his policies regarding emancipation and African-American enlistment evolved and reflected changing political circumstances.

220.   Huch, Ronald K. "Fort Pillow Massacre: The Aftermath of Peducah." *Journal of the Illinois State Historical Society,* 66, 1 (Spring 1973): 62-70.

The Confederate defeat at the battle of Peducah, and its direct connection to the massacre at Fort Pillow, is explored in this intriguing cause-and-effect study. On March 25, 1864 Confederate General Nathan Bedford Forrest, as part of a large-scale cavalry raid through Tennessee and Kentucky, attacked Peducah, a city located on the banks of the Ohio River in northern Kentucky. The town's Union garrison, stationed at Fort Anderson, consisted of 665 men, including 274 soldiers of the African-American Heavy Artillery (eventually re-designated the 8th U.S. Colored Heavy Artillery). Before attacking, the Confederates demanded the fort's surrender coupled with the chilling warning that "if I have to storm your works, you may expect no quarter." Colonel Stephen G. Hicks, the garrison commander, refused to be intimidated and rejected the surrender demand.

Three separate assaults were made; all three were repulsed with black artillerymen playing a leading role in the Confederate setback. According to the author, the defeat at Peducah, particularly by black troops, infuriated the defeated Confederates and lead directly to the massacre 17 days later at Fort Pillow. Huch maintains that "it is reasonable to argue that the frustration the Confederate forces experienced ... led them to seek revenge at the first opportunity." And the defeat at Peducah was "sufficient cause to turn Forest and his men from angry, battle-weary warriors into mass murderers at Fort Pillow." White superiority over African-Americans had to be re-asserted and "that is why, from the Southern viewpoint, the killings at Fort Pillow was a tragic necessity." The article includes a map, two illustrations, and 21 notes.

221. Hudson, Leonne M. "A Confederate Victory at Grahamville: Fighting at Honey Hill." *South Carolina Historical Magazine,* 94, 1 (January 1993): 19-33.
The little-known Battle of Honey Hill, South Carolina, fought on November 30, 1864, was a small-scale affair by Civil War standards. Originally conceived as a strategic move to aid General Sherman by cutting the Charleston & Savannah Railroad, it was a battle characterized by inexcusable Federal tactical blundering, poor planning, poor execution, and even worse leadership. Hudson's straightforward essay examines the battle from both the Confederate and Union perspective. After analyzing the tactics employed by both sides, Hudson concluded that flawless Confederate defense coupled with inept Union leadership resulted in Rebel victory. As a result, a numerically superior Union Army was defeated by a small Confederate force consisting mainly of Georgia militiamen. Several black regiments participated in the battle including, in the 1st Brigade, the 32nd, 34th, and 35th United States Colored Troops. The all black 2nd Brigade consisted of the 54th and 55th Massachusetts and the 102nd United States Colored Troops. Union losses in the battle were reported as 750 men; Confederate losses were less than 50. The article contains two maps and 58 notes based on primary sources including a number of contemporary Southern newspaper accounts.

222. _____. "Valor at Wilson's Wharf." *Civil War Times Illustrated,* 37, 1 (March 1998): 46-52.
Fort Pocahontas was an earthen fort located at Wilson's Wharf, Virginia on the north bank of the James River. As part of Grant's Overland Campaign, the fort was constructed and garrisoned by two regiments of Brigadier General Edward A. Wild's African Brigade. It was attacked on May 24, 1864 by a large force of Confederate cavalry commanded by Fitzhugh Lee. Lee believed the black troops, many of whom were former slaves, would be easily defeated. Events soon proved otherwise. After repeated and

persistent attacks Lee was forced to withdraw. To his chagrin, he found that black soldiers could fight and were quite willing to do so. This article by Leone Hudson describes the often overlooked affair at Wilson's Wharf and explains its wider implication: black troops could fight as well as white troops. The article is illustrated with period photographs and paintings. A map would make the battle narrative easier to follow; unfortunately, none is provided.

223. _____. "The Role of the 54th Massachusetts Regiment in Potter's Raid." *Historical Journal of Massachusetts*, 30, 2 (2002): 181-197.

Well-researched and based mainly on primary source materials, this is a comprehensive account of the Union's April 8-21, 1865, raid into the interior of South Carolina in the waning days of the war. Commanded by Brigadier General Edward E. Potter, and consisting of two brigades, one mainly black, the other white, the raid destroyed much of South Carolina's railroad system, liberated thousands of bondsmen, and generally wreaked havoc throughout interior South Carolina. The raid is described on a day-by day basis with particular emphasis on the 54th Massachusetts. The only encounter of significance for the 54th was at Boykins Mills on April 18, 1865 in which the regiment lost two killed and 13 wounded, including Lt. Edward L. Stevens, who may have been the last officer killed in the war. It was also the regiment's last battle of the Civil War.

224. Huffstodt, James. "Campaigning for Mobile." *Civil War Times Illustrated,* 21, 1 (March 1982): 8-17.
Fought in the waning days of the war, the campaign for Mobile is described including a fleeting description of the part played by the African-American division. According to one observer, many Confederates "were shot down because they would not surrender to a black man." The article is illustrated with period photographs, drawings, and several maps.

225. _____. "River of Death." *Lincoln Herald,* 84, 2
(Summer 1982): 70-83.
In order to divert Confederate attention from Sherman's march on
Meridian, Mississippi, in 1864, Union forces launched a
diversionary expedition via steamboat up the Yazoo River. The
author has provided a detailed and well-written account of this little-
known January to March 1864 affair. The Union forces involved
included two regiments of African-American soldiers: the 8th
Louisiana Regiment (African Descent) and the 1st Mississippi
Colored Cavalry. The fighting at both Liverpool Heights and Yazoo
City is described. During the engagement both African-American
regiments "lost approximately 100 killed, wounded and captured."
A number of period drawings and photographs are included in the
article.

226. Humphreys, Margaret, and Truls Østbye, Kerry L. Haynie,
Idrissa Boly, Philip Costanzo, and Frank Sloan. "Racial
Disparities a Century Ago: Evidence from the Pension Files of
U.S. Civil War Veterans." *Social Science and Medicine*, 64, 8
(April 2007): 1766-1775.
Utilizing veteran's pension files, the authors compare Type 2
diabetes rates between black and white Civil War veterans circa
1900. They found that African-American veterans had a lower rate
of Type 2 diabetes. This lower rate may be attributed to the
physically demanding labor engaged in by most black veterans as
compared to their white counterparts. The article contains a number
of highly detailed charts and graphs

227. Hunt, Jeffrey. "The Battle of Palmito Ranch May 12-13,
1865." *E.C. Barksdale Student Lectures*, 10 (1987): 178-202.
The last battle of the Civil War, fought in Texas and fought a month
after Lee surrendered, is recounted. One African-American
regiment, the 62th USCT, took part in the affair.

228.   Huntington, Tom. "Freedom Fighters." *America's Civil War*, 22, 4 (September 2009): 38-45.

The 1st South Carolina Volunteers was the first African-American regiment organized during the war. It was established without government approval by Major General David Hunter, at that time commanding officer of the Union Department of the South. Many of its recruits were forcibly impressed into army service; as a result, many subsequently deserted. Washington refused to authorize the regiment and it was dissolved except for one company. Later a new department commanding officer had the regiment rebuilt and formally inducted into Federal service under the leadership of abolitionist Thomas W. Higginson. Under his command the regiment grew in size and experience. The article provides a history of the 1st South Carolina Volunteers from its original establishment to discharge. Included are several period photographs and an impressive full- page, full-color portrait of the regiment's first uniform.

229.   Indiana Historical Bureau. "Indiana's 28th Regiment. Black Soldiers for the Union." *Indiana Historian*, 65 (February 1994): 1-16.

The 28th USCT (also known as the 28th Indiana Colored Regiment) was the only African-American regiment raised in Indiana during the war. The history of the regiment is told both in narrative form and through the reproduction of military documents used throughout the regiment's service. For example, a copy of the letter authorizing the regiment is reproduced. The article also includes reproductions of a muster role, a present for duty report, a regimental statistical abstract, and a copy of the regiment's casualty report. Extracts from letters written by Garland White, the regiment's chaplain, are also included in the text. The 28th fought at the Crater where it sustained heavy casualties. Transferred to Texas, the 28th was mustered out in late 1865.

230.   James, Felix. "The Attitudes toward the Recruitment of
Black Troops in Ohio, 1862-1863." *Journal of Afro-American
Issues*, II (1974): 49-58.
In 1862 Cincinnati, Ohio African-Americans were not allowed to
enlist in the state militia or serve in the Union Army. Prejudice
against the city's black population was widespread and often
violent. However, in September 1862, due to a threatened attack by
Confederate forces, African-Americans were impressed, sometimes
forcibly, to construct fortifications to defend the city. Thus, "the
first grouping of black people for military service was the Black
Brigade of Cincinnati." The Confederate attack failed to materialize
and several months later the state raised the black 127th Ohio
Volunteer Infantry (later re-designated as the 5th USCT).

231.   Johnson, Charles, Jr. "Frazier A. Boutelle: Military Career
of a Black Soldier." *Journal of the Afro-American Historical
and Genealogical Society*, 3, 3 (1982): 99-104.
This is a biography of Frazier A. Boutelle, from his early enlistment
in the Civil War's 5th New York Cavalry, his commission as a 2nd
Lieutenant in the regiment, his post-war service on the western
frontier, his appointment as acting superintendent of Yellowstone
National Park, and his service with the Washington State National
Guard. Boutelle was appointed brigadier general of the guard by
Governor John H. McGraw and charged with the responsibility of
streamlining the organization. The author strongly suspects that
Boutelle was dismissed from his post when his partial African-
American ancestry became known. After leaving the guard,
Boutelle served as an army recruiting officer.

232.   Johnson, Mary E., editor. "Letters from a Civil War
Chaplain." *Journal of Presbyterian History,* 46, 3 (September
1968): 219-235.
Written by an astute but somewhat starry-eyed observer, this
collection of letters from a Civil War chaplain begin on May 6,
1864, and end almost a year later on May 20, 1865. Thomas Scott
Johnson was a recent graduate of Princeton Theological Seminary
who first worked for the U.S. Christian Commission at Fortress

Monroe, Virginia, before accepting the chaplaincy of the 127th U.S. Colored Troops. His letters, which were edited and arranged by his daughter, describe Chaplain Johnson's work among the wounded, the condition of exchanged prisoners, African-American religious services, frequent encampment changes before Petersburg, his successful efforts to organize a regimental school, and his assignment to supervise the school system for all the regiments in the division.

233.   Jones, Hari. "The Color of Bravery: United States Colored Troops in the Civil War." *Hallowed_Ground*, 14, 2 (Summer 2013): 26-33.

In this article, Hari Jones, the curator of the African American Civil War Museum in Washington, DC, briefly describes black participation in the Civil War. Sketches of black regiments recruited in Louisiana, South Carolina, and Louisiana are provided. Additionally, the impact of Lincoln's Emancipation Proclamation on black recruiting is examined. The article also includes a one-page synopsis of the attack of the 54th Massachusetts on Fort Wagner in Charleston Harbor.

234.   Jones, Howard J., editor. "Letters in Protest of Race Prejudice in the Army during the American Civil War." *Journal of Negro History*, 61, 1 (1976): 97-98.

Two short letters protesting discrimination by an African-American officer in the 2nd Louisiana Native Guards are reprinted in this article. In the first, dated March 3[d], 1863, Lieutenant Robert Hamlin Isabelle, as a protest against military racial prejudice, resigned his commission. In the second letter, dated approximately three months later, Isabelle broadly hints of accepting another commission. According to the editor, Isabelle was soon "back in military service with the rank of Captain."

235.   Jones, Terry L. "'The Enemy Cried No Quarter:' Courage and Controversy at Milliken's Bend." *Civil War, The Official Magazine of the Civil War Society*, 68 (June 1998): 38-50.

As part of his Vicksburg operations, Grant established a temporary supply depot at Milliken's Bend, Louisiana. Because of its vulnerability, and in order to protect the base, slaves from neighboring plantations were recruited and assigned as garrison troops. Most of the black soldiers at Milliken's Bend were only recently enlisted and all were poorly trained. One regiment did not receive its rifles until the day before the Confederate attack. The clash that later occurred was one of the most savage small engagements, man for man, in the Civil War. Hand-to-hand combat was not unusual and black battle casualties were substantial. One regiment — the 9th Louisiana Infantry (Colored) — sustained one of the highest casualty rates "for a regiments in a single engagement" in the war. The stubborn resistance of the untrained and only recently enlisted black soldiers is recounted. Even the Confederate commander had to admit that the black soldiers fought with "considerable obstinacy."

Jones describes in workmanlike fashion the Confederate assault, the Federal defense, and the battle's aftermath. Well written and easy to understand, this article is a fine account of the battle and is a valuable addition to the literature of this June 7, 1863, engagement. The article contains several illustrations and a map.

236. _____. "'A Disagreeable Dilemma:' Black P.O.W.s." *Civil War, The Official Magazine of the Civil War Society,* 68 (June 1998): 50-54.
"The Battle of Milliken's Bend did not end when the shooting stopped." After the battle, Confederate military authorities had to face the "harsh unpleasantries" of what do to with captive black prisoners and white officers. Theoretically, white officers were to be executed and African-American prisoners turned over to the Louisiana state government. That, of course, was the theory; reality was much different. Some black prisoners were turned over to state authorities; others were sent to prisoner-of-war camps in Texas, and a number, including several white officers, were probably murdered. "Texans," the author writes "did not go out of their way to take prisoners."

237.   Jones, Thomas L. "The Union League and New York's First Black Regiments in the Civil War." *New York History*, 87, 3 (Summer 2006): 312-343.

Using archival sources, the efforts of New York City's Union League Club to raise African-American regiments is intensively documented. The effort was often stymied by state and Federal officials and at times experienced internal discord. Nevertheless, on March 5, 1864, the 20th USCT marched down Broadway to the cheers of thousands of onlookers. Eight months earlier, Irish mobs had hanged "Colored" men from lamp posts in the same city to protest the national draft. Though not the first organization in the city to attempt to raise black regiments, the Union League was the most successful. Founded by 500 wealthy men, the League ultimately raised three regiments in the Empire State: the 20th, 26th, and 31st USCT. The article contains 146 primary and secondary notes.

238.   Jordan, Weymouth T., Jr. and Gerald W. Thomas. "Massacre at Plymouth April 20, 1864." *North Carolina Historical Review,* 72, 2 (April 1995): 125 193.

Was there a massacre of black soldiers and civilians as well as white Unionists when Plymouth, North Carolina was captured by Confederate forces on April 20, 1864? The controversy has raged for years. Often arguments for or against massacre cited evidence that was inconclusive, contradictory, or in some cases fraudulent. In this comprehensive study the authors extensively researched "military reports, orders, telegrams, and service records, contemporary letters and diaries, regimental records and histories, Federal gunboat logs, prisoner-of war records, newspaper accounts, reminiscences, and Federal pension applications." They concluded that a massacre, even if limited in scope and involving no more than 50 persons, did indeed take place. Containing 137 notes, this essay is a painstakingly documented account of an often-overlooked battle and a forgotten massacre.

239. Joshi, Manoj K., and Joseph P. Reidy. "'To Come Forward and Aid in Putting Down This Unholy Rebellion': The Officers of Louisiana's Free Black Native Guard during the Civil War Era." *Southern Studies,* 21, 2 (Fall 1982): 326-342.

In this well-documented study, the author explores the tortuous relationship of black officers of the Louisiana Native Guards with the Union Army. Originally recruited by Ben Butler to augment his existing forces, free men of color were granted commissions in the three regiments of Louisiana Native Guards; they were also promised the same pay as white officers. Unfortunately, Butler was replaced as commander of the Gulf Department by General Nathaniel P. Banks. Banks considered free black men, regardless of their education or professional background, as unqualified to serve as officers and proceeded to systematically "remove them from the service, by persuasion if possible, by force if necessary." How and when they were removed over a period of 18 months is described. The author also examines the profound post-war cultural, economic, and political differences that existed between free men of color, often from a privileged background and very often former officers of the Native Guards, and the newly freed slaves.

240. Kashatus, William C. "A Gallant Rush for Glory." *American History*, 35, 4 (October 2000): 22-28.

Though written for a popular audience, this is an excellent summary of the role the 54th Massachusetts played in the acceptance of African-Americans as soldiers. Early agitation for enlisting black soldiers, the role of Governor John A. Andrews of Massachusetts in organizing the 54th, a history of the regiment, and the assault on Fort Wagner are all examined. The article contains several photographs and a map of Morris Island.

241. Kaufman, A. F. "The Fifty-Fourth U. S. Colored Infantry: The Forgotten Regiment." *Ozark Historical Review*, 16 (Spring 1987): 1-8.

The 2nd Arkansas Volunteer Infantry (African Descent), later re-designated as the 54th U.S. Colored Infantry, was an African-American regiment whose war-time service was, according to the author, "relegated to obscurity." One of only five black regiments raised in Arkansas, its organizational history typified that of most African-American military units recruited during the war – particularly in the South or border states. In order to bring the regiment to full strength, escaped slaves, at the direction of white recruiting officers, were forcibly impressed into service. Its officer corps was a mixed bag; no better and certainly no worse than that of any other African-American regiment. As a military unit it served primarily as a labor force, though it did see limited active service in western Arkansas where two privates were captured by Confederates and murdered. After the end of hostilities the regiment was stationed at Little Rock where it performed guard, provost, and labor duties until mustered out in August 1865. According to the author the 54th U.S. Colored Infantry "regiment had a minimal impact on the Civil War itself, but it was representational of the black military units of that time." A good unit history of an unheralded regiment that did its duty and then quietly slipped into obscurity.

242. Keenan, Jerry. "Disaster in Mississippi: The Battle of Brice's Cross-Roads." *By Valor & Arms: The Journal of American Military History*, 1, 3 (Spring 1975): 41-47.
The battle of Brice's Cross-Roads is recounted by the author. The pivotal role played by several African-American regiments in preventing the Union disaster becoming worse than it was is never mentioned.

243. King, Lisa Y. "In Search of Women of African Descent Who Served in the Civil War Navy." *Journal of Negro History*, 83, 4 (Autumn 1998): 302-209.
This article explores the role of African-American women serving in various capabilities aboard U.S. Navy ships during the Civil War. According to the author, Ann Stokes, a nurse and pensioner, "may well be the first African-American women enlisted in the United States Navy." Based principally on pension records, naval muster rolls, and other primary sources. The article contains 21 notes.

244. _____. "'They called us Bluejackets:' The Transformation of Self-emancipated Slaves from Contrabands of War to Fighting Sailors in the South Atlantic Blocking Squadron during the Civil War." *International Journal of Naval History*, 1, 1 (April 2002): www.ijnhonline.org.
The process by which contrabands escaped to the South Atlantic Blockading Squadron and ultimately freedom is described. Because of their intimate knowledge of the local waterways, contrabands often served as pilots and guides on Union vessels; others provided intelligence concerning Confederate fortifications, and still more served on integrated ships as naval ratings with the same pay as their white counterparts.

245. Knight, Glenn. "Black Sailors from Lancaster." *Journal of the Lancaster County Historical Society*, 107, 3 (Winter 2005): 134-139.
A compilation and short service history of 32 African-American Civil War sailors who were born in Lancaster County, Pennsylvania. Information noted includes name, age and place of enlistment, naval rating, and pre-war occupation.

246. Krech, Shepard, III. "Participation of Maryland Blacks in the Civil War from Oral History." *Ethnohistory,* 27, 1 (Winter 1980): 67-78.
The Civil War oral history, as recalled by Joseph Sutton, a resident of Talbot County on Maryland's Eastern Shore, is compared to existing written documentation. The author concludes that oral history frequently overlaps its written counterpart.

247. Kynoch, Gary. "Terrible Dilemmas: Black Enlistments in the Union Army during the American Civil War." *Slavery and Abolition,* 18, 2 (August 1997): 104-127.
The decision to volunteer for the Union Army, as the article indicates, was a terrible dilemma for many African-Americans. The incentives to volunteer were often offset by disincentives to stay at home. The reaction of free blacks in the North was often different from slaves residing in the border states or the South. For those in bondage "the benefits of enlisting to gain freedom and in the fight

against slavery had to be weighed against the dangers ... of abandoning friends and families to the abuse of enraged masters." For the Northern black elite, a primary disincentive to enlisting was the lack of officer commissions. During the war only a handful of commissions were awarded to African-Americans, many in the Louisiana Native Guards and these were subsequently revoked. Nevertheless, many of the black elite campaigned tirelessly to encourage enlistments as a practical matter in attaining hoped for post-war equal rights. However, "not all well-to-do blacks supported the idea of enlistment. Having attained a certain station in life, military service in an army that refused to accept blacks as officer held little appeal..." There was also an economic disincentive. The Northern economy had boomed during the war and for African-American jobs were available. And for those in Union Army occupied areas "military labor often paid substantially more than a soldier's wage." Then, too, potential recruits had to deal with discrimination, institutional racism, unequal pay, and the knowledge that if captured they faced an uncertain future in the hands of Confederate authorities All these factors acted as deterrents to enlisting. Nevertheless, encouraged in the North by the black elite, and motivated by an overwhelming desire to end slavery, prove their manhood, and obtain the full rights of citizenship, thousands of African-Americans joined the Union Army. This is an excellent and well-documented study of an often overlooked aspect of black enlistments during the Civil War.

248.   Langley, Louden S. "From the 54th Mass. (Colored) Regt." *Rutland Historical Society Quarterly*, 22, 2 (1992): 37-39.
In this letter to the *Burlington Free Press*, dated March 9, 1864 and sent from Jacksonville, Florida, Langley comments on broken government promises regarding pay and bounty and the Battle of Olustee. Included in the article is a fold-out map of the operations area of the 54th Massachusetts from 1863 – 1865.

249.   Larson, Douglas E. "Private Alfred Gales: From Slavery to Freedom." *Minnesota History*, 57, 6 (Summer 2001): 274-283.
Based mainly on primary sources, this article documents the Civil War service and post-war life of Alfred Gales, a runaway Arkansas

slave who subsequently enlisted as an "undercook of African Decent" in Company B, 3rd Minnesota Volunteer Infantry. The 3rd, unlike most white Civil War regiments, had a reputation for enlisting African-Americans rather than turning them away to the uncertainties of the contraband camp. Gales served until mustered out with the regiment in Minnesota on September 2, 1865. Shortly after arriving in his adopted home state, he changed his name to Alfred Miller forsaking his slave name of Alfred Gales. The article is illustrated with reproductions of Gales' enlistment papers and muster record and contains 22 notes.

250. Lasorda, Jesse. "Orrin Edgar Wilson: The Life of an African-American Civil War Veteran." *Chronicle: The Quarterly Magazine of the Historical Society of Michigan*, 35, 3 (Fall 2012): 24-25.

Wilson's early life, service with the 102nd USCI, and postwar career is briefly described. Interestingly, Wilson, an African-American, served as the commander of an all-white Grand Army of the Republic post located in St. Johns, Michigan.

251. Lause, Mark. "Turning the World Upside Down: A Portrait of Labor and Military Leader, Alonzo Granville Draper." *Labor History*, Issue 2, 44 (2003): 189-204.
New England-born Alonzo Granville Draper was a Massachusetts labor leader and social reformer who fervently believed in the ideology of trade unionism and free labor. He was actively involved in the great shoe strike that gripped New England shoe manufacturers in 1860. With the advent of war, Draper obtained a commission as a captain in the 14th Massachusetts Volunteer Infantry. Later, he became commanding officer of the 2nd North Carolina Colored Volunteers (re-designated as the 36th USCT) at New Bearn, North Carolina. Under his leadership the regiment, which was part of Wild's African Brigade, raided interior Virginia and North Carolina to free slaves and suppress Confederate guerilla activity. After a short stint as prison guards at Point Lookout, Maryland, the regiment became part of Benjamin Butler's Army of the James. As a brigade commander, Draper led his African-American regiments in the bitter fighting for New Market Heights,

a battle in which the brigade sustained substantial casualties. Following its evacuation by Confederate forces, black regiments under his command became the first Union Army contingent to enter Richmond. Transferred to Texas, he was killed by the accidental discharge of a loaded weapon. The article contains 36 copious notes almost all based on primary source material.

252. Lawson, Brenda M., editor. "The Letters of Robert Gould Shaw at the Massachusetts Historical Society." *Proceedings of the Massachusetts Historical Society*, 3rd series, 102 (1990): 127-147.

Nine letters by Robert Gould Shaw, and a draft of a tenth, are reprinted here in there entirety. The chief recipient was Charles F. Morse, a fellow officer and friend from Shaw's former regiment, the 2nd Massachusetts. Most of the letters touch lightly upon various aspect of the 54th Massachusetts. Two, however, are of particular interest: the first is a draft of a letter to Governor John A. Andrew of Massachusetts discussing the possible piecemeal deployment of the regiment, a move Shaw opposed; the second dated July 3, 1863, and postmarked St. Helena's Island, South Carolina, contains a pithy word portrait of Colonel James Montgomery, the fervent and often violent abolitionist commander of the 2nd South Carolina Regiment. Edited with an introduction by Brenda M. Lawson, the letters are part of the collection of the Massachusetts Historical Society.

253. Ledbetter. Judith F. "Regimental Descriptive Books: A Way to Identify Virginia Blacks who Served in the Union Army." *Charles City County Historical Society Newsletter*, 12 (September 1997): 9-10.

Regimental Descriptive Books, located in the National Archives in Washington, DC, are a rich and often overlooked source of information regarding individual African-American soldiers. Descriptive Books were kept by all regiments in the Union Army, both black and white. They contain information for each soldier serving in the regiment, including age, height, weight, complexion, age, place of birth (if known), occupation upon enlisting, place of enlistment, and general remarks. Sample descriptive details for several African-American soldiers from Charles City, Virginia who served in the 1ˢᵗ and 2ⁿᵈ U.S. Colored Cavalry and the 38ᵗʰ U.S. Colored Troops are provided.

254.   Lee, Chulhee. "Socioeconomic Differences in the Health of Black Union Soldiers during the American Civil War." *Social Science History*, 33, 4 (Winter 2009): 427-457.
This article examines the socioeconomic differences in the mortality rate of African-American soldiers during the Civil War. The study is based on the military service records of 5,677 black Union soldiers. Some of the conclusions reached by the author were that "lighter-skinned men were less likely to contract and die of disease" and former slaves engaged in non-field occupations "were less likely to . . . be killed by disease than field hands." In addition, slaves that had resided in an urban area, or had lived on large plantations, had a "much lower risk of contracting and dying of disease." Other factors affecting the health of black soldiers such as age, climate, height, occupation, type of disease, and pre-war nutritional standards are also addressed. The article contains six data filled tables and 12 notes.

255.   Leeke, Jim. "The Black Brigade." *Timeline: A Publication of the Ohio Historical Society*, 18, 4 (July – August 2001): 42-54.
In early September 1862, the threat of a Confederate attack across the Ohio River into Cincinnati prompted Major General Lew Wallace to declare martial law. He closed every business in the city and halted ferry traffic across the river to Kentucky. All able-bodied men were instructed to rally to the city's defense. Citizens were to report for work to dig trenches and prepare fortifications. African-Americans ignored the emergency measures "because they did not feel themselves addressed in them." If they had asked, they were told "Niggers ain't citizens." However, Wallace wanted every man to work, regardless of skin color. Arbitrarily, Cincinnati police on September 2 forcibly rounded up African-Americans for service, often at the point of a bayonet. Wallace, as the author points out, was alarmed by these circumstances and moved swiftly to remedy the situation. He appointed William Martin Dickson, a 34 year old

lawyer, abolitionist, and well-connected Republican, to fairly organize black volunteer citizens into a single body. Dickson permitted those who had had been earlier seized by the police to return home. As a result, hundreds of African-Americans freely volunteered for service the next day. Ultimately the black volunteers were organized into 17 companies, the equivalent of three understrength regiments. Though an irregular organization, while marching or preparing entrenchments, the African-Americans labored under their own battle flag which proudly declared them to be the Black Brigade of Cincinnati. On Saturday, September 20, 1862, the brigade was disbanded as "an unqualified success." Heavily illustrated with period drawings and photographs, this article highlights the often overlooked contribution that African-American civilians made to the Union war effort.

256. _____. "The Earth Seemed to Tremble. *America's Civil War*, 19, 5 (May 2006): 22-28.
This is a well-written general account of the July 30, 1864, Battle of the Crater. The use of African-American troops in the battle enraged the counter-attacking Confederates and led to a large number of battlefield atrocities. Southern "accounts written in the days following the battle rarely shied away from including vivid descriptions of the harsh treatment and executions of surrendered black soldiers." The undocumented text is supplemented by several period photographs and a map.

257. _____. "Until Every Negro has been Slaughtered." *Civil War Times,* 49, 5 (October 2010): 32-37.
The July 1864 Battle of the Crater witnessed the largest massacre of black soldiers during the Civil War. Levin estimates that "between 200 and 300 or more USTCs were executed in the battle's aftermath" since Confederates were enraged at the sight of armed African-Americans in uniform. Black soldiers were viewed as an aberration of the exiting social order and invoked, in Confederate minds, the long-existing fear of slave insurrection with its intendant riot, black rape, and white massacre. For Southerners, the maintenance of the existing social order required swift and merciless retribution. The result was cold-blooded murder during

and after the battle. The author, utilizing primary source documents, describes a number of these killings in horrific detail. The article contains several illustrations and two-full color maps.

258.   Levstik, Frank R., editor. "The Civil War Diary of Colonel Albert Rogall." *Polish American Studies,* 27, 1&2 (Spring/Autumn 1970): 33-79.
Albert Rogall was a Polish nobleman who immigrated to the United States a decade before the Civil War. He fought at Shiloh and Corinth as an officer of the 54th Ohio Volunteers before accepting a commission as a captain in the 27th U.S. Colored Troops. From March 27, 1864, until his resignation from Federal service on April 5, 1865, Rogall kept a diary that is reprinted here in its entirety. The diary portrays a perennially homesick malcontent who had little good to say about his fellow officers, the commissary and quartermaster corps, medical doctors, the Army of the Potomac, the Christian and Sanitary Commission, the Federal government, and the African-American soldiers he commanded. There are, occasionally, nuggets of revealing insights tucked away in his diary, as for example his statement that the regiment was stoned by the "low people" of Pittsburg and spit upon while marching through the national capital. Rogall was commissioned as a lieutenant colonel of the 118th U.S. Colored Troops on December 9, 1864; he resigned, evidently with the army's wholehearted approval, three months later.

259.   _____. "The Fifth Regiment, U.S. Colored Troops, 1863-1865." *Northwest Ohio Quarterly,* 42, 4 (Fall 1970): 86-98.
The 127th Ohio Volunteer Infantry, later re-designated the 5th U.S. Colored Troops, was the first African-American regiment raised in Ohio. The regiment's recruitment, training, Federal discriminatory pay policies, and military service are described. All the officers were white but some details concerning the regiment's black enlisted men are provided: most were recruited in southern Ohio, three-fifths were between 18 and 25, the youngest was 15 and the oldest was age 52. The regiment served in Virginia and North Carolina. As part of the Army of the James, four members of the

regiment, all sergeants, received the Medal of Honor for conspicuous gallantry at the Battle of New Market Heights, Virginia, on September 29, 1864. Not a true in-depth regimental study, but a good, introductory overview of the 5th U.S. Colored Troops. The article has 84 notes based mainly on contemporary newspaper accounts and the Official Records.

260. _____, editor. "From Slavery to Freedom: Two Wartime Letters of One of the Conflict's Few Black Medal of Honor Winners." *Civil War Times Illustrated*, 11, 7 (November 1972): 10-15.

Civil War first person accounts by African-American soldiers are rare. This article reproduces two wartime letters written by Sergeant Major Milton M. Holland, 5th U.S. Colored Troops, to the Athens, Ohio *Messenger*. In his letters, dated January 19th and July 24th, 1864, Holland describes the regiment's organization and early engagements, enemy guerillas, the murder of a black soldier by Confederate partisans, the liberation of slaves from masters both loyal and in rebellion, the controversial pay issue, and combat before Petersburg. Years after the war Holland, who won the Medal of Honor at New Market Heights, Virginia, on September 25, 1864, founded Alpha Insurance, one of the nation's first African-American insurance companies.

261. _____. "Robert H. Pinn: Courageous Black Soldier." *Negro History Bulletin*, 37, 6 (1974): 304-305.

This is a straightforward biography of Sergeant Major Robert A. Pinn, 5th U.S. Colored Troops. Pinn was a Medal of Honor recipient for distinguished service during the Battle of New Market Heights, Virginia, post-war Ohio lawyer, GAR booster, and staunch Republican.

262. Lindberg, Kip and Matt Matthews. "To Play a Bold Game." *North & South*, 6, 1 (December 2002): 56-69.

The Battle of Honey Springs, fought on July 17, 1863, is considered a mere footnote to Civil War studies, even though it was the largest engagement fought in Indian Territory. The clash at Honey Springs is unique for two reasons: both armies were at the very end of their supply lines and because of the incredible racial mix of the combatants. Confederate Indian regiments fought Union Indian regiments; whites fought whites. Added to the racial mix was the storied African-American 1st Kansas Regiment (Colored), probably the largest organization on the field that day and perhaps the first African-American unit to see combat in the Civil War. (The *perhaps* is contingent upon the fight at Island Mound, Missouri, on October 28, 1862, when portions of the unit saw combat against Confederate guerrillas. At the time of Island Mound the 1st Kansas Colored was not officially mustered into service. Consequently, it was not carried as a regimental organization on Union Army roles.)

The pivotal role played by the 1st Kansas Colored in the decisive Union victory at Honey Springs is recounted in this excellent study of a forgotten frontier battle fought quite literally in the middle of nowhere. The article describes the overall encounter in detail and is supplemented by a large number of period photographs, a first-rate full color map, orders of battle, and 44 notes.

263.   Lockett, James D. "The Lynching Massacre of Black and White Soldiers at Fort Pillow, Tennessee, April 12, 1864." *The Western Journal of Black Studies,* 22, 2 (Summer 1998): 84-93.
Lockett assigns responsibility for the murder of black soldiers at Fort Pillow to a shared white Southern culture that regarded African-Americans as inferior beings "naturally endowed for slavery." The sight of armed black soldiers in blue, for both Forrest his soldiers, was enough to unleash a violence that knew no bounds. Contrary to the article's title, little attention is paid to the fate of white Union soldiers at the fort.

264.   Logue, Larry M. and Peter Blanck. "'Benefit of the Doubt': African-American Civil War Veterans and Pensions." *Journal of Interdisciplinary History,* 38, 3 (Winter 2008): 377-399.
Ostensibly the Federal pension system enacted during and after the Civil War applied to all veterans regardless of race. However, as both authors discovered during their research "race was never far from the minds of the men who administered the pension laws." Black veterans, under the provisions of the general pension law,

received "more outright rejections and smaller pension awards than did whites." Research pointed to biased pension examiners "and documentation rules that were more difficult for black veterans than white veterans to satisfy." Black pension applications were affected by number of other factors including illiteracy, poverty, residency in the rural South, and living under a new, non-slave name. Black veterans lacked the experience and resources necessary to negotiate the complex bureaucratic maze of the pension office. But racism played its part. Unlike their white counterparts, African-American veterans were most often not given the "benefit of the doubt." However, application successes increased with the passage of the Disability Act of 1890. This act granted a pension to surviving veterans based simply on old age and was not connected to war-related disabilities. The article contains six statistical tables and 34 notes.

265. Longacre, Edward. "Port Hudson Campaign." *Civil War Times Illustrated,* 10, 10 (February 1972): 20-34.
This is an account of the Union siege and eventual victory at Port Hudson, Louisiana in 1863. A few paragraphs are devoted to African-American soldiers who "answered every expectation" and whose conduct was "heroic."

266. _____. "Brave Radical Wild: The Contentious Career of Brigadier Edward A. Wild." *Civil War Times Illustrated*, 19, 3 (June 1980): 8-19.
Born in Brookline, Massachusetts, in 1825 and educated as a homoeopathic doctor, one-armed Edward A. Wild was both a dedicated abolitionist and a contentious officer, often bitterly feuding with both superior and subordinate officers. Wild served as a doctor in the Crimean War but, with the outbreak of civil strife in America, obtained a commission as a captain in the 1st Massachusetts Infantry. Losing his left arm at South Mountain, he returned to duty as a brigadier general authorized to raise African-American regiments in North Carolina. Known as Yazoo City he conducted his own version of hard war against North Carolina guerillas, foraging liberally, burning the houses of known guerilla supporters, taking hostages, and, in one case, personally hanging an

accused guerilla. Removed from service in North Carolina because of his difficult behavior he was transferred to Butler's Army of the James in Virginia. While on picket duty at Wilson's Wharf, Virginia, his brigade withstood as attack by 3,000 Confederates under the command of Major General Fitzhugh Lee. It was a resounding victory for Wild and his black soldiers. After the war Wild pursued a career in the mining industry. The article contains a number of period photographs and drawings and an impressive reproduction of a Burlington County, New Jersey, "colored" recruiting poster.

267. _____. "Black Troops in the Army of the James, 1863-65." *Military Affairs*, 45, 1 (February 1981): 1-8.
Reviled by the South as a beast because of his administrative policies in occupied New Orleans, mistrusted by many in the North because of his Democratic Party affiliation, always controversial Benjamin Butler proved to be one of the highest ranking champions of the "sable arm." Unlike most Union Army commanders Butler, as commander of the Army of the James, welcomed black troops in his command. The Army of the James had more African-American soldiers than any other in the Union Army and contained the first and only all-black army corps – the XXV – in American military history. Butler, an able administrator but an ineffective combat commander, repeatedly demonstrated a genuine concern for "the physical, intellectual, and moral welfare" of his African-American troops. Incompetent officers or officers who abused African-American soldiers were dismissed from the service, education was encouraged, dependents were cared for, a small bounty was paid to enlistees, a freedmen's savings bank was established, and black troops were used in responsible combat positions and not as laborers or garrison troops. Butler even threatened drastic retribution if black soldiers of his command were murdered by Confederates. An illuminating article about a flawed general who, unlike his contemporaries, overcame the politics of race. Most of the article's extensive documentation is based on primary sources.

268. _____, editor. "Letter from Little Rock of Captain James Bowler, 112th United States Colored Troops." *Arkansas Historical Quarterly*, 40, 3 (Autumn 1981): 235-248.

A collection of eight letters from Captain James M. Bowler, 112th U.S. Colored Troops, are reprinted in this article. Generally of a commonplace nature, the letters are to his wife and mother and begin in July and end in December, 1864. In several letters Bowler describes living accommodations for the regiment's officers. Longacre's introduction provides some background notes regarding the 112th and African-American regiments in general.

269. Lovett, Bobby L. "The Negro's Civil War in Tennessee, 1861-1865." *Journal of Negro History*, 61, 1 (January 1976): 36-50.

The records of African-American infantry regiments and artillery organizations recruited in Tennessee are summarized and a concise service history of each is provided. Several battle histories are also included. Particularly noteworthy is a chart listing each unit and its Civil War experience. The article contains 54 notes based on primary and secondary sources.

270. _____. "The West Tennessee Colored Troops in Civil War Combat." *West Tennessee Society Papers*, 34 (October 1980): 53-70.

The Civil War service of African-American army units that served or were raised in West Tennessee is summarized. The author describes the organizational history and service record of several of these units including their participation in the battles fought against Confederate General Bedford Forrest at Fort Pillow, Brice's Crossroads and Tupelo. Overall, African-American troops suffered a "total of 2,242 casualties fighting against the Confederate forces under General Forrest." The article contains 39 notes based principally on primary source materials.

271. _____. "Nashville's Fort Negley: A Symbol of Black's Involvement with the Union Army." *Tennessee Historical Quarterly,* 41, 1 (Spring 1982): 3-22.
The building of Fort Negley in Nashville, mostly by forced black laborers, the construction of the Northwestern Military Railroad by blacks, and the recruiting of African-American regiments in the Nashville area are all discussed. The article is extensively footnoted.

272. _____. "African Americans, Civil War, and Aftermath in Arkansas." *Arkansas Historical Quarterly*, 54, 3 (Autumn 1995): 304-358.
Most of this excellent article describes the slave experience in Arkansas during and immediately following the Civil War. The military participation of the states' African-Americans in the Union war effort receives considerable attention.

273. Lowe, Richard. "Battle on the Levee: The Fight at Milliken's Bend." In *Black Soldiers in Blue: African American Troops in the Civil War Era*, edited. John David Smith. Chapel Hill: University of North Carolina Press, 2002, pp-107-135.
Alan Nevins, in his multi-volume study of the Civil War, devoted a handful of words to the Battle of Milliken's Bend. Likewise in James Fiske's 1902 history of the Vicksburg campaign Milliken's Bend garners not a single mention. Yet in many respects the June 7, 1863 battle at Milliken's Bend was of pivotal significance for the Union and African-Americans: it demonstrated that "black Americans could fight and die for Union and freedom as well as anyone, white or black, famous or obscure."

The black regiments that fought and carried the day at Milliken's Bend were recruited only weeks before. They were untrained former slaves; many were not even familiar with their weapons. Indeed, one regiment received its weapons the day before the engagement. Yet they stubbornly defended the levee at Milliken's Bend in one of the "bloodiest small engagements of the war." Vicious assaults by equally untrained Texas troops degenerated into close-quarter "skull bashing" toe-to toe fighting. Union victory marked only the second time in the Civil War that organized regiments of black soldiers "had stood and fought under the American flag in a general engagement."

In this excellent account, the author provides a vivid description of the battle. Events leading up to Milliken's Bend, the battle itself, and its aftermath, are all explored in detail. Individual unit histories for each of the black regiments that fought at Milliken's Bend are provided as well as detailed regimental causality figures. This well-researched and well-written, the essay contains 50 notes and an informative map.

274.   Lufkin, Charles L. "'Not Heard From Since April 12, 1864.' The Thirteenth Tennessee Cavalry, U.S.A." *Tennessee Historical Quarterly*, 45, 2 (Summer 1986): 133-151.
Forceful, thoroughly researched, and well-written, this article presents another view of the controversial Fort Pillow affair, this time from the perspective of the 13th Tennessee Cavalry, a white Union regiment that shared garrison duties at the fort with a detachment of African-American artillerymen. While focusing primarily on the 13th Tennessee, the author demolishes Southern assertions regarding the battle – most of which were voiced considerably after the incident. The fort was not defended by "a mongrel garrison of blacks and renegades." Nor were the white soldiers of the 13th drawn from the dregs of West Tennessee society. Indeed, "an examination of the background of individual soldiers of the Thirteenth Cavalry uncovered no significant differences between them and their adversaries." Charges that black and white soldiers plundered through the countryside, and that "negro soldiers were especially insulting to the wives and families of confederate soldiers," are without merit. African-Americans had only arrived at Fort Pillow two weeks before and "during this time they were installing their artillery and preparing defenses. Moreover, they were not cavalry." The accusation against the 13th, according to the author, is also without merit; they were not at the post long enough to be guilty of the depredations Confederate forces later charged them with. Frequently overlooked in the Fort Pillow debate is the

fate of the 13th Tennessee Cavalry (Union): out of the 286 officers and men present at the fort on April 12, 1864 only 60 or 70 survived the war. Most lost their lives in Confederate captivity. The article contains 62 notes based on primary and secondary sources.

275.   Lutz, Stephen D. "The 1st Kansas Colored Infantry Was the First Black Regiment to Strike a Personal Blow for Ending Slavery." *America's Civil War,* 16, 1 (March 2003): 62-64.
This article provides a generalized account on the 1st Kansas Colored Regiment "the first black regiment to strike a blow for personal freedom" in the Civil War. Organized by Senator Jim Lane of Kansas without Federal authorization, the regiment first clashed with Confederate guerillas near Island Mound, Missouri, on October 29, 1862 – three months before the War Department began accepting African-American regiments into Federal service. The various battles of the regiment are recounted including Cabin Creek, Honey Springs, and Poison Springs. Later in the war the 1st Kansas Colored was re-designated as the 2nd USCT.

276.   MacDonald, Sharon S. and W. Robert Beckman. "Foster's a Humbug." *North & South,* 11, 5 (October 2009): 24-42.
Inconclusive Federal operations against Charleston in early July 1864 are described in this copiously footnoted and well-illustrated study. Union Army casualties were minimal and numbered less than 300. African-American regiments that took part in the operation included the 54th and 55th Massachusetts and the 26th and 33rd U. S. Colored Troops. Included in the article is an extract from the journal of Major John Appleton, 54th Massachusetts, describing the effects of sunstroke. Three explanatory full color maps help to explain the operation.

277.   _____. "Heroism at Honey Hill." *North & South,* 12, 1 (February 2010): 20-30, 35-43.
Drawing extensively on primary source materials, the authors have written a well-researched study of the Union military debacle at Honey Hill, South Carolina, on November 30, 1864. Several African-American regiments participated in the battle, including the 55th Massachusetts Infantry, a regiment which soldiered long in the

shadow of its more illustrious sister regiment, the 54th. Years later the battle was described by a Union Army participant as one in which "the generalship displayed in the fight was not equal to the soldierly qualities of the troops engaged." A full-color map with unit locations marked makes the unfolding tactical maneuvers easy to follow. Overall, an excellent summary description of a battle in which the 55th proved itself equal in courage to the 54th. The article contains a number of contemporary photographs, three maps, and 49 notes.

278. MacMaster, Richard K. "The Colonel Died with His Men: Led by Shaw, Negro Troops Proved Courageous and Reliable under Fire." *New York State and the Civil War*, 2, 4 (September – October 1962): 26-35.

This is a brief but nevertheless excellent account of the life of Robert Gould Shaw. The author describes Shaw's earliest days in Massachusetts, his education at home and abroad, his extensive family connections, and his military service with the 7th Regiment, New York State Militia, the 2nd Massachusetts Infantry, and as commanding officer of the 54th Massachusetts Infantry.

279. McAfee, Michael J. "The 108th U.S.C.T." *Military Images*, 25, 4 (January/February 2004): 36-37.

This two-page article features a Civil War era photograph of Louis Troutman, 108th USCT. No other particulars regarding Troutman's life are provided. As befitting a publication of this nature, a description of Troutman's Quartermaster issued uniform, accouterments, and firearm is provided. The article also contains an unflattering 1867 *carte de visite* portraying African-American soldiers in the new post-war black regiments as "ragged buffoons."

280. McBride, W. Stephen. "Camp Nelson: A Fortified Union Supply Depot, Recruitment Center, and African American Refugee Camp in Central Kentucky." *Journal of America's Military Past*, 25, 3 (Winter 1990): 24-35.

Camp Nelson was a major Union Army supply and recruitment depot located in Kentucky's Bluegrass Country. Established in June 1863, Camp Nelson swiftly grew into a sprawling military encampment of over 300 wooden buildings, numerous tents, forts, warehouses, horse and mule corrals, quartermaster workshops, two taverns, and sutler stores. Its facilities even included a bakery, a military hospital, and a military prison. Staffed by 2,000 civilian employees, and garrisoned with between 3,000 – 8,000 troops, Camp Nelson served as a massive supply and logistical base for Union operations in Kentucky, eastern Tennessee, and southwestern Virginia. However, Camp Nelson's chief significance, according to the author, was as a recruitment and training center for African-American soldiers. Fully 40% of all African-American soldiers recruited in Kentucky passed through the camp. Eight black regiments were raised within its confines including four infantry, two cavalry, and two heavy artillery regiments. It was the largest training and recruitment center for African-Americans in Kentucky and the third largest in the country.

Also included in the article is an account of Brigadier General Speed S. Fry's abrupt order expelling black dependent women and children from the camp. Overall, the author provides a historically sound overview of an often-overlooked but important aspect of Civil War Kentucky.

281. _____. "Camp Nelson and Kentucky's Civil War Memory." *Historical Archaeology*, 47, 3 (2013): 69-80.
Camp Nelson, Kentucky, was established in 1863 and soon became one of the largest Federal recruiting and training centers for African-American soldiers. Overall Kentucky contributed 23,000 black soldiers to the Union Army, the second largest of any state. That contribution, and the existence of Camp Nelson and what it symbolized for black Americans, was intentionally forgotten in slave holding Kentucky after the war. The reasons for this historical forgetfulness are neatly explored by the author and include racism, the Lost Cause narrative, and a desire for white sectional reconciliation and reunion. Nevertheless, through the use of historical documents, archaeological findings and oral histories, Camp Nelson's history is being restored to its rightful place in the story of emancipation and black military service. Archaeological evidence enables the historian to compare barracks, equipment,

rations, clothing, and cooking arrangements between white and black soldiers, and to determine black refugee family quarters and occupations.

282. McConnell, Catherine T. and Roland C. McConnell. "Selected African American Musicians and Bands in the United States Military from Colonial Times through the Civil War." *Journal of the Afro-American Historical and Genealogical Society*, 12, 1&2 (Spring/Summer 1991): 1-27.
The authors provide an excellent overview of African-American bands in the military from the Revolution to the Civil War. Most of the article describes African-American bands associated with the 54th and 55th Massachusetts and various regiments of the United States Colored Troops.

283. McConnell, Robert C., editor. "Concerning the Procurement of Negro Troops in the South during the Civil War." *Journal of Negro History*, 35, 3 (1950): 315-319.
Dated December 24, 1863, this reprint of a report from Brigadier General Lorenzo Thomas may be the earliest statistical summary "showing the exact condition" of African-American regiments and detachments. The report, addressed to Secretary of War Edwin M. Stanton, lists most units by state designation and aggregate strength.

284. _____. "The Corps d'Afrique: A Chapter in the Development of the Black Soldier in the U.S. Military Establishment." *Journal of the Afro-American Historical and Genealogical Society*, 12, 1&2 (Spring/Summer 1991): 43-56.
The Corps d'Afrique, an African-American Louisiana military organization, was authorized by Major General Nathaniel Banks on May 1, 1863. By Bank's order, the Corps d'Afrique incorporated Ben Butler's Louisiana Native Guards, black units in the process of organization in Louisiana, and those black regiments recruited by General Daniel Ullman. The author describes the organizational and administrative history of the Corps d'Afrique in some detail. Ultimately the Corps d'Afrique was administratively dissolved by the Adjutant General; its component regiments were numbered

seriatim and became part of the United States Colored Troops. Several of the regiments participated in the Port Hudson campaign.

285. _____. "The Maryland Infantry Regiments of the U. S. Colored Troops in the Civil War." *Journal of the Afro-American Historical and Genealogical Society*, 12, 1&2 (Spring/Summer 1991): 57-68.
Though Maryland was a slave state, it contributed over 9,000 African-Americans to the Union Army. Grouped into six black regiments, they served chiefly in Virginia and Florida. The service history of each regiment is described primarily through excerpts from Frederick H. Dyer's *A Compendium of the War of the Rebellion.* Maryland abolished slavery by constitutional amendment effective November 1, 1864.

286. McCurry, Stephanie. "'In the Company' with Susie Taylor." *America's Civil War,* 27, 2 (May 2014): 26-27.
The life of Susie King Taylor is chronicled. Born a slave in Georgia, she escaped to Union-occupied St. Simon's Island in early 1862. Unlike most slaves, she was literate and was soon officially employed as a regimental laundress. In fact she was a teacher of contraband children and African-American soldiers; later she performed front-line service as a nurse. In 1902 she wrote and self-published *Reminiscences of my Life in Camp with the 33rd United States Colored Troops,* a "tribute to the memory and heroism" of Company E and the regiment. In the post-war years she was instrumental in organizing Corps 67 of the Women's Relief Corps, "the women's auxiliary to the Grand Army of the Republic."

287. _____. "Army Wives' Emancipation Complications." *America's Civil War*, 27, 3 (July 2014): 24-25.
The difficulties faced by the wives of African-American soldiers are recounted. Most black soldiers were former slaves and marriage between slaves was illegal in the American South. As a result, "if the marital route to emancipation was difficult for those African-American women who were not soldiers' wives, it could be almost as impassable for those who were."

288.   McDonald, Rod. "Negro Troops." *Virginia Tidewater Genealogy*, 29, 2 (June 1997): 77-78.

Though the author grossly misstates the number of black soldiers who served during the war, he does provide a comprehensive list of battles in which African-Americans played a prominent part.

289.   McGehee, C. Stuart. "Military Origins of the New South: The Army of the Cumberland and Chattanooga's Freedmen." *Civil War History*, 34, 4 (December 1988): 323-343.

The transition of Chattanooga, Tennessee, from a small pre-war town to a Norther- style "New South" city is traced. The article also discusses the many Northern officers who served in occupation duty in Chattanooga and saw opportunity in the city's future. These men, and the city's unskilled black laborers, were responsible for Chattanooga's post-war industrial boom. The enlistment of the five back regiments raised in the city is also recounted. Interestingly, impressment was often the key to recruitment. Local army regulations stated that: "All male negroes coming into our line, who, after examination, shall be found capable of bearing arms, will be mustered into companies and regiments of colored troops." Five regiments, the 14th, 16th, ^{h} 42nd, 101st, and 44th USCT were eventually raised. Though they served mostly as labor troops, these regiments helped to transform the city's infrastructure by constant labor on the roads and railways. They also assisted in bridge building over the Tennessee River. One general remarked that it was just as well that the army "initially provided the black troops with shovels rather than muskets, and the men's basic training had consisted only of manual labor."

290.   McKnight, Brian. "The Winnowing of Saltville: Remembering a Civil War Atrocity." *Journal for the Liberal Arts and Sciences*, 14, 1 (Fall 2009): 34-51.

How many African-American soldiers were murdered at Saltville, Virginia on October 3, 1864? "Whether the numbers exceed one hundred ... or fewer than half-dozen" the debate still continues unabated to this day. The events leading up to the battle and subsequent shootings are described in the article. Conflicting interpretations for and against the massacre argument are reviewed.

According to the author, a newly discovered document found in the National Archives, by a research team of Civil War historians, concluded that between 45 to 50 black solders listed as missing at Saltville "are presumed to have been murdered by Confederate renegades."

291.   McMurry, Richard. "The President's Tenth and the Battle of Olustee." *Civil War Times Illustrated*, 16, 9 (January 1978): 12-24.

Republican maneuvering to create a loyal state in Florida, the battle of Olustee, which is described in detail, and the treatment of black prisoners by their Southern captors are all addressed. The author maintains that, with few exceptions, black prisoners were not mistreated. The article is illustrated with period photographs, drawings, and two maps.

292.   McPherson, James M. "The 'Glory' Story: The 54th Massachusetts and the Civil War." *The New Republic,* 202, 2&3 (January 8 & 15, 1990): 22-23, 26-27.

Ostensibly a commentary on the movie *Glory*, this article by Pulitzer Prize winner James M. McPherson recounts the achievements the 54th Massachusetts with several revealing insights. For example, while the attack on Fort Wagner was a military defeat it was, in a larger sense, a victory of revolutionary proportions: it forever disabused the Northern public of the idea that the African-Americans were incapable of fighting for their own freedom. Other black units had fought mostly in obscurity long before the 54th Massachusetts assaulted Fort Wagner. However, no African-American unit had received the attention lavished on the 54th, and in that sense their commitment to combat was still considered a "risky experiment." Their success in failure enabled the Lincoln administration to change the direction of the war: it was no longer a war to preserve the Union but one to abolish slavery.

The author also comments on what is right and what is wrong about the movie; most of the important details are right with a few exceptions: for instance, most men who served in the 54th were born in the North and had never been slaves. Thankfully, *Glory*, according to McPherson, has finally replaced the cinema's moonlight and magnolias interpretation of the Civil War with "the most powerful and historically accurate movie about that war ever made."

293. _____. "'We Were to Give up our Guns, who Belonged to the Band': Diary of William Woodlin, 8th U.S. Colored Troops, Company C." *OAH Magazine of History*, 19, 4 (July 2005): 41-47.
William Woodlin enlisted in Company C, 8th U.S. Colored Troops at Syracuse, New York in August 1863. While diaries by white Civil War soldiers are common, war-time diaries kept by African-Americans are rare. Woodlin and his diary are an exception. For most of his military service he compiled a "near-daily" diary recording his activities and those of his regiment. Woodlin's 123-page diary entries began in November 1863 and continued until December 1864. Excerpts of several diary pages, beginning with the first few months of army service and his participation in the regimental brass band, are reprinted in this article. The article text, which is introduced by James M. McPherson, is supplemented by a facsimile reproduction of actual diary pages. The original diary is part of the Gilder Lehman Collection on deposit at the New-York Historical Society.

294. McRae, James S. "David G. Cooke Joins the United States Colored Troops." *Tennessee Historical Quarterly,* 64, 3 (Fall 2005): 179-185.
David Grant Cooke, a white minister and schoolteacher, joined the 92nd Illinois Volunteer Regiment as an enlisted man in the fall of 1862. In August 1863 he sought and obtained a commission as a 1st lieutenant with the 12th U.S. Colored Troops. Captured by Confederate cavalry shortly after the Battle of Nashville in December 1865, he was subsequently brutally murdered by his captors. Using letters Cooke wrote to his wife, the author examines the factors that prompted Cooke to seek a commission in a black regiment; a commission that carried with it enormous risks for white officers if captured on the field of battle.

According to his letters, Cooke supported the destruction of slavery and the Emancipation Proclamation. While he was impressed by the ability and professionalism of the black soldiers under his command, he still considered them "very childish" and almost never mentions any by name in his letters. The author concluded: "Abolitionist ideals were not at the core of his decision." There is strong evidence, however, that financial considerations played a significant if not a dominant part in Cooke's pursuit of a commission, since officer status in an African-American regiment led to an almost ten-fold increase in pay. According to his correspondence, pre-war debts and the need for a financially secure future were very much on his mind. Service with a black regiment provided an opportunity for advancement and prestige simply not available in the 92nd Illinois. Ultimately, Cooke's decision to seek a commission was motivated by several factors: an abhorrence of slavery, debts, the need for financial security, and the desire for increased prestige and pay that came with promotion from the enlisted ranks: "Promotion provided the chance to regain a sound financial footing." Cooke's motivations, according to the author, were probably no different than scores of other whites who sought commissions in the Colored Troops. An excellent article that contains 31 notes based primarily on letters in the privately owned D.G. Cooke Collection.

295.   McRae, Norman. "Camp Ward, Detroit: Home of the First Michigan Colored Infantry Regiment." *Bulletin of the Detroit Historical Society*, 24 (May – June 1968): 4-11.
The 1st Michigan Colored Regiment, later re-designated as the 102nd U.S. Colored Troops, was raised in Detroit from local residents and former slaves living in nearby Canada. The article describes the regiment's early history at Camp Ward, vicious racial attacks on African-American soldiers by the local Democratic press, abysmal barrack accommodations, and racial animosity between soldiers and white civilians. Over 1,400 men served in the regiment; 10% lost their lives. The regiment participated in the bungled Union action at Honey Hill, South Carolina, on November 30, 1864. Based primarily on Detroit newspaper accounts, the article contains a map

of the U.S. Barracks and Camp Ward, several period photographs, and 22 notes.

296.   Maciejewski, Jeffrey. "Shock, Awe, and a Colossal
    Failure." *America's Civil War*, 23, 2 (May 2010): 28-35.
A well-illustrated recounting of the July 1864 Petersburg Crater disaster. The planning and preparation for the attack, the attack and its ghastly aftermath, and the decision not to use black troops in the initial assault are discussed.

297.   Mainfort, Robert C., Jr. "A Folk Art Map of Fort Pillow."
    West Tennessee Historical Society Papers, 40 (1986): 73.81.
Reproduced in full color, this folk art representation is the only known contemporary map of Fort Pillow. Drawn with colored pencils by William D. Power, Co. I, 32nd Iowa Volunteer Infantry, the map identifies prominent features of the fort including camps, batteries, fortifications, officers' quarters, contraband housing, and surrounding roads. The 32nd Iowa was withdrawn from Fort Pillow prior to the April 12, 1864 Confederate attack.

298.   Majher, Patricia. "The Later and Sometimes Illustrious
    Careers of 12 Civil War Figures." *Michigan History*, 95, 6
    (November/December 2011): 47-53.
The careers of 12 Michigan Civil War era personalities are discussed. Included in this list is Joseph Clovese who, at age 17, enlisted as a drummer in the 63rd United States Colored Infantry. Clovese, who passed away in 1951, was the last surviving black Civil War veteran.

299.   Maness, Lonnie E. "Fort Pillow under Confederate and
    Union Control." *West Tennessee Historical Society Papers*, 38
    (1984): 84-98.
The author traces the history of Fort Pillow, from its establishment and evacuation by Confederate forces to Union Army occupation. Included is a description of the April 12-13, 1864 Confederate attack on Fort Pillow. Describing the battle, Maness studiously avoids the term "massacre" and maintains that the death toll "was not an extraordinarily high rate for a fort that had to be taken by

assault." The article contains 49 notes based mainly on the Official
Records, both naval and military, as well as primary and secondary
sources.

300. _____. "The Fort Pillow Massacre: Fact or
Fiction." *Tennessee Historical Quarterly*, 45, 4 (Winter 1986):
287-315.

Based on a comprehensive re-examination of the exiting primary
documents, the author maintains that "Fort Pillow was a horrible
slaughter – a great victory for Forrest – but not a massacre."
Superior tactics by Forrest won the battle and there was no massacre
of "a large number of troops who were unresisting and defenseless."
An exhaustive description of the battle and its subsequent aftermath
is provided. The article contains a number of illustrations and 62
notes.

301. Margo, Robert A. "Civilian Occupations of Ex-Slaves in
the Union Army, 1862-1865." In *Without Consent or Contract:
The Rise and Fall of American Slavery, Vol. 1. Markets and
Production: Technical Papers,* edited by Robert W. Fogel and
Stanley L. Engerman. New York: W.W. Norton Co., 1992, 170-
185.

In an attempt to determine the pre-war occupations of ex-slaves in
the Union army, the author analyzed black enlistment records found
in regimental muster rolls. These muster rolls contain information
regarding each individual soldier's military rank, eye and hair color,
complexion, place of birth and place of enlistment, height, age, term
of service, civilian occupation, and much more. Using this data, and
applying sophisticated statistical tools, the author determined the
distribution of civilian occupations among a sample of ex-slaves
serving in the Union Army."

302. "Marking Time." *Pennsylvania Heritage*, 36, 4 (Fall 2010):
48.

This one-page article discusses the role of Pennsylvania African-
Americans in the 54th Massachusetts Infantry.

303.   Marvel, William. "The Battle of Saltville: Massacre or Myth?" *Blue & Gray Magazine,* 8, 6 (August 1991): 10-19, 46-60.

Marvel has provided a comprehensive almost minute-by-minute recounting of the Federal defeat at Saltville, Virginia on October 2, 1864. Of particular interest is the author's controversial assertion that, contrary to popular belief, no widespread massacre of black soldiers occurred after the battle. He maintains, that however reprehensible the killing of black prisoners may be, only "five ... were definitely murdered at Saltville...and as many as seven more may have suffered the same fate."

304.   _____. "Last Hurrah at Palmetto Ranch." *Civil War Times,* 44, 6 (January 2006): 66-73.

The last armed clash of the Civil War was fought in a remote corner of Texas and resulted in a one-sided Confederate victory. When the battle of Palmetto Ranch was fought on May 12-13, 1865, the principal armies of the Confederacy had already surrendered and Jefferson Davis was a prisoner of the Federal government. Arrogant ambition led an over-eager and glory-seeking Union commander to initiate a needless battle. One of the Union regiments participating in the battle was the 62nd United States Colored Infantry. Ironically, not only was the last battle of the war a Confederate victory, but the last prisoner of war to fall into Confederate captivity was Sergeant David Clark of the 62nd Colored Infantry. The article is illustrated with a map and contains several photographs.

305.   Mauldin, Curtis A. "Unassuming Valor: Sergeant William H. Carney and the Awarding of the Medal of Honor." *Proceedings and Papers of the Georgia Association of Historians,* 12 (1991): 46-80.

This work offers an account of the awarding of the Medal of Honor to Sergeant William H. Carney, Company C, 54th Massachusetts Infantry. Carney's medal was awarded 36 years after his exploits in saving the flag at Fort Wagner, South Carolina, on July 18, 1863. Though severely wounded he carried the national flag to safety. In actuality, the first Medal of Honor for an African-American was awarded to Robert Blake, a navy Landsmen. Blake received the medal for extraordinary courage while serving aboard the U.S.S. *Marblehead* during an engagement with Confederate shore batteries on the Stono River in South Carolina on December 25, 1863. However, Carney's medal was backdated to July 1863, so he is considered the first African-American Medal of Honor recipient. Ironically, the impetus for Carney's medal rests with former Sergeant Major Christian Fleetwood, 4th USCT, another recipient of the medal. Fleetwood was instrumental in bringing Carney's actions at Fort Wagner to the attention of the government "because he wanted justice done for a personal friend." On May 9, 1900, justice was done and the medal was awarded. The article contains a brief biography of Carney, a description of the attack on Fort Wagner, and an account of Carney's role in the battle.

306.　Mayo, Thomas D. "The Battle of Saltville." In *Black Soldiers in Blue: African American Troops in the Civil War Era*, edited by John David Smith. Chapel Hill: University of North Carolina Press, 2002, 200-226.
The late September early-October 1864 Federal attack on Saltville, Virginia is recounted. Among the Union forces making the assault were 600 men of the hastily organized and ill-trained 5th U.S. Colored Cavalry. The October 2, 1864 battle is described in detail. That night, Union forces retired from the battlefield leaving behind a number of wounded black soldiers. In the ensuing days, according to the author, many of these men were murdered by rage-filled Confederate soldiers. The author uses both Union and Confederate sources that "demonstrate that the murders at Saltville were among the worst atrocities of the American Civil War." While most historians agree that the murder of captive black soldiers did occur at Saltville, they disagree on the number murdered. Mayo provides no casualty estimate since "it is difficult to make an exact judgment as to how many were murdered at Saltville." The article is illustrated and contains 82 notes.

307.   Meier, Judith A. H. "Citizens of Color: Biographical Sketches of Montgomery County's Black Soldiers in the Civil War." *The Bulletin of the Historical Society of Montgomery County*, 29, 2 and 3 (Spring & Fall, 1994): 3-145.

Using church records, wills, marriage certificates, census reports, county documents, newspaper accounts, and military and pension records, Meier has identified and provided biographies for almost every Montgomery County African-American who served in the Civil War. Copies of original documents regarding many of the individuals profiled are incorporated in the text.

308.   Meier, Michael T. "Lorenzo Thomas and the Recruitment of Blacks in the Mississippi Valley, 1863-1865. In *Black Soldiers in Blue: African American Troops in the Civil War Era*, edited by John David Smith. Chapel Hill: University of North Carolina Press, 2002, 249-275.

The Civil War recruiting efforts of Adjutant General of the Army Lorenzo Thomas is related. Thomas, described as an arrogant, desk-bound, paper-pusher, was despised by Secretary of War Edwin A Stanton, his immediate superior. To remove him from Washington, Stanton dispatched Thomas on an inspection tour of the Mississippi Valley. He was to assume the immense task of raising and administering black regiments throughout the valley. Surprisingly, Thomas became a strong advocate for the enlistment of black soldiers. He approached his task with unusual gusto and tireless energy. Many of his addresses to groups of contraband and white troops were said to resemble an old fashion camp meeting. Thomas "brought uniformity to the size of the new black regiments, involved many commands in their recruitment, and eased the path of their acceptance into a skeptical U.S. Army." Eventually more than 70,000 African-Americans were recruited under his supervision. The difficulties in recruiting African-American soldiers in Kentucky in the teeth of intense popular opposition is also discussed in detail. The article contains 126 notes of both a primary and secondary nature.

309.   Messner, William F. "Black Violence and White Response: Louisiana, 1862." *Journal of Southern History,* 41, 1 (February 1975): 19-38.

Benjamin Butler, the first Union general officer in charge of occupied southern Louisiana, was responsible for maintaining social order, restoring sugar plantations to productivity while, at the same time, controlling the fugitive slave population and the potential for racial violence. Threats of civil disorder by African-Americans were countered by a system of contraband programs designed to put former slaves back to work as wage earners on government run plantations. Butler, woefully short of troops, also recruited both free men and later fugitive slaves as soldiers in the Louisiana Native Guards. Military discipline, it was assumed, would give former slaves a much needed sense of military discipline while controlling "the dangerous proclivities of Afro-Americans." Military and racial considerations - the supposed immunity of African-Americans to climatic diseases - dictated that the Native Guards, and later black units raised in Louisiana, be used only on fatigue duties or as garrison troops. From a number of perspectives, economic, social, and military, a well-written and thought-provoking article.

310.   Metzer, Jacob. "The Records of the U.S. Colored Troops as a Historical Source: An Explanatory Examination." *Historical Methods*, 14, 3 (Summer 1981): 124-132.

Records kept by the National Achieves in Washington are a rich source of statistical information regarding African-American Civil War soldiers. According to the author company roles are of particular importance since "these records contain systematic information on the physical, demographic, occupational, and military characteristics of a large segment of the black population." The article contains ten tables illustrating how this information can be utilized in historical analysis. As for example, Table 4 shows how black noncommissioned officers were taller and lighter in complexion than black privates. Other tables include information on state residence upon enlistment, occupation by height and complexion, age, mortality, mobility, and military rank by previous civilian occupation.

311.   Miller, Edward A., Jr. "Angel of Light: Helen L. Gilson, Army Nurse." *Civil War History*, 43, 1 (March 1997): 17-37.

Helen Gilson, a Boston-born teacher and Civil War nurse with the U.S. Sanitation Commission, is profiled. Gilson, in the face of institutional opposition and little support, established the Colored Hospital Service at City Point, Virginia, to care for wounded and sick African-American soldiers. The hospital she organized and administered was "known as the best in that department of the army."

312.   _____. "Garland H. White, Black Army Chaplain." *Civil War History*, 43, 3 (September 1997): 201-218.

The life of Garland H. White is chronicled. White was a self-educated runaway slave and one of only fourteen black chaplains commissioned by the Union Army. White served with the 28th USCT until mustered out in 1866. His post-war career is briefly described.

313.   Miller, Edward A. "Volunteers for Freedom: Black Civil War Soldiers in Alexandria National Cemetery." *Historic Alexandria Quarterly*, Part I, (Fall 1998): 1-14; Part II, (Winter 1998): 1-14.

Based almost entirely on primary sources, this is an extraordinary well-researched study of African-American burials in the Alexandria (not Arlington) National Cemetery. Part I deals with the early history of black of enlistments in the Union Army and the establishment of military hospitals and cemeteries – both black and white – in Alexandria, Virginia. Part II contains an Appendix listing the Name, Rank, Regiment, and Date of Death of 277 black soldiers buried in the segregated plots in the Alexandria National Cemetery.

314. _____. "The Black Civil War Soldiers of Illinois: The Story of the Twenty-Ninth U.S. Colored Infantry." *Prologue: Quarterly of the National Archives and Records Administration*, 30, 4 (Winter 1998): 269-274.

Civil War histories of African-American regiments are few in number. Most African-Americans soldiered in obscurity performing garrison duty or functioning as a readily available military labor force. The 29th U.S. Colored Infantry was typical in this respect except for one terrible exception in July 1864. Raised in Illinois and brought to full strength by recruited and drafted men from the slave states, it saw little combat until its deployment in the Battle of the Crater outside Petersburg on July 30, 1864. Fully a third of the regiment was lost; many captured African-Americans "were killed by Confederate soldiers who resented the encounter with soldiers of a despised race." After the war the regiment performed garrison duty in Texas along the Rio Grande before mustering out in November 1865.

Unusual for studies of this nature, Miller examined 200 pension applications from veterans who served in the 29th (over 60% of the officers and men applied for pensions). Utilizing records in the National Archives, Miller concluded that "black and white pensioners were treated equally." However, almost all the enlisted men were former slaves, even those recruited in Illinois. As a consequence, African-American pension requests were hampered by illiteracy, marriage laws, the unavailability of personal information such as date and place of birth, and frequent and often bewildering name changes. Miller found that most black veterans of the 29th seeking a pension were day laborers barely making a subsistence living; as a result "black civil war veterans benefited very little by their army service."

Miller has provided a valuable and out of the ordinary unit history of an almost forgotten African-American Civil War regiment. Particularly noteworthy is his analysis of the post-war travails of the unit's veterans. The article contains several period photographs, a statistical appendix, and 11 notes based primarily on pension records found in the National Archives.

315.   Miller, Randall M. and Jon W. Zophy. "Unwelcome Allies: Billy Yank and the Black Soldier." *Phylon: The Atlanta University Journal of Race and Culture*, 39, 3 (September 1978): 234-240.

In this essay the authors maintain that racial prejudice and racism were all too common among both officers and enlisted men in the Union Army. Many whites bitterly opposed the enlistment of African-Americans as soldiers; many viewed armed blacks as a threat to the exiting social order and many more feared they could not be trusted in combat. Even when black units performed well, their accomplishments, while acknowledged by whites, were soon forgotten. "The surprising fact revealed in a review of Union soldiers' diaries and letters is not that so many held anti-Negro beliefs; rather, it is that these ideas persisted for so long . . . and anti-Negro sentiments proved so resilient."

316.   Miller, Richard F. "For His Wife and His Widow, and his Orphan: Massachusetts and Family Aid during the Civil War." *Massachusetts Historical Review*, 6 (2004): 70-106.

During the Civil War, Massachusetts provided public and private support for dependent families of Civil War soldiers. State aid was seen as a means of maintaining soldiery morale and spurring enlistments. Unfortunately, family aid, in the form of public assistance, only extended to soldiers who were residents of the state upon enlistment. The majority of black soldiers recruited in the three Massachusetts African-American regiments (the 54th, 55th Massachusetts Infantry and 5th Massachusetts Cavalry) were out-of-state residents. Consequently, their dependent families were not entitled to state aid and "the majority of the state's black soldiers, as residents of other states, never gained the full benefits accorded to their fellow Massachusetts troops." The article contains several illustrations and 67 notes based on newspaper accounts as well as primary and secondary sources.

317.   Mohr, Clarence L. "Before Sherman: Georgia Blacks and the Union War Effort." *Journal of Southern History,* 45, 3 (August 1979): 331-352.

The focus of this study is an examination of Georgia slave escapes to the Union controlled Sea Islands and their subsequent contributions, as freed men, to the Union war effort. Many of these escapes were initiated by black individuals; others were the result of "rescue" operations conducted by the Union Army or Navy along the coast or inland waters. Many of the escapes were in family groups, and Union Army recruiters "discovered early that the prospects of securing the freedom of friends and relatives was a powerful inducement for blacks to join Union ranks." According to the author the liberation of family and friends was only one of many reasons to enlist in the army. "Nearly all Negro soldiers shared a basic hatred of bondage and a desire to strike out directly at the slave system." The author also examines the individual exploits of African-Americans in rescuing those still in bondage, their efforts in obtaining valuable intelligence for the Federal cause, and their service as pilots. The self-defense of many black settlements on the Sea Islands is also described. Self-defense measures, which meant armed resistance, were necessary to counter Confederate raiding expeditions. The article contains 47 notes based on manuscripts, newspaper accounts, letters, and both primary and secondary sources.

318.   Moneyhon, Carl H. "White Society and African-American Soldiers." In *All Cut to Pieces and Gone to Hell: The Civil War, Race Relations, and the Battle of Poison Spring,* edited by Mark K. Christ: Little Rock: August House, 2003, 31-57.

Why did Confederate soldiers react so violently to the idea of African-American soldiers under arms? This intriguing essay explores the cultural circumstances that lead Confederate soldiers, on numerous occasions, to murder black solders that fell into their hands. African-Americans soldiers were considered by Confederates as an affront to the established social order, an armed form of servile insurrection, and "the ultimate threat" to the survival of Southern society and white supremacy. In order to redress the social balance and make matters right strong measures were necessary; even murder could be justified. "In the end, the idea of confronting black soldiers produced anger and outrage among most Confederate soldiers." As a result a number of atrocities occurred, some of which are recounted in the essay. The essay is extensively documented.

319.   Mountcastle, Clay. "Saltville's Dark Legacy." *The Civil War Monitor*, 4, 3 (Fall 2014): 28-29, and 72.
The execution of wounded black soldiers after the battle of Saltville, Virginia on the morning of October 3, 1864 is recounted.

320.   Montgomery, Horace. "A Union Officer's Recollection of the Negro." *Pennsylvania History,* 28, 2 (April 1961): 156-186.

In 1916, John McMurray, a former officer in an African-American infantry regiment, privately printed his *Recollections of a Colored Troop*. It was subsequently published serially in a Pennsylvania newspaper, and still later printed as a separate pamphlet. The author of this article has provided an excellent summary of these recollections. Murray's service as a captain in Company D, 6th United States Colored Troops is outlined from his first day with the regiment at Camp William Penn (located north of Philadelphia) through its campaigns before Petersburg and in North Carolina. Particularly noteworthy is the description of the September 1864 regimental assault on New Market Heights before Petersburg. In the attack Company D suffered 12 killed and 15 wounded out of 30 men making the assault. Overall, in 40 minutes the 6th USCT lost 210 men killed, wounded, and missing out 367 men committed to the battle. According to the author "McMurray's feeling toward his men was a composite of sorrow, pride, concern, and sincere gratitude."

321.   Moore, Alicia L. and La Vonne I. Neal. "African Americans and the Civil War: Brave Standard Bearers." *Black History Bulletin*, 73, 2 (Summer/Fall 2010): 4-7.
This is an introductory overview for an issue of the Black History Bulletin dedicated to teaching students about Civil War era African-Americans. Particular attention is paid to the exploits of Sergeant William H. Carney, the first black recipient of the Medal of Honor,

and the poem by Olivia Ward Bush Banks commemorating that achievement.

322.   Moore, John Hammond, editor. "The Last Officer April — 1865." *South Carolina Historical Magazine*, 67, 1 (January 1966): 1-14.

Potter's raid took place in the waning days of the war when two Union brigades – one white the other black – set out to destroy rail communications between Camden and Florence, South Carolina. Edward L. Stevens, a lieutenant in the 54th Massachusetts Infantry, kept an account of the raid in his diary. These entries are reprinted in full along with the official after-action report of Colonel E. N. Hallowell, his brigade commander. Stevens describes contrabands, looting by white and black troops, hard marching, the destruction of bridges and rail equipment, and feeble Confederate resistance. Stevens, may have been "the last officer killed in action during the Rebellion." He was shot and instantly killed on April 18, 1865.

323.   Moore, Kenneth Bancroft. "Fort Pillow, Forest, and the United States Colored Troops in 1864." *Tennessee Historical Quarterly*, 54, 2 (Summer 1995): 112-123.

Moore's article focuses on the combat role of African-Americans following the massacre of black troops at Fort Pillow. In its report concerning the massacre, the Joint Committee on the Conduct of the War was guilty of gross exaggeration; nevertheless, black soldiers, as well as their white officers, were well aware they could expect little in the way of quarter from Forest or his men. According to the author, Fort Pillow served as a motivating factor for black soldiers to even accounts. Thus, at Brice's Crossroads, Tupelo, Pulaski and Nashville, African-Americans fought with determination, confidence, hard-won experience, and the memory of a massacre to be avenged. They were, by the summer of 1864, seasoned and tough soldiers, soldiers that were more than willing to take on the man they considered responsible for what happened on the banks of the Mississippi only months before. Based on primary and secondary sources, the article includes 62 notes, six photos, and a map.

324. Moore, Wilma L. "Everyday People: Researching the Civil War." *Traces of Indiana and Midwestern History*, 22, 3 (Summer 2010): 22-24.

Research into the activities of Indiana's African-American soldiers is discussed. The article also includes capsule summaries of letters written by white officers and enlisted men regarding blacks as soldiers.

325. Morgan, Michael. "Surprise at Ocean Pond." *America's Civil War*, 18, 1 (March 2005): 46-52.

The Battle of Olustee, or Ocean Pond, was the largest and bloodiest battle in Florida. Fought on February 20, 1864, it was a resounding Southern victory. Morgan's article offers a highly detailed account of the battle and the part played by several African-American regiments in the encounter. The article includes period photographs and illustrations as well as a map.

326. Morris, Roy, Jr. "Fort Pillow: Massacre or Madness?" *America's Civil War*, 13, 5 (November 2000): 26-32.

Forrest's capture of Fort Pillow on April 12, 1864, and the controversial events that followed, are described. While never actually calling the events at Fort Pillow a massacre, the author does conclude that a number of factors – racial animosity, hatred of Tennessee Unionists, physical exhaustion, and fear – all combined to produce "a brief but deadly spasm of vengefulness." Southern eyewitness accounts of the battle are used uncritically; nor is the role of Forrest in the aftermath at Fort Pillow explored in any depth. The article contains several illustrations, a map, but no documentation.

327. Moss, Juanita Patience. "Forgotten Glory: The Civil War's Black Soldiers in White Regiments." *Journal of the Afro-American Historical and Genealogical Society*, 23, 2 (Fall 2004): 117-126.

Undoubtably, black soldiers served in white regiments during the Civil War. Using the index to the Compiled Military Service Records as a basic research tool, the author has provided selected examples of these occurrences.

328.　Mulderink, Earl F, III. "A Different Civil War: African American Veterans in New Bedford, Massachusetts." In *Union Soldiers and the Northern Home Front: Wartime Experiences, Postwar Adjustments*, edited by Paul A. Cimbala and Randall M. Miller. New York: Fordham University Press, 2002 417-441.

This article recounts the vain efforts of African-American Civil War veteran in Bedford, Massachusetts, to keep alive the collective memory of black military service and their contribution to Union victory. These efforts included parades, encampments, Memorial Day celebrations, and Grand Army of the Republic (GAR) membership. The article is profusely documented.

329.　Murray, Donald M. and Robert M. Rodney. "Colonel Julian E. Bryant: Champion of the Negro Soldier." *Illinois State Historical Society Journal,* 56, 2 (Summer 1963): 257-281.

The efforts of Julian E. Bryant in obtaining "recognition and justice" for African-American soldiers are recounted. Bryant had previously served in the 33rd Illinois before being commissioned as a major in the 1st Regiment, Mississippi Infantry, African Descent (later redesignated as the 51st USCT). He saw combat with that regiment during the brutal Battle of Milliken's Bend on June 7, 1863. He was later lieutenant colonel of the 51st USCT and still later colonel and commanding officer of the 46th USCT, a regiment described as difficult to handle. A proponent of the employment of African-Americans as soldiers, Bryant was outraged at the use of black soldiers either in demeaning roles or as laborers suitable only for fatigue duties. He agitated forcefully - and continuously - for equitable treatment of black soldiers. His uncle, William Cullen Bryant, was the crusading editor of the *New York Evening Post*. Several letters he wrote to his uncle concerning the treatment of black troops were later used in a number of scathing editorials published by the paper, though without attribution to Colonel Bryant. As a result, several reforms regarding the employment of African-American soldiers were subsequently implemented. Bryant drowned at the age of 28 while on occupation duty in Texas on May

14, 1865. The article contains 49 notes and several illustrations including several drawings by Colonel Bryant.

330.   Musick, Mike. "Research Room." *Civil War Times*, 49, 4
    (August 2010): 17.
Personal letters, diaries, and unit histories written by black Civil War soldiers are rare. However, documentation found in the National Achieves and Records Administration (NARA) regarding African-American soldiers is extensive. Records kept by the Bureau of Colored Troops, and on file at NARA, include the individual soldier's Compiled Military Service Record, as well as inspection reports, regimental record books, unbound regimental unit files, and hospital reports. In addition, pension files for individual black Civil War soldiers are also on file.

331.   Newmark, Jill L. "Face to Face with History." *Prologue*,
    41, 3 (Fall 2009): 22-25.
During the Civil War only 13 men of color served the Union Army as surgeons. As rare as that was, the discovery of a photograph of an African-American contract surgeon is even rarer. A black-and-white photograph of William J. Powell, Jr., who served as a contract army surgeon, was discovered in his pension file application. Powell, who was born in Massachusetts and studied at the College of Physicians and Surgeons in London, applied for and received a surgeon's contract in May 1863. He served in the Contraband Hospital in Washington until the end of his service in November 1864. Later in life Powell was unsuccessful in his efforts to receive a pension since he served under contract and not as a commissioned officer. Included in this short but interesting account is an 1863 photograph of Powell in uniform and a copy of his contract as an acting assistant surgeon.

332.   Nichols, Ronnie A. "The Changing Role of Blacks in the
    Civil War." In *"All Cut to Pieces and Gone to Hell:" The Civil
    War, Race Relations, and the Battle of Poison Spring*, edited by
    Mark K. Christ: Little Rock: August House, 2003, 31-59.
The changing role of African-Americans in the Civil War, from slaves to soldiers, is discussed in this brief overview article.

333.   Nofi, Albert A. "Knapsack: Profile: African-Americans in Union Service." *North & South*, 3, 3 (March 2000): 9-11.
This article provides background information regarding African-American military participation in the Civil War. It contains two tables; one provides a listing of black regiments and batteries as of 1865, the other a breakdown of black enlistments by state and territory.

334.   _____.. "Knapsack: Black Troops from New York State." *North & South*, 8, 3 (May 2005): 11, 93-94.
During the Civil War the state of New York provided three regiments of African-American troops to the Union cause. A capsule history of each regiment – the 20th, 26th, and 31st USCT – is provided by the author. Only the 31st USCT saw considerable combat; for all three, however, "the war was mostly one of hard fatigues and tedious garrison duty."

335.   _____. "Knapsack: Incidents of War: The Battle of Palmetto Ranch." *North & South*, 11, 5 (October 2009): 9-11.
The Battle of Palmetto Ranch, Texas, fought on May 13, 1865, six weeks after Lee had surrendered at Appomattox Court House, was the last battle of the Civil War and a Union defeat. One of the regiments that took part in the Union debacle was the 62nd U. S. Colored Infantry, a unit that remained on garrison duty in Texas until March 1866. Ironically, the last Union soldier wounded in the Civil War was Sergeant Crocker of the 62nd.

Before mustering out, the 62nd contributed money for establishing a college for African-American men in Missouri, the original state in which the regiment was recruited. Today that institution is Lincoln University of Missouri. In general, far too brief but still a good overview of a battle that never should have been fought.

336.   Nolin, Kelly. "The Civil War Letters of Sgt. J. O. Cross, 29th Connecticut Volunteer Infantry (Colored)." *The Connecticut Historical Society Bulletin*, 60, 2-4 (Summer-Fall 1995): 211-235.

A collection of letters written by Sergeant Joseph Orin Cross to his wife are reprinted. Cross enlisted in the 29th Connecticut Volunteer Infantry (Colored) on April 30, 1864. Serving mainly on the Petersburg front, he was mustered out on October 24, 1865. Genealogical information and a short biography of Cross is also provided.

337.   Northcott, Dennis, compiler. "55th Massachusetts Infantry: Letters from Alfred S. Hartwell." *Gateway Heritage*, 22, 3 (Winter 2001-2002): 32-35

A series of four letters written by Lt. Colonel Alfred S. Hartwell of the 55th Massachusetts Infantry to St. Louis attorney and friend Lucian Eaton are transcribed in their entirety. The letters provide a description of Union operations in and around Charleston, the demoralizing influence of unequal pay on the regiment, duty in Florida, weather, disease, incompetent and competent officers, the hoped for commissioning of an African-American soldier, the Battle of Honey Hill, South Carolina, and officer losses during the battle. The letters are part of a collection of 39 addressed by Hartwell to Eaton and are part of the Lucian Eaton Papers preserved in the archives of the Missouri Historical Society.

338.   Noyes, Edward. "The Negro in Wisconsin's Civil War Effort." *Lincoln Herald*, 69, 2 (Summer 1967): 70-82.

According to the 1860 census the total black population of Wisconsin was only 1,171. Wisconsin African-Americans could testify in court but were denied the franchise, were not citizens and, initially, could not serve in the military. Nevertheless, 353 African-Americans were eventually credited to Wisconsin's war roster by the states' Adjutant General. Approximately 20% of this number may have been enrolled in other states but credited to Wisconsin. The number who served "is modest in comparison with the total of troops Wisconsin furnished the Union, but it represents a proportion to the state's Negro population greater than that of white soldiers" in the state. Early efforts by African-Americans to serve in the military are reviewed as well as the changing dynamics of war which created a critical need for additional manpower, either black or white. Individual Wisconsin African-Americans served in the 5th, 12th, 14th, 21st, 29th, and 49th U.S. Colored Troops. The only organized unit wholly credited to Wisconsin was Company F, 29th U. S. Colored Troops. The article is heavily footnoted largely from primary sources.

339.   Ochs, Stephen J. "'American Spartacus': Captain Andre' Cailloux of the 1st Louisiana Native Guards." *American Legacy: Celebrating African-American History and Culture*, 7, 3 (Fall 2001): 31-36.
Boasting that he was the "blackest man in the Crescent City," Afro-Creole Andre Callioux was born a slave but prospered as a free man of color in antebellum New Orleans. French in religion, language, and culture, the bi-lingual Cailloux was killed while bravely leading Company E, 1st Louisiana Native Guards on an impossible assault on Confederate fortifications at Port Hudson, Louisiana, on May 27, 1863. This very readable account of Cailloux's life, and his impact on Civil War black America, is adapted from the author's full-length study *A Black Patriot and a White Priest: Andre Cailloux and Claude Paschal Maistre in Civil War New Orleans*.

340.   O'Den, Jeffrey and Raymond Herek. "Michigan's Soldiers of Color." *Michigan History*, 95, 4 (July/August 2011): 53-56.
The 1st Michigan Colored Infantry, later re-designated as the 102nd United States Colored Troops, is profiled. This was the only black regiment raised in Michigan during the war. First Lieutenant Orson Bennett of the regiment won the Medal of Honor for gallantry at Honey Hill, South Carolina.

341.   Omenhausser, John Jacob. "Blacks & Whites in Color."
Civil War Times, 53, 6 (December 2014): 38-45.
Six watercolor paintings by Private John Jacob Omenhauser, a
Confederate prisoner at Point Lookout, Maryland, are reproduced.
The watercolors "portray a range of interactions" between
Confederate prisoners and their African-American guards.

342.   "The 102nd United States Colored Infantry." *Chronicle: The
Quarterly Magazine of the Historical Society of Michigan,* 35,
3 (Fall 2012): 25.
This is a half-page summary of the Civil War service of the 102nd
United States Colored Infantry (formally known as the 1st Michigan
Colored).

343.   Paradis, James. "Flexing the Sable Arm: Emancipation,
Black Troops, and Hard War." *Transactions of the American
Philosophical Society,* 97, 4 (2008): 5-25.
This essay examines the evolution of Lincoln's war policy from
conciliation and restraint to hard war. "The conflict was
transformed," under Lincoln's leadership, "from a war of civility to
a remorseless war of exhaustion." According to Paradis, a
substantial part of this policy change involved the enlistment of
African-Americans as soldiers. Black emancipation, and African-
American military service, became linked administration objectives
to save the Union. Paradis provides a brief history of black military
accomplishment during the war and discusses the thorny issue of
retribution for the murder of black soldiers. The author also
addresses Lincoln's early opposition to arming black soldiers. This
is an excellent summary highlighting the important role
emancipation and black military participation played in Lincoln's
evolving strategy for subduing the South and winning the war. The
article contains 39 notes.

344. _____. "Men of Nerve." *Military Images*, 34, 1 (Winter 2016): 10-15.
Selected *cartes de visite* of members of the 5th Massachusetts Cavalry, one of only seven black cavalry regiments raised during the war, are featured. All of the images save one are of white officers; the only exception is a *carte de visite* of an African-American trooper identified only as "Booth." The images are from the collection of Captain Andrew F. Chapman of the regiment. A short history of the 5th is also provided.

345. Peyton, Westmore. "War Within and Without: A Study of the Black Man's Role in the American Civil War." *Lincoln Herald*, 86, 2 (Summer 1984): 93-100.
The military participation of African-Americans in the Civil War is recounted.

346. Phillips, Geraldine N. "Civil War Pension Files in the National Archives: Windows on the Lives of African-Americans." *Journal of the Afro-American Historical and Genealogical Society*, 12, 1/2 (Spring/Summer 1991): 28-32.
A succinct but informative review of the rules governing Civil War pension applications coupled with actual examples filed by former African-American soldiers or their immediate survivors.

347. Pinkett, Harold T. "A Brother's Fight for Freedom." *Maryland Historical Magazine*, 86, 1 (Spring 1991): 39-50.
The wartime chronicle of the four Pinkett brothers from the Eastern Shore of Maryland is described by one of their descendants. The four brothers – Sandy, Stephen, Adam, and Wilson Pinkett – were born to a free black father but a slave mother. In all, there were 12 children in the family. However, under Maryland law children born to a slave mother were considered slaves. Though slaves, one brother fled from his master and enlisted in Company G, 7th United States Colored Troops. The other three, without consent of their pro-Southern owners, joined the 9th Regiment, USCT. The shared wartime experience of both regiments is described. Together they served principally in the Virginia theater and saw action at Fort

Gilmer, Deep Bottom, New Market Heights, Darbytown Road, Fair Oaks, and post-war border service in Texas. During the war two Pinkett brothers were wounded in action, two were promoted to corporal, and two learned to read and write. In 1864, by constitutional amendment, Maryland abolished slavery. For the Pinkett brothers, "Their mother, sisters, and brothers were no longer slaves."

348.   Plant, Trevor K. "Researching African Americans in the U.S. Army, 1866-1890: Buffalo Soldiers and Black Infantrymen." *Prologue*, 33, 1 (April 2001): 56-61.
For the genealogists and researchers, this article provides information regarding African-Americans who enlisted in the new black regular army regiments authorized by Congress after the Civil War. Initially, many of the men who enlisted were former soldiers in the USCT. Information regarding these troops, such enlistment papers, regimental returns, medical records, pensions, service records, and decorations are available at the National Archives Records Administration (NARA) building in Washington, DC. Information can also be obtained by mail. Mail inquiries should be addressed to: Old Military and Civil Records, National Archives and Records Administration, 700 Pennsylvania Avenue, NW, Washington, DC 20408-001. The article contains several photographs and 15 notes.

349.   Poole, Scott W. "Memory and the Abolitionist Heritage: Thomas Wentworth Higginson and the Uncertain Meaning of the Civil War." *Civil War History,* 51, 2 (June 2005): 202-217.
The intellectual disillusionment of radical abolitionist Thomas Wentworth Higginson is examined. Higginson, a Unitarian minister and former commanding officer of the 1st South Carolina Infantry of African Descent, grew progressively disenchanted in post-war America. At a Decoration Day speech at Harvard on May 29, 1904, he chose "to participate in the conspiracy of forgetfulness" by embracing the idea of sectional reconciliation. He asserted that the war had not been about liberating the slaves but rather a struggle between two contending theories of government: states' rights and the sovereignty of the Federal government. As Poole notes "the

aging abolitionist warrior helped shape a memory of the war friendly to the white South, unwittingly giving ground the historical amnesia that haunts us still."

350.	Popchock, Barry. "A Shower of Stars at New Market Heights." *Civil War Magazine,* 46 (August 1994): 30-31, 34-39.
Thirteen African-American soldiers were awarded the Medal of Honor for conspicuous gallantry during the engagement at New Market Heights, Virginia on September 29, 1864. The attack was launched by Major General Benjamin Butler, commander of the Army of the James. Its purpose was twofold: to open the road to Richmond while proving the "combat worthiness" of black soldiers. The first objective did not succeed; the second did. The battle is described in considerable detail by the author. The African-American regiments committed to the assault suffered over 900 casualties. Included in the article are several photographs and a full-color period map.

351.	Possemato, Joseph Anthony. "'Ain't you glad your husband is an officer in a 'Nigger Reg't?': The Letters of Captain Richard Henry Lee Jewett of the 54th Massachusetts." *New England Journal of History,* 65, 2 (Spring 2009): 1-23.
Excerpts from the wartime letters of Richard Jewett, an officer in the 54th Massachusetts Infantry, are the basis for this dual account of a committed abolitionist and one of the war's most celebrated regiments.

352.	Powles, James M. "South Carolina Slave Robert Smalls Put His Ship-Piloting Skills to Good Use in an Audacious Break for Freedom." *America's Civil War,* 13, 4 (September 2000): 8, 24, 62 and 64.
The author has written a fascinating account of the life and times of an extraordinary African-American, Robert Smalls. Though written for a general Civil War audience, the article provides considerable information regarding Smalls' early life, his escape with his family and friends aboard the captured Confederate steamer *Planter,* his experience as a Union pilot along the South Carolina coast, and his

subsequent career in public life. The article includes a black and white photograph of Smalls.

353.   Quarles, Benjamin. "The Abduction of the 'Planter.'" *Civil War History,* 4, 1 (1958): 5-10.
Another account of the legendary Robert Smalls, this time by one of the early pioneers of African-American studies. Unfortunately, details are sparse regarding Smalls' early and later life. The author's description of the abduction of the *Planter* is adequate but light on details. Unlike most commentators, Quarles does elaborate on the ship's cargo: cannon for Fort Ripley in Charleston Harbor.

354.   Rafferty, Colleen F. "The Records of Camp William Penn." *Pennsylvania Magazine of History and Biography*, 135, 4 (October 2011): 547-548.
The recent addition of Camp William Penn's records to the National Archives in Philadelphia is discussed. "Surviving records detail conditions at the camp and the personal and familial circumstances of many" of the enlisted men and offer insight into prevailing Philadelphia and Pennsylvania race relations. Camp William Penn, outside of Philadelphia, was purposely built for the exclusive training of African-American soldiers.

355.   Rampp, Lary C. "Negro Troop Activity in Indian Territory, 1863-1865." *Chronicles of Oklahoma*, 47, 1 (Spring 1969): 531-559.
As the title suggests, this article offers a fairly comprehensive account of African-American regiments that served and fought in the Indian Territory during the Civil War. Concerned mainly with the 1st Kansas Colored Regiment, the multi-ethnic clashes at Elk Creek, Honey Springs, Iron Bridge, and both battles of Cabin Creek are described in considerable tactical detail. The article contains 44 notes based on primary and secondary sources.

356. _____. "Incident at Baxter Springs on October 6, 1863." *Kansas Historical Quarterly*, 36, 2 (Summer 1970): 183-197.

On October 6, 1863, one company of the 2nd Kansas Colored Infantry took part in the defense of the Union post at Baxter Springs, Kansas, when it was attacked by Confederate guerrillas under the command of William Clarke Quantrill. The narrative provides little additional information regarding the company. The author does mention one African-American soldier who was murdered after the battle by his former master, a Confederate guerrilla.

357. Redding, Saunders. "Tonight for Freedom." *American Heritage*, 9, 4 (June 1958): 52-55, 90.

Written for a popular audience, this article is a well written and moving account of the assault on Battery Wagner in July 1863 by the 54th Massachusetts Infantry.

358. Redkey, Edwin S. "Rocked in the Cradle of Consternation. A Black Chaplain in the Union Army Reports on the Struggle to take Fort Fisher, North Carolina, in the Winter of 1864-1865." *American Heritage,* 31, 6 (October-November 1980): 70-79.

The two Union attempts to capture Fort Fisher, North Carolina are recounted by the Reverend Henry M. Turner, the first African-American commissioned as a chaplain in the Union Army. Turner's lucidly written journal entries describing both attempts (only the second assault was successful) were published shortly after the second battle in *The Christian Recorder*, the journal of the Methodist Episcopal Church.

359. _____. "Black Chaplains in the Union Army." *Civil War History,* 33, 4 (December 1987): 331-350.

"Of the 133 men who served as chaplains in black units, only 14 were black." And, as the author points out, the government only allowed these few to serve with great reluctance. According to army regulations, chaplains were elected by officers, and white officers in black regiments, with few exceptions, did not relish the idea of sharing their mess with men of color. Those who did obtain commissions as chaplains did so because of their success as recruiting agents or because of political connections. The latter was particularly true for the black regiments raised under Massachusetts state sponsorships. Regardless of how they obtained their commissions, black chaplains faced the same racial hostility as the men they served. But they faithfully performed a number of functions. They were teachers and preachers; they conducted worship services, wrote letters home for those who were illiterate, distributed religious tracts, counseled those who awaited execution for crimes, and comforted the sick and wounded in hospitals. And, as commissioned officers without command responsibilities, they still held "highly visible and prestigious positions." The article contains 44 notes, much of it based on correspondence. An appendix listing the names, religious affiliation, regiment and residence of all 14 black chaplains is also provided.

360. _____. "They Are Invincible: Two Black Army Chaplains Get a Look At Sherman's Army." *Civil War Times Illustrated*, 28, 2 (April 1989): 32-37.

The observations of two black army chaplains regarding Sherman's army are reprinted. Both chaplains were literate, free born, African-American, and seminary trained. The first, William Waring, was chaplain of the 102nd U.S. Colored Troops, a regiment composed of free black men recruited in Michigan. Writing from South Carolina to a black newspaper published in New York, Waring recorded his impressions when encountering Sherman's soldiers. They were, he wrote, hard-bitten, disheveled in appearance, manifesting little regard for private property, and lacking in what he considered soldierly discipline. Nevertheless, he found them, as an army, to be supremely self-confident and imbued with an aura of invincibility. Their treatment of black civilians, he observed, varied from cruel to humane.

The second black chaplain who recorded his observations was Henry M. Turner of the 1st U.S. Colored Troops. A Methodist minister, later a bishop, and still later a black nationalist, he observed Sherman's soldiers after meeting them in North Carolina.

Writing to an African-American newspaper in Philadelphia, he found Sherman's soldiers ill-clothed, ill-disciplined, and deliberately destructive of civilian property. In comparison, black soldiers of his command, Turner remarked "manifested more feelings for the rebels than did the white soldiers." The correspondence of both chaplains is extensively quoted. The article contains a number of period photographs.

361. _____. "Brave Black Volunteers: A Profile of the Fifth-fourth Massachusetts Regiment." In *Hope & Glory: Essays on the Legacy of the 54th Massachusetts Regiment*, edited by Marti H. Blatt, Thomas J. Brown, and Donald Yacovone: Amherst: University of Massachusetts Press, 2001, 21-34.

Utilizing military service records and government pension files, the author has constructed a statistical profile of the men who served in the 54th Massachusetts Regiment. Originally 1,007 black enlisted men and 37 white officers served; during the war an additional 286 enlisted men and 27 officers reinforced the regiment for a total of 1,357 men. Most of the enlisted men were not from Massachusetts. To fill the ranks, it was necessary to recruit throughout the North and border states. The largest number of recruits – 294 – hailed from Pennsylvania followed by New York with 183. Altogether the regiment enlisted men from 24 states and from as far away as Canada and the West Indies. The average age was 24.3 years. As for occupations "about a quarter enlisted as farmers, and a third called themselves laborers." There were no teachers and no mechanics; one was a preacher and two were peddlers. Approximately 152 men died as a result of combat, 326 were wounded, and 164 men discharged for reasons of health. Lucid, incredibly well researched and well written, this is an outstanding in-depth statistical study of one of the Civil War's most celebrated regiments.

362. _____. "Henry McNeal Turner: Black Chaplain in the Union Army." In *Black Soldiers in Blue: African American Troops in the Civil War Era*, editor. John David Smith. Chapel Hill: University of North Carolina Press, 2002, 336-360.

The life of Henry McNeal Turner is recounted from his earliest days to his post-Civil War career. Turner was born free in South Carolina and learned to read and write at his grandmother's knee and at a law office in Abbeville, South Carolina. At 17 he had a religious conversion; years later he was licensed as a Methodist preacher. Redkey's article discusses Turner's Civil War experience where he was one of only 14 black chaplains commissioned in the Union army. He served for two years as chaplain of the 1st United States Colored Troops, an experience that provided "an intense, invigorating crucible for his energetic talents." A gifted journalist, he wrote often to African-American newspapers in the North attacking the institution of slavery while also deploring the inequities black soldiers were forced to endure. In his dispatches he celebrated African-American victories on the battlefield and proselytized for the African Methodist Episcopal Church (AME). Turner's post war career as a Georgia politician and AME bishop from 1880 to 1915 is discussed. The theological challenges he faced from other competing black religious groups, and his position as national spokesmen for African-Americans, are all explored in depth. The author states that Turner "found his life's work in his two years as an army chaplain." It was in the army that Turner "refined his thinking about the African race and its future."

363. Reed, Moses. "Report of Lieut.-Col. Moses Reed, 56th U S Colored Troops." *Tri-County Genealogical Society*, 16, 1 (Spring 2001): 20-21.

This is a reprint of an after-action report by Lieutenant Colonel Moses Reed, 56th U.S. Colored Troops. Reed's report describes the engagement at Wallace's Ferry on Big Creek, Arkansas, fought on July 26, 1864. Casualties suffered by the 56th and 60th U.S. Colored Troops and the 2nd U.S. Colored Artillery are described.

364.   Reid, Richard M. "Black Experience in the Union Army: The Other Civil War." *Canadian Review of American Studies*, 21, 2 (1990): 145-155.

In this well-documented and eye opening study, the author concludes that the African-American military experience in the Civil War was vastly different from that of white Union soldiers. Civil wars by their very nature are often pitiless conflicts with quarter seldom asked or given. In this respect the American Civil War was unique: both North and South exercised restraint and in general the rules of war were observed – for white soldiers. As the author points out "for one group of Americans, however, the conflict ... included a strikingly brutal and savage side." The "other war" experienced by black soldiers was often characterized by forcible conscription into military service by Union recruiting officers, discrimination in pay, indifferent treatment by military officials, and denial of commissions as officers. What markedly differentiated the experience of blacks from their white comrades-in-arms was the treatment they received as prisoners of war or as wounded soldiers left on the field of battle. Often African-American soldiers were murdered after capture or shot "while attempting to escape." Often, too, their families suffered greatly at the hands of vengeful slave owners or, in many cases, indifferent and prejudiced Union officers. From the perspective of the African-American soldiers and their families, it was a war far different than the white man's war. The article contains 47 notes based on private letters, unpublished records, official documents, and secondary sources.

365.   _____. "Government Policy, Prejudice, and the Experience of Black Civil War Soldiers and Their Families." *Journal of Family History*, 27, 4 (October 2002): 374-398.

Reid has written an excellent summation of government financial assistance to African-Americans both during and after the Civil War. His study examines the impact of these efforts upon black military dependents, military pay and bounties, and pensions of African-American soldiers and veterans. Particularly informative is the treatment of dependent families left behind during the war. While treatment differed from region to region, and community to community, in slave-holding areas families of black soldiers often faced harsh and vindictive retaliation from slave owners as punishment for a man's enlistment. Even in the North support for black families was often lacking. Often they were herded into unsanitary, overcrowded, and disease ridden camps. While some officials vainly attempted to alleviate the suffering of black military dependents others were indifferent to their well-being. As Reid observes, "The families with the greatest chance of community and government support resided in New England." The author also addresses the unequal pay and bounties received by black soldiers in the war. The pension system, particular the 1890 Dependent Pension Act, is described. The 1890 Dependent Pension Act allowed veterans, regardless of race or disability, to apply for a government pension. Honorable service during the war was all that was required. However, notes Reid, "While more than 90 percent of white veterans were able to make at least one successful application, the rate for blacks was only 75%." The rate of acceptance was even lower for the widows and children of black veterans. While the 1890 act may have guaranteed a pension based solely on service, many African-Americans were unable to apply because of cost, illiteracy, poverty, lack of documentation, rural residence, and government prejudice. Reid's wide-ranging article contains 92 notes based on primary and secondary sources

366. Reid, Richard. "General Edward A. Wild and Civil War Discrimination." *Historical Journal of Massachusetts,* 13, 1 (January 1985): 14-29.

Edward A. Wild was a Harvard trained physician and fervent abolitionist who distinguished himself as an officer in the Union Army early in the war. Though suffering from several grievous wounds, one of which required the amputation of his left arm, he was asked by Massachusetts Governor John Andrew to recruit freedmen as soldiers in New Bern, North Carolina, a black refugee center. A fervent advocate of arming African-Americans, he recruited several regiments that later became known as Wild's African Brigade. The brigade saw service in North and South Carolina and in the Overland Campaign in Virginia where it distinguished itself in the Battle of Wilson's Wharf on May 24, 1864. Wild's recruiting of freedmen led to a number of confrontations with racist white officers and lead to his court martial and subsequent demotion.

367. _____. "Raising the African Brigade: Early Black Recruitment in Civil War North Carolina." *North Carolina Historical Review*, 70, 3 (July 1993): 266-297.
This article discusses the recruiting of African-Americans as soldiers in Union-occupied coastal North Carolina. The recruiting of blacks as soldiers in the state was strongly encouraged by abolitionist in Massachusetts and in particular by John Andrew, the state's governor. They believed that black soldiers led by hand-picked, competent, and abolitionist-inspired officers would lead the way in proving to the nation at large the fighting potential, value, and usefulness of African-American troops. To command this effort, the governor selected Colonel Edward Wild. Wild was a Massachusetts-born doctor, Harvard educated, a much experienced and horribly wounded officer who "was sympathetic to the problems facing black Americans." Unlike other white officers who were appointed to serve in black regiments, officers in Wild's African Brigade did not have to face a board of examiners in order to receive a commission. Officers were appointed directly by Wild if they met his exacting standards for fairness and professionalism. Several regiments were raised and originally designated as North Carolina Colored Volunteers. The composition, background, organization, occupation, and average age of soldiers in the 1st and 2nd North Carolina Colored Volunteers are described. Service histories for all the regiments in the short-lived African Brigade are provided. Later black North Carolina regiments were re-designated as United States Colored Troops. Ironically, whether ex-slaves would fight and whether white soldiers would grudgingly accept them was settled by the end of 1863. The question had been answered at Port Hudson, Fort Wagner, and Milliken's Bend.

The article contains 134 notes based on the *War of the Rebellion: A Compilation of the Official Records of the Union and Confederate Armies*, records in the National Archives, and particular Record Group 94, Colored Troops Division, personal papers and secondary sources. The article also contains three appendixes and a number of illustrations.

368. _____. USCT Veterans in Post-Civil War North Carolina." In *Black Soldiers in Blue: African American Troops in the Civil War Era*, edited by John David Smith. Chapel Hill: University of North Carolina Press, 2002, 391-421.

The postwar residency of African-American soldiers recruited in North Carolina is examined. Reid maintains that settlement patterns of black veterans from the state were dictated by place of service during the war. The author argues "the more extensive service ...outside the state, the less likely it is that one can locate the veterans within North Carolina in later years." Veterans who served exclusively in North Carolina, generally continued to reside in the state long after the war.

369. Reid, Robert D. "The Negro in Alabama during the Civil War." *Journal of Negro History*, 35, 3 (July 1950): 265-288.

Most of this dated study concentrates on the African-American experience in Civil War and post-war Alabama. Considerable attention is paid to the activities of African-American regiments recruited and raised throughout the state. According to one source quoted in the study, the total number of black soldiers enlisted in Alabama during the war was almost double the official government estimate.

370. Reidy, Joseph P. "Black Men in Navy Blue during the Civil War." *Prologue, Quarterly of the National Archives and Record Administrations* 33, 3 (Fall 2001): 155-167.

Utilizing records in the National Archives, primary sources, and academic studies, Reidy has written an in-depth examination of African-American sailors serving in the Union Navy during the Civil War. Unlike the army, sailors did not serve in segregated units. However, there was a concentration of black sailors on support and supply vessels. "Black men filled an inordinately large number of the enlisted billets on the barks and schooners that served as colliers and ordnance storeships." As in the army, no African-Americans were commissioned as officers and none received warrants.

Miniscule numbers were promoted to petty officers ratings. Mostly these were men who were free born, had previous maritime experience, and hailed from port cities along the Atlantic seaboard. The majority of African-American sailors were former slaves and were assigned to lowly ship board positions and were paid and rated accordingly. However, Reidy cautions that the black naval experience varied from fleet to fleet and ship to ship and generalizations about their role often contained a number of exceptions and contradictions.

During the war African-Americans constituted close to 20% of the Union Navy's enlisted ranks, a not inconsiderable number. And while they often served under racist officers and suffered blatant discrimination, they did man integrated gun crews and three received the Medal of Honor. In addition, naval tradition and naval regulations prescribed "a degree of uniformity over judicial proceedings." According to the author, "black sailors particularly welcomed the impartiality of the regulations." It was, after all, a measure of equality with their fellow white shipmates.

Characterized by a high standard of scholarship, this outstanding article contains 61 extensive footnotes, several tables, and seven photos.

371.   Renard, Paul D. "Rueben Delavan Mussey: Unheralded Architect of the Civil War's U. S. Colored Troops." *Military Collector & Historian*, 58, 3 (Fall 2006): 181-184.
This article provides a thumbnail sketch of abolitionist and regular army officer Reuben Delavan Mussey, who, according to the author, "may be the man who had the greatest impact on the formation of the USCT." Mussey, "an advocate for and organizer of African-American units," is credited with the concept of Federal sponsorship of U.S. Colored Troops. Mussey served as assistant and later Commissioner for Organization of U.S. Colored Troops and coordinator of the Nashville examination board for white officers. At war's end he was promoted brevet brigadier general of Volunteers and was, for a short time, military secretary to President Andrew Johnson. After resigning from the army, Mussey practiced

law in Washington, DC. The article relies extensively on quoted material.

372.   Renard, Paul. "With the XXV Corps along the Rio Grande in 1865: Two U.S.C.T. Officers in Postwar Texas." *Military History of the West,* 38 (Spring 2008): 29-50.

Drawing on primary sources, the author describes the experiences of two white officers of the all-black XXV Corps performing postwar occupation duty in south Texas. One officer, George Tate, was appointed a lieutenant in the 41st U.S. Colored Infantry at the end of the war; the other, Oliver Willcox Norton, was a veteran of the 83rd Pennsylvania and the 8th U.S. Colored Infantry, a battle-hardened African-American regiment. Each man reacted differently to the harsh environment along the Rio Grande; an environment in which water was scarce, heat was unbearable, and sand flies and snakes infested the landscape. Tate resented his service and did as little as possible; Norton, a quartermaster with a "sunny" personality kept active and freely mingled with the local Hispanic population. Tate resigned his commission in September while Norton remained with his regiment until it was mustered out in November 1865. Both men had little to say about the black troops they commanded or the role the XXV Corps in thwarting French imperialism and Emperor Maxmillan's government just across the Rio Grande in Mexico. However, the author does discuss the XXV Corps from its initial organization in Virginia to its deliberate deployment along the border.

373.   Rhodes, Sonny. "Opposite Extremes: How Two Editors Portrayed a Civil War Atrocity." *American Journalism*, 22, 4 (Fall 2005): 27-45.

The Battle of Poison Spring, Arkansas, fought several days after the carnage at Fort Pillow, has been described by one historian as "the worst war crime ever committed on Arkansas soil." How two Arkansas newspaper editors reported the battle is examined and contrasted in this article. One newspaper, published in Washington, Arkansas was pro-Confederate; the other, printed in Fort Smith, was pro-Republican. Their accounts were substantially different. The battle, and the subsequent slaughter of members of the 1st Kansas

Colored Infantry, is described in gruesome detail in the *New Era*, the Republican paper. The *Washington Telegraph*, its Confederate counterpart, makes "no mention of shooting prisoners or scalping" while extoling the valor of the Southern troops involved in the battle. The only allusion to a massacre is a vague justification published in the *Washington Telegraph* that appeared several months after Poison Spring. In it the paper's editor wrote "we cannot treat Negroes taken in arms as prisoners . . . without a destruction of the social system for which we content."

374.   Rice, Charles. "The Bullwhip Mutiny." *Civil War Times Illustrated*, 40, 7 (February 2002): 38-43, 62
This article focuses on the mutiny that occurred in the ranks of the 4th Louisiana Native Guards at Fort Jackson, Louisiana, on December 11, 1863. The mutiny was prompted by the whipping of two enlisted men by Lieutenant Colonel Augustus Benedict, an officer with a reputation for harsh and often sadistic disciplinary measures. The mutiny is described as is the subsequent measures taken by the army to restore order and punish the perpetrators. After an investigation, 14 men were subsequently charged and faced court- martial, including Benedict. Based on the testimony of eye witnesses, several African-American soldiers were sentenced to imprisonment, several were found not guilty of mutiny; Benedict was found unfit for command and dishonorably discharged from the army. The regiment was later re-designated as the 76th U.S. Colored Troops and distinguished itself at the battle of Fort Blakely outside of Mobile in April 1865. During the battle the regiment lost "2 officers and 11 enlisted men killed and 3 officers and 75 men wounded." The article contains several period photographs.

375.   Richards, Ira Don. "The Battle of Poison Spring." *Arkansas Historical Quarterly*, 18, 4 (Winter 1959): 338-349.
This is a summary account of the Battle of Poison Spring, Arkansas, fought on April 18, 1864. The participation of the 1st Kansas Colored in the battle, and the subsequent slaughter of wounded black soldiers, receive scant attention. The author does concede that surviving evidence supports the assertion "that wounded Negroes

were shot down without mercy." The article contains 41 notes and two maps.

376. _____. "The Battle of Jenkins' Ferry." *Arkansas Historical Quarterly*, 20, 1 (Spring 1961): 3-16.

Fought less than two weeks after Poison Spring, the Union defensive stand at Jenkins' Ferry, Arkansas on April 30, 1864, coupled with poor Confederate tactical deployment, permitted Federal forces to escape to Little Rock and end the luckless Camden Expedition. The tactical description of the battle is generally from the Confederate perspective; only a single reference is made to the 2nd Kansas Colored Infantry. Overall the article is of little value to students of the African-American Civil War military experience; it is included only because it provides a summary description of the Battle of Jenkins' Ferry, a battle in which the 2nd Kansas Colored Infantry played a pivotal role.

377. Richardson, Heather Cox. "Stopped at Olustee." *Cobblestone*, 35, 1 (January 2014): 8-9.

The Battle of Olustee, and the role played by the 54th Massachusetts and 35th U.S. Colored Troops in covering the Union retreat, is succinctly recounted.

378. Riley, Steven T. "A Monument to Colonel Robert Shaw." *Proceedings of the Massachusetts Historical Society*, 75 (January - December): 27-38.

The fits and starts surrounding Augustus Saint-Gaudens's bas-relief tribute to Colonel Robert Gould Shaw and the men of the 54th Massachusetts Infantry is described. Years in the making, the monument was finally dedicated on May 1, 1897. Approximately 65 surviving officers and men of the 54th attended the ceremony.

379. Ripley, C. Peter. "The Black Family in Transition: Louisiana, 1860-1865." *Journal of Southern History*, 41, 3 (August 1975): 369-380.

This is a study of slave families and slave marriages in Civil War Louisiana. A number of factors which negatively impacted the stability of war time black families are reviewed, including the effects of military service in the Union Army. According to the author, the greatest crisis facing the black family in Louisiana, and black family stability, "resulted from married males serving in the army." Many black soldiers were forcibly recruited at bayonet point and promptly marched off to military camps. To the Union Army and its recruiters African-American men were "soldiers and laborers first, husbands and fathers second." Isolated and separated from their loved ones, many attempted to leave the army and rejoin their families. This practice "was common enough to force the military to place guards over recruits to prevent their escape."

Concern for their families' welfare was a major anxiety for black soldiers. Wives and children left behind were often subjected to physical abuse by their former masters; many were turned out of plantation quarters once it was discovered their husbands were serving in the army. The Union Army made a number of only partially successful attempts to remedy the situation. In the end, however, "Union officials were never able to protect or provide adequately for families of black soldiers."

380.   Ritter, E. Jay. "Congressional Medal of Honor Winners." *Negro History Bulletin,* 26, 4 (January 1963): 135-136.
This is a very brief account of several African-Americans who won the Medal of Honor during the Civil War. Included is a brief description of the September 29, 1864, assault on New Market Heights, Virginia, by Medal of Honor recipient Christian A. Fleetwood, 4th U.S. Colored Troops. Contrary to the author's assertion, the July 18, 1864, Union assault on Fort Wagner, led by the 54th Massachusetts Infantry, did not "succeed in carrying the fort."

381.   Robbins, Gerald. "Recruiting and Arming of Negroes in the South Carolina Sea Islands." *Negro History Bulletin*, 28, 7 (April 1965): 150-151, 163-167.
This study is concerned primarily with the activities of Major General David Hunter who, as commander of the Department of the South, unilaterally emancipated the Sea Island slaves and attempted to raise a regiment of African-American soldiers. His emancipation

pronouncement was nullified by President Lincoln, and his heavy-handed and forceful recruiting practices left a deep psychic scar on the black inhabitants of the Sea Islands. Though a regiment was raised, it was neither paid nor sanctioned by the War Department and, except for one company, was disbanded. Later, Brigadier General Rufus Saxton was directed by the Secretary of War to raise a regiment of black soldiers on the Sea Islands; only after recruiting difficulties, the regiment mustered on June 25, 1863, as the 1st South Carolina Volunteer Regiment commanded by Colonel Thomas Wentworth Higginson. The article contains 77 notes based mainly on primary sources.

382.   Robbins, Peggy. "The 54th Massachusetts' War within a War." *Military History*, Supplement (2003): 62-70.
The history of the 54th Massachusetts from its beginning to its trial by fire before Fort Wagner, South Carolina on July 18, 1863 is recounted. The author maintains that the assault, though a military failure, was, for black Americans, a moral victory because it demonstrated that black soldiers would fight with bravery and tenacity. The article includes several photographs.

383.   Robertson, Brian K. "'Will They Fight': United States Colored Troops at Big Creek, Arkansas, July 26, 1864." *Arkansas Historical Quarterly*, 66, 3 (Autumn 2007): 320-332.
With the exception of the Union disaster at Poison Spring, little has been written about black soldiers in Arkansas during the Civil War. This study partially rectifies that shortcoming. During the war at least six African-American regiments were raised in Arkansas, one of which – the 56th U.S. Colored Infantry – is the subject of this first-rate account. Organized in St. Louis in the summer of 1863, the regiment was originally enrolled as the 3rd Arkansas Infantry, African Descent. (In March 1864, in order to reflect its Federal service, the regimental designation was changed to the 56th U.S. Colored Infantry.) As each company was enlisted, organized, and mustered, they were shipped to Helena, Arkansas, to perform the humdrum role of garrison troops in a forgotten backwater of the war. The monotony of garrison duty was abruptly interrupted in the wake of the Union Army's disastrous Camden expedition. As a

result of the Federal defeat, Confederate forces launched a series of destructive hit-and-run raids throughout eastern Arkansas. In order to determine the location of Confederate forces in the area, six companies of the 56th U.S. Colored Infantry were dispatched some 20 miles west of Helena as a reconnaissance force. Accompanying the expedition was a 42- man section from Battery E, 2nd U.S. Colored Light Artillery and a detachment from the 60th U.S. Colored Infantry. For most, if not all of the African-American rank and file, this would be their first experience of combat.

On July 26, 1864 the Union force of black troops and white officers clashed with a superior Confederate force at Wallace's Ferry on Big Creek, Philips Country, Arkansas. Heavy fighting took place throughout the day, fighting which the author describes in commendable detail. Although almost overwhelmed on several occasions, the 56th tenaciously fought off each Rebel attack until reinforced by the 15th Illinois Cavalry. The combined Federal force made a fighting retreat to the safety to Helena. Casualties for the 56th were reported as 13 men killed, 26 wounded, and three missing. The 60th U.S. Colored Infantry had four killed and ten wounded while the light artillery section reported 2 men killed. Confederate casualties were estimated at 150.

By this stage of the war atrocities were increasing in the Trans-Mississippi and there is evidence that three wounded African-American soldiers were murdered after the battle, especially since Confederates forces reported capturing no prisoners. Writing years after the war one former Confederate "remarked that it was well that the black troops fought as hard as they did, as none of them would have been given any quarter had they surrendered." After the battle, the 56th returned to garrison duties at Helena for the remainder of the war. Prior to discharge from Federal service, the 56th was devastated by a cholera epidemic which took the lives of 178 enlisted men and one officer.

The article contains 35 notes based mainly on the Official Records and several secondary sources.

384.   Robertson, James I., Jr. "Negro Soldiers in the Civil War."
Civil War Times Illustrated, 7, 6 (October 1968): 21-32.
Robertson's article provides an overview account of the African-
American Civil War soldier, a soldier that "was neither a saint nor
sinner" but whose "camp and battle behavior ultimately compared
well with his white compatriots." Robertson attributes the success
of enlisting and arming mostly ex-slaves to three factors: the
unstinting recruiting efforts of Lorenzo Thomas, changing attitude
among high-ranking army officers, and the performance of African-
American soldiers in combat.

385.   Robertson, William Glenn. "From the Crater to New
Market Heights: A Tale of Two Divisions." In *Black Soldiers
in Blue: African American Troops in the Civil War Era,* edited
by John David Smith. Chapel Hill: University of North Carolina
Press, 2002, 168-199.
A perceptive comparison of two all-black Union Army divisions is
provided. One division was in the Army of the James commanded
by General Benjamin Butler; the other in the Army of the Potomac
commanded by General George G. Meade. According to Robertson,
Butler believed in the fighting potential of African-American
soldiers, he treated them fairly, and brought them along in a number
of engagements. As a result, as an experienced unit, they performed
with admirable steadiness during their fight at New Market Heights.
To Meade, however, black troops were seen simply as a large labor
reservoir capable not of combat but suited only for performing
commonplace fatigue duties. Robertson argues that black soldiers
of the Army of the Potomac were led indifferently and their
divisional commander did "not provide his men the training they
needed to survive" in combat, particularly at the Crater. An
interesting assessment, not only of how two different divisions
performed in combat, but how two general officers looked upon the
African-American soldiers in their respective commands.

386.   Roca, Steven Louis. "Presence and Precedents: The USS 'Red Rover' during the American Civil War, 1861-1865." *Civil War History*, 44, 2 (June 1998): 91-110.
The *Red Rover* was a damaged Confederate Mississippi steamboat captured after the Battle of Island No. 10 in April 1862. Repaired and refitted, it became the navy's first hospital ship and served throughout the war in support of the Mississippi gunboat service. "Everything . . . considered essential for the treatment of sick and wounded was carried on board." According to the author contraband women employed and mustered on the *Red Rover* were "the first female naval personnel." In addition, numerous contraband men were employed as coal heavers, cooks, stewards, and landsmen. Many eventually obtained official naval ratings. The article contains an appendix and 58 extensive notes.

387.   Romero, Patricia W. "A Witness to War." *American Legacy, Celebrating African-American History & Culture*, 8, 2 (Summer 2002): 97, 99-102.
Excerpts from Susie King Taylor's account of service with the 1st South Carolina Volunteers (later the 33rd U.S. Colored Troops) are reprinted in this article. Taylor was a company laundress, cook, nurse, and teacher as well as the only African-American woman who "participated both early and actively" in the regiment's campaigns. Reprinted excerpts are from Taylor's "My Life in Camp with the 33rd United States Colored Troops, Late 1st S.C. Volunteers." The article is edited with an introduction by Patricia W. Romero.

388.   Roser, Robert. "Respect Is for Those for Whom it is Due." *America's Civil War*, 15, 1 (March 2002): 38-43.
Erasmus W. Jones was the Welsh-born chaplain of the 21st U.S. Colored Troops. In this September 20, 1864, letter from Morris Island, South Carolina, written in Welsh (and addressed to a Welsh-American language magazine), Jones reflects on the thirst for knowledge demonstrated by the former slaves in the regiment, his duties as minister and schoolmaster, drunkenness among many white officers in white regiments, the Union forts on Morris Island,

the coming presidential election, and the irrefutable fact "that the black man has given proof enough to the country that he is capable of true military endeavors."

389.   Rutherford, Philip. "Revolt in the Corps d'Afrique." *Civil War Times Illustrated,* 24, 2 (April 1985): 20-23, 42-44.

A dramatic and detailed account of a mutiny by black soldiers of the 4th Regiment, Corp d'Afrique in December 1863 is provided. The mutiny, which occurred at Fort Jackson, Louisiana, was precipitated by the actions of a sadistic martinet, Lieutenant Colonel Augustus Benedict. Benedict, second in command of the regiment, regularly subjected African-American soldiers to mistreatment and brutal punishments. The severe whipping of two privates, however, proved to be the regiment's breaking point and on December 9, 1863, "all hell broke loose." Almost the entire garrison participated in the mutiny. Order was restored the following day with no loss of life. Several African-American soldiers who participated in the revolt were sentenced to prison terms of hard labor; two were sentenced to be executed by firing squad, though the order was evidently never carried out. Benedict was court-martialed and dishonorably dismissed from the service for "inflicting cruel and unusual punishments." The regiment, later re-designated as the 76th U.S. Colored Infantry, subsequently "served honorably until the end of the war."

390.   Ryan, David M. "The All-American Battle." *Civil War Times,* 42, 6 (February 2004): 44-48, 50, 52.

The little-known engagement of Honey Springs, on July 17, 1863, was the largest battle fought in Indian Territory (present day Oklahoma). It was an "all-American battle" that saw Confederate Cherokees, Creeks, Choctaws, Chickasaws and Texas Cavalry pitted against several regiments of Union Indian Home Guards, Northern white volunteers, and the African-Americans of the hard-fighting 1st Kansas Colored Infantry. The battle resulted in a decisive Union victory. The article includes a fairly detailed description of the battle and the part played by the 1st Kansas, a map, and several photographs.

391.   Samito, Christian G. "The Intersection between Military Justice and Equal Rights: Mutinies, Courts-martial, and Black Civil War Solders." *Civil War History*, 53, 2 (June 2007): 170-202.

Making extensive use of courts-martial records found in the National Archives, Samito determined the causes for African-American mutinies in the Civil War and, most importantly, the nature of the courts-marital proceedings that followed. Most black grievances were centered on military bigotry and frustration associated with pay inequality. Indeed "pay disparity undermined army discipline and also energized black soldiers' demands for equal treatment." However, the generalized assumption that institutional racism pervaded the military justice system, according to Samito, is unfounded. While individual white court officers may have been racist, African-American defendants generally received judicial due process, an opportunity for legal counsel, and the ability to question witnesses. In capital crimes, black soldiers received equal treatment and equal justice and "enjoyed rights and opportunities denied them in civilian life because they were entitled to uniform application of the Articles of War." As the author concludes: "rather than sanction a different disciplinary scheme for African- American troops, the Federal government held black soldiers were entitled to the same application of military justice and court-martial procedures that whites enjoyed." Many of the article's 60 notes are based on courts-martial records.

392.   Schafer, Daniel L. "Freedom was as Close as the River: The Blacks of Northeast Florida and the Civil War." *El Escribano*: *The St. Augustine Journal of History*, 23, (1986): 91-116.

Because of the presence of Union forces along the coast, thousands of slaves in northeastern Florida fled from captivity whenever they had the opportunity. Many who escaped subsequently volunteered for service in the 1st, 2nd, and 3rd South Carolina Infantry (later re-designated as the 33rd, 34th, and 21st U.S. Colored Troops). The author uses extensive primary sources to document the impact of runaway slaves on the local plantation economy. The military exploits of Florida's ex-slaves in the three Union regiments are also described. Interestingly, Schafer also documents the post-war occupations of many former Florida bondsmen who served in the Colored Troops.

393.   Scharnhorst, Gary. "From Soldier to Saint: Robert Gould Shaw and the Rhetoric of Racial Justice." *Civil War History,* 34, 4 (December 1988): 308-322.

The fame of Robert Gould Shaw, commander of the black 54th Massachusetts Infantry, and his canonization as "a saint in the pantheon of American heroes" is related. Shaw, who was not a fervent abolitionist and, as a commanding officer, often accused of mistreating his black soldiers, became an instant celebrity with his death before Confederate guns at Fort Wagner. His death and subsequent fame, according to the author, "was less deserved than an accident of history." He was wildly celebrated throughout the North as the *beau ideal* New England Brahmin and a representative of "the flower of the Anglo-Saxon race." He was part of a profound social revolution that demonstrated that black soldiers could stand and fight just as well as their white comrades. A bas relief bronze memorial executed by Augustus St. Gaudens was unveiled in 1897 on Boston Commons as a tribute to Shaw and his soldiers. Over time, however, the eulogies declined and the rhetoric of racial justice they represented were forgotten. "Since the 1940s, the Shaw Memorial has been routinely vandalized…and its honors have faded from memory."

394.   Schroeder, Patrick. "One of the 'Checker-board.'" *Civil War Times*, 54, 2 (April 2015): 60-63.

Until recently, most historians believed that no more than 2,000 USCTs were present at Appomattox Court House to witness Lee's surrender. However, new research among the Compiled Military Service Records of black regiments that took part in the April 1865 campaign has increased that number to between 4,000 and 5,000. In addition, research uncovered, for the first time, a photographic image of a black soldier who was present at the Appomattox surrender. The photograph is that of Sergeant John Peck, Company E, 8th United States Colored Troops. Peck, who enlisted at Meadville, Pennsylvania served his entire enlistment with the 8th and saw combat at Olustee, before Petersburg, and during the pursuit of Lee's army to Appomattox. The article outlines the tactical movements of all six black regiments that participated in Lee's pursuit and contains a reproduction *carte de visite* photograph of Sergeant Peck.

395.   Schultz, Jane E. "Seldom Thanked, Never Praised, and Scarcely Recognized: Gender and Racism in Civil War Hospitals." *Civil War History*, 48, 3 (September 2002): 220-236.

Almost the entirety of this compelling article is concerned with the racial interaction between white and African-American women working in Civil War military hospitals either as nurses, matrons, maids, or cooks. However, the article does contain several significant observations regarding African-American soldiers and black and white hospital workers. As an example, the author maintains that black nurses were not allowed in white hospitals but "military hospitals serving black soldiers were willing to employ black women as nurses, with or without the title." More interesting, however, is the notion that white female hospital staff honored black soldiers entrusted to their care "as they did the white rank and file" and most "had nothing but praise for black soldiers." Hospitalized black soldiers were often described "in the language of valor that came to be associated ... with men in arms." Ironically, African-American women working in military hospitals continued to be stigmatized because of race by the same white observers who admired the courage of black soldiers.

396.   Scott, Donald. "Camp William Penn's Black Soldiers in Blue." *America's Civil War,* 12, 5 (November 1999): 44-49, 82.

Built on land leased to the Federal government, and located approximately ten miles north of downtown Philadelphia, Camp William Penn was the largest training facility for African-American soldiers during the Civil War. Under the leadership of German-born Colonel Louis Wagner, over 11,000 men received their training at the camp while facing overt hostility from many Philadelphians; indeed, it was not uncommon for African-Americans leaving the camp to be attacked by white mobs. Scott provides a campaign history of the African-American regiments from the camp and recounts the Medal of Honor award to three members of the 6th USCT, a regiment raised and trained at Camp William Penn. All three were awarded the medal for conspicuous gallantry during the Battle of New Market Heights. The article is illustrated with several period drawings and photographs.

397. Sellers, John E. "The Union Soldier Meets the Freedman." *Maine Historical Society Quarterly*, 33, 2 (Summer 1993): 88-105.

According to the author, an historical specialist at the Library of Congress, "the average Union soldier seemed either blind or indifferent to the condition and aspirations of Freedmen" and were unsympathetic or even openly hostile toward African-Americans they encountered. Nor were black soldiers viewed any differently. Black volunteers, "regardless of how hard they trained or how well they fought, were looked upon as inferior or unreliable by white units, if not viewed with open derision." Indeed, many white soldiers even considered black battle casualties less worthy of hospital attention. Sellers' harsh assessment of Union Army racial sentiments is based on his first-hand observation of hundreds of Civil War manuscripts.

398. Seraile, William. "The Struggle to Raise Black Regiments in New York State, 1861-1864." *New-York Historical Society Quarterly*, 58, 3 (July 1974): 215-233.

New York Governor Horatio Seymour's adamant refusal to recruit African-Americans for the Union war effort is documented. Seymour, a Democrat, as well as New York City Democrats, were united in their opposition to the employment of black troops. This article describes the persistent efforts of the white Association for Promoting Colored Volunteers, working closely with the city's Union League, to persuade the War Department to enlist black volunteers. Eventually three African-American regiments totaling over 4,000 men were recruited. "Due to disease, battle wounds, mistreatment by the enemy, and other factors, 14 percent of these soldiers died." The article contains 40 notes, many based on primary source materials, and several illustrations.

399.   Shaffer, Donald R. "'I Do Not Suppose That Uncle Sam Looks at the Skin:' African Americans and the Civil War Pension System 1865-1934." *Civil War History,* 46, 2 (June 2000): 132-147.

Pension laws enacted by Congress for Civil War veterans were race neutral and did not discriminate. "This meant that black and white Union veterans and their families theoretically enjoyed the same eligibility." Shaffer concluded, however, based on an extensive examination of pension applications in the National Archives, that this was not the case. A number of factors prevented black applicants from having the same success in obtaining a pension as their white counterparts. To begin with, many African-American applicants were often former slaves, illiterate, poverty stricken, and lived in rural areas. "Poverty hampered the application process because pursuing a pension claim cost money." Surnames were often inconsistent. Upon enlisting in the army many slaves used their master's name; after discharge they often took a new name based on personal family connections. As a result, unit muster roles often did not match the pension applicant's name. In addition, black applicants could not always supply the written documentation required by the Pension Bureau. This was particularly true in determining birth dates. Institutional racism on the part of the bureau's examining agents, and fraudulent claims agents, also hindered black applications. When comparing white and black application success, the author concluded that 92.6% of all white pension applications were successful; for African-Americans the success rate was75.4%. The article contains one table, and 36 notes, most of which are based upon pension records in the National Archives.

400.   _____. "'I would Rather Shake Hands with the Blackest Nigger in the Land': Northern Black Civil War Veterans and the Grand Army of the Republic." In *Union Soldiers and the Northern Home Front: Wartime Experiences, Postwar Adjustments,* edited by Paul A. Cimbala and Randall M. Miller. New York: Fordham University Press, 2002, 442-462.

The Grand Army of the Republic, the GAR, was the largest Union veterans' organization founded after the war. Unusual for Gilded Age America, the organization was not race based; the only criteria for membership were honorable service during the war. Shaffer's analysis about the degree of black acceptance by the nationwide organization presents a mixed picture. "Gratitude to black soldiers in their Civil War service moderated the racism of many white veterans in the North but did not eliminate it." A few African-Americans were admitted to all-white chapters in the North, and a few, actually rose to leadership positions. Generally, however, African-American membership was limited to segregated local chapters. And in the South white veterans attempted to exclude African-Americans from the organization. In the end, as the author observes, white GAR members did not share the vision of racial equality and the right to vote championed by the usually poor all-black GAR chapter members. Shaffer's essay contains 33 notes based on primary and secondary sources.

401.   Shaffer, Donald R., and Elizabeth Regosin. "Voices of Emancipation: Union Pension Files Giving Voice to Former Slaves." *Prologue*, 37, 4 (Winter 2005): 22-31.

For years the slave narratives collected by the Depression-era Works Progress Administration were considered the definitive first-hand accounts of African-American slavery and, by extension, the black Civil War experience. According to authors Shaffer and Regosin, however, pension applications and records originally kept by the U.S. Bureau of Pensions are far superior as an historical resource. Unlike the narratives, most of which were collected in the mid-1930s, the majority of pension applications and records were compiled and filed from the early 1880s to 1910. Many include interviews with former soldiers that touch on such "issues as military service, identity, health and disability, marital and family relationships, employment, economic circumstances, and previous ownership." Included in the case files are first hand accounts of former black soldiers discussing their Civil War service. Often moving, these personal accounts give "a voice to those whom history has silenced" and, as a result, "provide a valuable window onto the lives of former slaves" and African-American Civil War soldiers. This is an excellent and highly recommended article.

402.   Shoaf, Dana B. "Sea Change." *Civil War Times*, 52, 1 (February 2013): 31.

According to the author the publication of General Orders 143 by the War Department "was one of the war's most important but little-known documents." Published on May 23, 1862, the document officially established the Federal government's program for recruiting and enrolling African-Americans as soldiers.

403.   Simmons, Sellano L. "Count Them too: African Americans from Delaware and the United States Civil War Navy, 1861-1865." *Journal of Negro History*, 85, 3 (Summer 2000): 183-190.

This study examines the contribution of African-Americans from Delaware who served in the U.S. Navy during the Civil War. Approximately 300 saw service, the majority enlisted at the lowest naval rating as landsmen, their average age was 25, and approximately 10% had previous maritime experience. The article contains a map of Delaware, a chart, and 33 notes.

404.   Simpson, Brooks D. "'The Doom of Slavery': Ulysses S. Grant, War Aims, and Emancipation, 1861-1863." *Civil War History*, 36, 1 (March 1990): 36-56.

Grant's evolving views regarding the preservation of the Union, slavery, emancipation, and the arming of African-Americans as soldiers are reviewed. Initially Grant, though not an Abolitionist, believed the Union could be saved without drastic changes to the social fabric of the country. His perspective changed over time until he concludes "By arming the negro we have added a powerful ally. They will make good solders and taking them from the enemy weaken him in the same proportion they strengthen us." The article contains 47 notes and is based primarily on Grant's personal papers.

405. _____. "Quandaries of Command: Ulysses S. Grant and Black Soldiers." In *Union and Emancipation: Essays on Politics and Race in the Civil War Era*, edited by David W. Blight and Brooks D. Simpson. Kent, Ohio: Kent State University Press, 1997, 123-149.

This insightful essay explores Grant's evolving views regarding the employment of African-Americans as soldiers in war, peace, in Reconstruction, and as part of the post-war regular army. Initially Grant had serious reservations about the employment of blacks as soldiers. Over time, and faced with stubborn Southern resistance, his opinion changed from reluctance to wholehearted acceptance. His demand for the equal treatment of both black and white prisoners, and the difficulties he faced by using African-American soldiers as occupation troops immediately after the end of hostilities are examined. The essay contains 54 notes.

406. Skaptason, Bjorn, editor. "West Tennessee U.S. Colored Troops and the Retreat from Brice's Crossroads: An Eyewitness Account by Major James C. Foster (USA)." *West Tennessee Historical Society Papers*, 60 (2006): 74-107.

This reprint was originally published by Foster in 1884. It was a response to an article that appeared in the *National Tribune,* a monthly journal and later newspaper that served as an organ of the Grand Army of the Republic, a Union Army veterans group. In this article Foster angrily denied accusations that African-Americans abandoned their weapons at Brice's Crossroads and led the retreat back to Memphis. He was particularly critical of certain white brigade commanders who, according to his observations, were more than willing to sacrifice black troops to save white soldiers. His eyewitness account is a significant addition to the literature regarding the battle and a forceful presentation of the important role played by black troops in the retreat. At the time of the Union Army defeat at Brice's Crossroads, Foster was a battle-hardened 22 year old acting major of the 59th U.S. Colored Infantry. He commanded much of the retreat's rear guard defense. Photographs of some of the regiment's officers are included as well as 46 heavily annotated notes.

407. Slawson, Robert G. "African American Physicians in the Union Army during the Civil War." *Journal of Civil War Medicine*, 7, 2 (April/May/June 2003): 47-52.

This useful and authoritative study that provides a biographical sketch of 10 black physicians who served in the U.S. Army during the Civil War. Of the 10, three obtained army commissions while the remaining 7 served as contract physicians. Contract physicians were usually hired by the army to perform services for a limited period, and while they wore uniforms they were not considered active duty personnel but civilians hired for a limited time period. Included in the article is a thumbnail portrait of Dr. Alexander Thomas Augusta who, as a brevet lieutenant colonel, held the highest rank of any African-American during the Civil War.

408. Slay, David. "Abraham Lincoln and the United States Colored Troops of Mississippi." *Journal of Mississippi History*, 70, 1 (Spring 2008): 67-86.

During the Civil War nine African-American regiments and two companies of light artillery were raised in Mississippi; additionally, thousands of the state's freedmen enlisted in regiments recruited in Louisiana. As soldiers they encountered white hostility and the threat of murder if captured, they guarded freedmen's camps, functioned as labor and fatigue battalions, performed garrison duty, and helped destroy the Confederacy in the Mississippi Valley. This article recounts the very successful formation of African-American troops in Mississippi and discusses the central role played in their recruitment and training by Lorenzo Thomas, U.S. Grant, Chaplain Lucian, General John P. Hawkins, and Colonel Isaac B. Shepard. These men, and others of like mind, "carried out Lincoln's policies in Mississippi during the formation of the USCT and defined Lincoln in the eyes of the freedmen." The article contains 33 notes based on primary and secondary sources.

409. Slotkin, Richard. "Hallowed Ground: Petersburg Crater, Virginia." *Military History* (March 2010): 76-77.

A succinct account noteworthy only for a present day picture of what remains of the Petersburg Crater.

410. Smith, Derek. "Potter's Raid." *North & South*, 10, 2 (July 2007): 64-77.

This is an excellent account of a Union expedition deep into the interior of South Carolina in the waning days of the Civil War. Tasked by Major General William T. Sherman with destroying Confederate rolling stock, the expedition marched over 300 miles during a 17 day period beginning on April 5 and ending on April 21, 1865. The Union force of approximately 2,500 infantry consisted of two brigades: one white, the other black. The black brigade, commanded by Colonel Edward N. Hallowell, consisted of the veteran 54th Massachusetts Infantry and companies from the 32nd and 102nd U.S. Colored Troops. The fighting at Swift Creek and Boykin's Mill by the 54th Massachusetts is described in some detail. The success of the expedition was overshadowed by the Confederate surrender at Appomattox and the assassination of President Lincoln. The article contains 42 notes and a superb full-color map.

411. Smith, Eric Ledell, editor. "The Civil War Letters of Quartermaster Sergeant John C. Brock, 43rd Regiment, United States Colored Troops." In *Pennsylvania's Civil War,* edited by William Blair and William Pencak. University Park: The Pennsylvania State University Press, 2001, 141-163.

This article presents nine letters written by Quartermaster Sergeant John C. Brock of the 43rd USCT to the *Christian Recorder*, the official newspaper of the African Methodist Church. Brock's letters, addressed to "Dear Recorder," describe the regiment's movements and organization, the desolation of the Virginia countryside, picket and fatigue duty, skirmishes with the enemy, and the lack of a regimental chaplain. As a black man, Brock was particularly pleased when his regiment received full pay – meaning they received the same pay as white soldiers. The article contains an introductory essay and commentary on each letter by the editor.

412.   Smith, John David. "The Recruitment of Negro Soldiers in Kentucky, 1863-1865." *Register of the Kentucky Historical Society,* 72, 4 (October 1974): 364-390.
Kentucky was both a loyal border and a slave holding state. As a result, President Lincoln could proceed only with caution regarding the Emancipation Proclamation and the recruitment of African-Americans into the Union Army. Both measures were strenuously opposed by leading government officials, politicians, newspaper editors, gubernatorial candidates, and the state's white population in general. The author describes this opposition which, in the case of army recruitment, was often of a violent nature. However, African-Americans, both free and slave were eventually recruited – sometimes by force. Loyal slave owners were promised compensation for their financial losses. Kentucky's white population reluctantly acquiesced to Federal policy when it became apparent that black enlistments counted against the state's draft quota. As a result, a considerable number of white citizens avoided military service. "Despite the intense opposition of many citizens of the state, 23,703 of the 178,895 Negroes who fought for the North came from Kentucky." Only Louisiana contributed more African-Americans to the Union Army. The article contains 103 extremely detailed notes; most are based on primary source materials.

413.   _____. "Kentucky Civil War Recruits: A Medical Profile." *Medical History,* 24, 2 (April 1980): 185-196.
Impressively documented and based on the wartime records of eight Union army medical examiners, this study provides fresh insights into the physical condition of Kentucky's Civil War soldiers, white and black. Overall, both white and blacks were found by the examiners to be in good health. Indeed, in many cases African-Americans were physically equal or superior to their white counterparts. While physically impressive because of their agricultural labors, widely held racial beliefs considered African-Americans in need of white leadership to function successfully in the army. Reflecting medical knowledge of the day, one examining

surgeon recommended that African-Americans perform only garrison duty in Southern forts since "neither a hot climate nor malarial fevers effect them in any material degree."

414. _____. Let us all be Grateful that we have Colored troops that will Fight." In *Black Soldiers in Blue: African American Troops in the Civil War Era*, edited by John David Smith. Chapel Hill: University of North Carolina Press, 2002, 1-77.

This essay provides an outstanding overview of Lincoln's decision making regarding not only the freedom of enslaved people, but his decision, over time, to enlist African-Americans as soldiers. The author maintains that "Lincoln charted a far more linear course" toward the twin objectives of emancipation and black military service than his critics appreciate. Well documented with 108 notes based on numerous primary and secondary sources.

415. Smith, Michael O. "Raising a Black Regiment in Michigan: Adversity and Triumph." *Michigan Historical Review*, 16, 2 (Fall 1990): 23-42.

During the Civil War recruiting an African-American regiment in a Northern free state – with a few exceptions – was a difficult process marked by white hostility, and in the case of Detroit's black regiment, bitter political controversy. Republican support for the idea was more than offset by unrelenting Democratic opposition. Nevertheless, after numerous setbacks the 1st Michigan Colored Regiment was organized and mustered into Federal service as the 102nd United States Colored Infantry. Obstacles encountered in recruiting and organizing the regiment is described as is the regiment's service in Florida and South Carolina. Mustered out on September 30, 1865, the regiment was considered by Detroit's black population as a potent political symbol that demonstrated their loyalty and courage. To its opponents the regiment "represented a threat to the superior social position of whites." The article contains 39 notes based on newspaper accounts, regimental records, and archival and secondary sources.

416. Smith, Steven D. "History and Archaeology: Edward Wild's African Brigade in the Siege of Charleston." *Civil War Regiments: A Journal of the American Civil War*, 5 (Number 2): 20-70.

During the course of residential construction on Folly Island, South Carolina in 1987, a relic hunter accidentally discovered several human remains. This monograph by Steven Smith, at that time an archaeologist with the South Carolina Institute of Archology and Anthropology, describes the results of the subsequent in-depth forensic investigation that took place. Eighteen bodies were discovered and disinterred. They were found in a scattered burial pattern and were identified as members of the all-black 55th Massachusetts Infantry, part of Wild's African Brigade. No battle wounds were discernible and they were probably men who died of disease while in a camp hospital. Most were between the ages of 20 and 30 and averaged 5 feet 6 inches in height and "many of their bones exhibited the features of a life of heavy labor." A number of skeletons were missing their skulls.

The author traces the Civil War battle history of the 55th Massachusetts, the less well-known brother regiment of the more celebrated 54th. He provides statistics regarding the age, occupations, civilian status (born free or slave), birthplace, and education levels of the regiment's soldiers and describes what military service was like on Folly island during the siege of Charleston. The bodies were subsequently reinterred with full military honors at the Beaufort National Cemetery in Beaufort, South Carolina, in May 1989. The monograph contains maps, photographs, 115 notes, and the most likely explanation of why several skeletons were missing their skulls.

417. Solomon, Irwin D. "Southern Extremities: The Significance of Fort Myers in the Civil War." *Florida Historical Quarterly,* 72, 2 (October 1993): 129-152.

The reactivation of Fort Myers, Florida, by Union Forces in January 1864 threatened the extensive cattle industry in south Florida, an industry the Confederate Army desperately depended on for supplies of fresh beef. As a further irritant to Southern sensitivities, according to the author, the garrison was largely staffed with two companies of the 2nd U.S. Colored Troops, and this "deployment of the USCT . . . dramatically changed the conduct of war in Florida." Black infantry companies, together with white Florida Unionists, raided deep into the interior of south Florida disrupting the cattle industry and scattering Southern forces. Solomon's study also describes the abortive February 20, 1865 Confederate attack on the fort, and racial tensions between African-American and white soldiers and civilians at Fort Myers. The article contains 52 notes based on primary and secondary sources, a map, and three period illustrations.

418. _____. "Fort Myers during the Civil War." *South Florida History Magazine*, 22, 1 (Winter 1994): 12-15.
Another, shorter account by Solomon describing the January 1864 re-activation of Fort Myers, its garrison of mostly African-American troops, and the subsequent attack on the fort by Confederate forces on February 20, 1865. After desultory skirmishing, Confederate forces retreated; combined casualties on both sides were less than 50. The affair at Fort Myers was probably the southernmost land action of the Civil War.

419. Solomon, Irvin D. and Grace Erhart. "Race and Civil War in South Florida." *Florida Historical Quarterly*, 77, 3 (Winter 1999): 320-341.
Much of this essay concerns race relations in antebellum and Civil War Florida. According to the authors, slaves in sparsely settled south Florida were treated differently from those that labored in Florida's northern plantation belt. Nevertheless, the article also contains a good deal of information regarding African-American regiments that served in Florida. Particular emphasis is placed on the activities of the 2nd USCT.

420. Sommers, Richard J. "The Dutch Gap Affair: Military Atrocities and the Rights of Negro Soldiers." *Civil War History*, 21, 1 (March 1975): 51-64.
The Dutch Gap Affair was prompted by the Confederate government's use of captured African-American soldiers as

laborers. As part of the defenses of Petersburg, captive black soldiers, together with impressed slaves, were employed in constructing fortifications along the Petersburg front. Outraged by this violation of the rights of black soldiers, Major General Benjamin F. Butler retaliated by ordering the employment of captured Confederate soldiers as laborers on the Dutch Gap Canal, an area often under Confederate artillery fire. To emphasis his order, the prisoners were guarded by Company G, 127th USCT with "orders to kill any who tried to escape." Fortunately, before an ugly confrontation escalated into mutual atrocities, both Lee and Grant arrived at a practical solution: black soldiers were removed from the labor details and the Confederates were returned to their prisoner camps.

421.   Soodalter, Ron. "Black in Blue." *America's Civil War*, 30, 3 (July 2017): 14-15.
This is a basic but still informative study of Civil War African-Americans serving in the Federal Navy. Commenting on the extensive research of Howard University professor Joseph P. Reidy, the author points out that approximately 20% of the navy's enlisted men were black. Of that number, "more than 11,000 had been slaves, while 4,000 were freeborn men." According to the author, though the navy was not officially segregated, it still relegated black sailors to the lowest naval ratings and pay. In addition, aboard ship black crews members were often assigned the most menial tasks. Nevertheless, they did serve on gun crews in battle and three, Aaron Anderson, Robert Blake, and James Mifflin, were awarded the Medal of Honor. This article is a solid synopsis of certain aspects of the African-American experience afloat.

422.   Stanchak, John. "A Legacy of Controversy: Fort Pillow Still Stands." *Civil War Times Illustrated*, 32, 4 (September/October 1993): 18, 25, 75-78.
The partially restored Fort Pillow State Historic Area is described in this short travel piece, coupled with a brief recounting of the April 12, 1864 battle, an encounter described as "one of the most controversial small battles in the Civil War." The author reaches no conclusion regarding what happened on that spring day in 1864.

423.   Stark, William C. "Forgotten Heroes: Black Recipients of the United States Congressional Medal of Honor in the American Civil War, 1863-1865." *Lincoln Herald*, Part I, 88, 4 (Winter 1985): 122-130; Part II, 88, 1 (Spring 1986): 5-11; Part III, 88, 2 (Summer 1986): 70-80.

A three-part series of articles discuss the circumstances under which African-Americans, in both the Union Army and Navy, were awarded the Medal of Honor. Part I provides a history of the medal, describes the actions of William H. Carney, the first African-American to receive the Medal of Honor, and recounts the ill-fated attack on Fort Wagner. Part II describes additional Union Army black recipients of the Medal of Honor. The battlefield circumstances that led to the award, as well as background information regarding each recipient, where possible, is provided. Part III provides similar information for the seven Civil War African-American sailors who were recipients of the medal.

424.   Stuart, Reginald. "A Proud Heritage." *Diverse Issues in Higher Education,* 27, 26 (February 3, 2011): 21-22.

The efforts of a small but growing group of historians to close the knowledge gap concerning the black Civil War experience is discussed.

425.   Straudenraus, P.J., editor. Occupied Beaufort, 1863: A War Correspondent's View." *South Carolina Historical Magazine,* 64, 3 (July 1963): 136-145.

Written by Noah Brooks, peripatetic reporter and friend of Abraham Lincoln, this is a vivid newspaper account of occupied Beaufort, South Carolina, which appeared in the Sacramento *Daily Union* on July 11, 1863. In his dispatch, Brooks describes the effects of Southern abandonment and Union Army occupation on the town. Only a few paragraphs are devoted to the African-American 1st South Carolina Infantry Regiment. Brooks does make an interesting comparison regarding the leadership techniques of Colonel Thomas W. Higginson of the 1st and Colonel James Montgomery of the 2nd South Carolina. Of limited value to students of the African-American military experience.

426.   Sturcke, Roger and Anthony Gero. "Zouave Dress for the 10th United States Colored Troops: A Probability." *Military Collector & Historian*, 49, 3 (Fall 1997: 132-133.

A series of letters are reprinted which suggest the 10th USCT "may have worn Zouave dress." Based on incomplete evidence, the authors believe that the uniforms were indeed issued. However, as the authors indicate "absolute documentation" regarding the style of dress is lacking. The article contains 11 notes.

427.   Suderow, Bryce A., editor. "The Suffolk Slaughter: We Did Not Take Any Prisoners." *Civil War Times Illustrated*, 23, 3 (May 1984): 36-39.

Reprints a letter that appeared in the March 22, 1864 edition of the Petersburg, Virginia *Daily Register*. In the letter the unknown Confederate correspondent comments on military operations around Suffolk, Virginia and clashes with the 2nd U.S. Colored Cavalry. According to the writer "we did not take any prisoners" and "Ransom's brigade never takes negro prisoners." The article is illustrated with period photographs.

428.   _____. "The Battle of the Crater: The Civil War's Worst Massacre," *Civil War History*, 43, 3 (September 1997): 219-224.

Using regimental and pension records, gruesome eyewitness testimony — both Confederate and Union — contemporary letters, and detailed casualty lists, the author concludes that the Battle of the Crater on July 30, 1864, outside Petersburg, Virginia, witnessed "the worst massacre of blacks during the Civil War." Two casualty tables are used to support the massacre argument. The first table contains a nominal list of African-American casualties. According to this table 410 men are listed as missing and presumed prisoners of war. However, Confederate records indicate that only 200 African-Americans were captured during and after the battle. The author maintains that a deliberate massacre explains the discrepancy. According to credible personal accounts, Confederate soldiers murdered black soldiers who attempted to surrender or who lay wounded on the field. Consequently, Suderow has provided an adjusted casualty table that lists a larger number of black soldiers as killed and a much smaller number as prisoners of war. In addition, during the Civil War the "normal ratio of killed to wounded was 1 to 4.8." Among African-Americans soldiers who participated in the Crater attack, the ratio was 1 to 1.7. A well-researched and persuasive study based principally on regimental records. The article contains 15 notes and 2 tables.

429.   Synnestvedt, Sig, editor. "The Earth Shook and Quivered."
    Civil War Times Illustrated, 11, 8 (December 1972): 30-37.
Containing vivid and well-written observations, this article contains edited extracts from the diary of Lieutenant Joseph J. Scroggs, 5th U.S. Colored Troops, describing the Petersburg Crater debacle and the Union attack on New Market Heights, Virginia. According to his September 29, 1864, diary entry, Scroggs began the New Market Heights assault with a 50 man company; at the conclusion of the battle, no more than ten remained. The article contains two contemporary photographs and four period drawings.

430.   Tap, Bruce. "These Devils Are Not Fit to Live on God's
    Earth: War Crimes and The Committee on the Conduct of the
    War, 1864-1865." *Civil War History*, 42, 2 (June 1996): 116-
    132.
As a result of Confederate actions at Fort Pillow, several members of the Committee on the Conduct of the War left Washington to investigate charges that black soldiers at the fort were massacred. Dominated by Radical Republicans, much of the information they collected was distorted or grossly exaggerated; however, the "committee did uncover significant abuses and atrocities" most of which have been substantiated by modern historians. The results of the committee's investigation were published and over 60,000 copies were printed. After reading the report, members of Congress, the cabinet, and the general public demanded that Lincoln adopt a policy of retaliation for Confederate atrocities. Lincoln demurred from adopting such a drastic measure. The article also includes an investigation by the committee on the condition of released Union prisoners and a general assessment of the committee's true aims and objectives.

431.   Taylor, Brian. A Politics of Service: Black Northerners' Debates over Enlistment in the American Civil War." *Civil War History*, 58, 4 (December 2012): 451-480.
The arguments for or against black enlistment in the Union Army, as manifested in four major Northern African-American newspapers, are examined in considerable depth.

432.   Taylor, John M. "The Crater." *MHQ: The Quarterly Journal of Military History*, 10, 2 (Winter 1998): 30-39.
An accurate and detailed history of what General Grant termed "a stupendous failure," the brutal July 30, 1864, Battle of the Crater. Of the total Union casualties, over one-third came from the black division. Confederate soldiers, enraged at facing African-American troops in combat, were reported to have cried "Take the white man – kill the nigger." The article is profusely illustrated with contemporary photographs and drawings.

433.   _____. "The Crater." Supplement 1864. *America's Civil War*, (2004): 50-58.
The same article as noted above but reprinted in its entirety several years later as part of a special magazine supplement.

434.   Thompson, Benjamin W. "Back to the South – Part III." *Civil War Times Illustrated*, 12, 7 (November 1973): 28-39.
Thompson was an officer in the 32nd U.S. Colored Troops and later served as a provost marshal. Thompson's regiment took part in the continuing Charleston campaign and later performed garrison duty at Hilton Head, South Carolina. Unfortunately, most of this "exceptionally interesting and informative" memoir is concerned with Thompson's responsibilities as provost marshal; little attention is paid to the 32nd U.S. Colored Troops. The article contains six drawings, seven period photographs, and an excellent war-time map of Hilton Head.

435.   Tobin, Richard L. "The Great Petersburg Mine." *Mankind: The Magazine of Popular History,* 1, 5 (1968): 26-33, 57-60.
A generic account of the July 30, 1864, mine explosion before Petersburg, Virginia, a battle described by the author as an "adventurous plan that failed" more from stupidity than any other factor. Little mention is made of African-American participation in the fighting. The article is illustrated with period photographs and artwork.

436.   Toppin, Edgar A. "Humbly They Served: The Black Brigade in the Defense of Cincinnati." *Journal of Negro History,* 48, 2 (April 1963): 75-97.
This is an excellent and detailed account of the role played by African-American civilian laborers, the Black Brigade, in the defense of Cincinnati in the summer of 1862. The treatment of blacks in the city of Cincinnati before, during, and after the Confederate threat are addressed. The article contains 55 notes, many based on contemporary newspaper accounts.

437.   Trudeau, Noah. "Kill the Last Damn One of Them." *MHQ: The Quarterly Journal of Military History*, 8, 3 (Spring 1996): 86-93.
For good reason the massacre at Fort Pillow on April 12, 1864, still resonates today. While Trudeau addresses what occurred that April day, he also presents several factors frequently overlooked. As an example, he points out that the Emancipation Proclamation authorized the military to employ African-Americans "to garrison forts, positions, stations, and other places." As a result, black troops often ended up guarding railroad bridges, supply depots, and isolated posts, all of which were vulnerable to attack by Confederate raiders. Fort Pillow was one such example. Secondly, the post was ordered closed and abandoned long before the battle. For reasons more to do with command greed than military considerations, the fort was re-opened. Lastly, the fort was tactically ill-suited for defense against determined attack. "In many ways Fort Pillow was a military disaster waiting to happen."

The author describes the battle and concludes beyond a doubt that Confederates massacred much of the garrison. He quotes the in-depth study conducted by John Cimprich and Robert C. Mainfort (which see). They determined, regarding the half black-half white garrison, that "nearly half were killed or morality wounded." Among African-American soldiers, the morality rate was an astounding 64 percent. Forrest's culpability for what occurred is in doubt. As the author indicates, for thirty minutes "Whether he knowingly allowed his men to run riot, or simply lost control ... will forever be an issue for debate." The article is supplemented by contemporary photograph, several drawings, and two maps.

438. _____. "Proven Themselves in Every Respect to be Men: Black Cavalry in the Civil War." In *Black Soldiers in Blue: African American Troops in the Civil War Era*, edited by John David Smith. Chapel Hill: University of North Carolina Press, 2002, 276-305.

Often overlooked by historians, the seven black cavalry regiments that were raised during the Civil War "saw more constant and active field service" than most African-American infantry regiments. Mounted regiments were expensive when compared to the cost of an average infantry regiment. Horses, equipage, lengthy training, and strenuous upkeep all worked to limit the number of Union cavalry regiments. In the case of mounted black soldiers, racial biases also came into play: many whites questioned if African-Americans possessed the necessary intellectual capacity to learn the intricate art of cavalry horsemanship. Eventually six regiments of black cavalry were authorized under Federal auspices; Massachusetts raised the only state numbered unit, the 5th Massachusetts Cavalry (Colored). While in Federal service, all generally performed credibly.

Trudeau's essay provides a wide-ranging operational overview for all seven African-American cavalry regiments. Of particular interest are the engagements of the 3rd U.S. Colored Cavalry in Mississippi, a unit that experienced considerable small scale combat. The author also provides a random sampling of several cavalry companies regarding place of birth and occupation of each cavalryman upon enlistment. The work is well documented with 66 notes.

439. _____. "Jungle War." *America's Civil War*, 16, 5 (November 2003): 26-33.

After the Union occupation of Fort Wagner, the siege of Charleston, South Carolina lapsed into a forgotten sideshow of the war. In 1864, in order to prevent Confederate forces from reinforcing the Virginia front, Major General John G. Foster, commanding officer of the Department of the South, was ordered by Washington to conduct a "demonstration" against the defenses of Charleston. In July Foster launched simultaneous assaults against several Confederate fortifications. The Union attacks were stymied by a combination of fetid swamps, marshlands, incessant heat, defective maps, bogs, swarms of mosquitos, and unpredictable tides. The jungle-like landscape did more to hinder Union operations than Confederate opposition. A number of African-American regiments took part in the affair including the 54th and 55th Massachusetts Volunteer Infantry. The article is illustrated and contains an informative map outlining the Union plan of attack.

440. _____. "Chaos in the Crater." *Civil War Times,* 43, 3 (August 2004): 26-33.

The July 30, 1864, assault on the Confederate defenses outside of Petersburg, the ill-fated Battle of the Crater, is recounted in workmanlike fashion by the author. Trudeau describes the construction of the tunnel, the original plan of attack, and the miscarried assault. Particular attention is paid to the conduct of Ferrero's all-black division and the slaughter of African-American soldiers who were murdered while attempting to surrender. The article is illustrated with several period drawings and photographs as well as a map outlining the assault.

441. _____. "A Stranger in the Club: The Army of the Potomac's Black Division." In *Slavery, Resistance, Freedom*, edited by Gabor Boritt and Scott Hancock, New York: Oxford University Press, 2007, 96-107.
A brief history of the only all-black division in the all-white Army of the Potomac is presented. Organized in January 1864 in Annapolis, Maryland, and commanded by Brigadier General Edward Ferrero, the division's recruits hailed from Maryland, Ohio, Pennsylvania, Connecticut, and later, in the war, Virginia. The division, officially designated as the 3rd Division, 9th Corps, saw limited combat in the opening phases of Grant's Overland Campaign. During these actions several African-Americans were captured by Confederate forces. A number were either shot on sight or hanged.

Considerable detail is provided by the author concerning the division and the role it played in the disastrous Crater attack outside Petersburg in January 1864. After the battle, fully a third of the division's complement was listed as casualties. Later the division was transferred to the all-black 25th Corps in the Army of the James. They left the Army of the Potomac as they had found it: an "elite white only club." The article contains 41 notes, most based on primary sources.

442. _____. "Needless Valor." *MHQ: Quarterly Journal of Military History*, 21, 1 (Autumn 2008): 56-65.
This article is a comprehensive account of the assault on New Market Heights, Virginia, on September 29, 1864 by several regiments of African-American soldiers. Militarily the attack was bungled by Benjamin Butler, the commander of the Union Army of the James, and was the second bloodiest battle fought by black soldiers in the war. According to the author, part of Butler's justification for the assault was to prove the reliability of black soldiers in combat. Indeed, 14 black soldiers at New Market Heights received the Medal of Honor for courage under fire and "the open fields opposite the heights are hallowed ground in the saga of black

soldiers in the Civil War." The well-written and easy to understand text is supplemented by several period photographs and map.

443.   _____. Blood Proof." *Civil War Times*, 52, 1 (February 2013): 44-51.

The pivotal role played by several African-American brigades in the decisive Union victory at Nashville, in December 1864, is recounted in this workmanlike tactical account. During the two-day battle black regiments were responsible for attacking the Confederate right flank. These attacks were strictly diversionary as the main Union assault was aimed at the opposite end of the Confederate line. Though ultimately successful, black soldiers sustained heavy casualties before victory was achieved. The article contains several period photographs and two excellent full-color maps that graphically illustrate the attacks made by the two black infantry brigades.

444.   Tucker, Philip Thomas. "The First Missouri Confederate Brigade's Last Stand at Fort Blakeley on Mobile Bay." *Alabama Review*, 42, 4 (October 1989): 270-291.

The day Confederate forces surrendered in Virginia saw the last great infantry action of the war in Alabama; Union forces, under the command of Major General Edward Canby, attacked and overwhelmed Fort Blakely as part of the Mobile Campaign. While this article is chiefly a study of the Missouri Brigade and the defense of the Fort Blakeley, the author does devote some attention to black soldiers. African-American troops are described as shouting "Remember Fort Pillow" as they stormed the defenses and "some black soldiers continued shooting into the huddled Confederates after they had surrendered." Other than a few paragraphs, this tactical study – detailed as it may be – is of little value to students of the African-American Civil War military experience.

445.   Turkel, Stanley. "The Remarkable Life of Robert Smalls." *Sea History*, 91 (Winter 1999-2000): 28-30.

A short but well-written biography of the remarkable Robert Smalls. The article traces Smalls early childhood as a slave in South Carolina, describes the seizure of the cotton steamer *Planter* and his

Civil War exploits, and concludes with a history of Smalls' post-war political career. Illustrated with 14 notes.

446.   Turnage, Sheila. "Stealing a Ship to Freedom." *American Legacy: Celebrating African-American History and Culture*, 8, 1 (Spring 2002): 70-73, 75-76.
Known as the "Gullah Statesman," Robert Smalls went from South Carolina slave to a post-Civil War seat in the United States House of Representatives. His career from early youth, through the abduction of the *Planter* in Charleston Harbor, as well as his post-war political triumphs and unfortunate travails are chronicled in this brief but workmanlike overview.

447.   Urwin, Gregory J. W. "I Want You to Prove Yourselves Men." *Civil War Times Illustrated,* 28, 6 (November/December 1989): 42-51.
This is a well-written and vivid account of the 54th Massachusetts from its inception to its July 1863 assault on Fort Wagner.

448.   _____. "'We Cannot Treat Negroes. . . as Prisoners of War': Racial Atrocities and Reprisals in Civil War Arkansas." *Civil War History*, 42, 3 (September 1996): 193-210.
The author convincingly argues that Arkansas witnessed some of the worst racial atrocities of the Civil War and the Battle of Poison Spring, fought on April 18, 1864, was probably "Arkansas's most notorious war crime." Days later at Marks' Mills African-American civilian employees and camp followers of the Union Army were indiscriminately slaughtered by Confederate soldiers. The author maintains that both incidents were not isolated examples of white racial violence but part of a "savage contest in which the central issue was race."

Southerners viewed African-Americans, and their employment by the Union Army, either as soldiers or civilians, as a direct threat to the economic and social position of white society. Black soldiers were considered in servile insurrection and their arming was a direct assault on a Southern social system based on white superiority and black subordination. The arming of former slaves as soldiers was considered a crime against humanity and, as a result, Confederates "felt absolved from any obligation to treat black soldiers and their white officers as honorable opponents." Extermination of rebellious slaves was necessary to reinforce the social order and "keep other blacks in their place."

Poison Spring was the first time that large numbers of African-American soldiers were engaged in a campaign as opposed to performing garrison and scouting duty in Arkansas. The Southern response was immediate and vicious. Wounded soldiers of the 1st Kansas Colored regiment left on the field were murdered and in many cases their bodies were horribly mutilated. Because of feared Union retribution, the policy of not taking black soldiers as prisoners was never officially articulated by the Confederate government or by the Trans-Mississippi Department. However it was "tacitly understood" by most Confederates that African-American soldiers were not to be taken as prisoners.

On April 30, 1864, at the Battle of Jenkins' Ferry African-American soldiers of the 2nd Kansas Colored responded to the atrocities committed at Poison Spring by slaughtering wounded Confederate soldiers left on the battlefield. While the reprisal was common knowledge throughout the army, it was never acknowledged by the Union command. The article contains 59 notes based on primary and published sources.

449. _____. "'Cut to Pieces and Gone to Hell': The Poison Spring Massacre." *North & South,* 3, 6 (August 2000): 45-57.

Gregory J.W. Urwin has written one of the best accounts of the Battle of Poison Spring to appear in article form. Fought on April 18, 1864, in southwestern Arkansas, the battle resulted in one of the worst racial atrocities of the Civil War. The author, in this excellent and meticulously detailed tactical study, describes the events leading up to the battle, the battle and massacre, and the battle's aftermath.

Poison Spring was a byproduct of Major General Frederick Steele's abortive march south from Little Rock in support of the Union's Red River Campaign in Louisiana. Deep in Confederate territory, dangerously overextended, and in desperate need of food and fodder, Steele dispatched a wagon train westward from Camden, Arkansas, with orders to forage liberally throughout the countryside. The Union forage party of 1,170 included 438 men of the 1st Kansas Colored Infantry, a "quick firing" regiment that had previously distinguished itself at Cabin Creek and Honey Springs. Even though it was ostensibly a Kansas unit, fully half its soldiers were runaway slaves from Arkansas. The wagon train was attacked and ultimately overwhelmed by superior Confederate forces on April 18, 1864, at Poison Spring, Arkansas.

As the 1st Kansas position was overrun, widespread and unrestricted slaughter of wounded black soldiers took place. "The Rebels celebrated their triumph with an orgy of barbarism." One Southerner boasted in his journal that "no black prisoners were taken." Most of the racial atrocities were committed by Confederates from Arkansas, and Texas, and by Choctaws from the Indian Territory. Atrocity breeds atrocity. At the Battle of Jenkins' Ferry, fought less than two weeks later, African-Americans of the 2nd Kansas Colored avenged Poison Spring by murdering wounded Confederates found on the field. The text is supplemented by order of battle information, a large number of period photographs, two full-color maps, and 39 notes.

450. _____. "Poison Spring and Jenkins' Ferry: Racial Atrocities during the Camden Expedition." In *All Cut to Pieces and Gone to Hell: The Civil War, Race Relations, and the Battle of Poison Spring,* edited by Mark K. Christ: Little Rock: August House, 2003, 107-133.
This is a revised and enlarged version of the article cited above.

451. _____. "Warfare, Race, and the Civil War in American Memory." In *Black Flag over Dixie: Racial Atrocities and Reprisals in the Civil War*. Carbondale: Southern Illinois University Press, 2004, 1-18.

In this thought-provoking essay, Urwin, a noted Civil War scholar, assesses the central role race played in the war. "The Civil War," he maintains," was not the chivalrous contest that white America prefers to remember." It involved numerous battlefield racial atrocities by Confederate soldiers which, in turn, provoked black reprisals. Tragically, this darker side of the Civil War is often lost in the complexities of remembrance which prefers "a sanitized picture of the most wrenching experience in American history." A well-written and insightful essay.

452. _____. "USCT Recruitment/Graph and USCT Strength Levels." *Civil War Times*, 53, 1 (February 2014): 16.

A map illustrating USCT recruiting areas and a chart listing USCT strength levels is provided.

453. Wagandt, Charles L. "The Army versus Maryland Slavery, 1862-1864." *Civil War History*, 10, 2 (June 1964): 141-148.

Though Maryland was a slave state, it remained loyal to the Union. Efforts by the state government to protect its "peculiar institution" were constantly undermined by Union Army recruiters who enlisted African-Americans, either slave or free. As the author indicates, some blacks were impressed into service and some volunteered, but in either case enlistment became a form of "preemptory emancipation." The ability of the Maryland governor to stop the practice came to naught, even after numerous appeals to the Lincoln administration. Finally, in November 1864 Maryland, abolished slavery.

454.   Walker, John. "Brice's Crossroads." *Military Heritage*, 10,
     1 (August 2008): 40-47.
The author presents a comprehensive account of the Confederate
victory at Brice's Cross Roads, Mississippi, on June 10, 1864.
Though receiving only cursory attention, approximately half the
Union soldiers killed in the battle were from African-American
regiments.

455.   Walker, Thomas. "Fought with the Desperation of Tigers."
     Journal of the West, 51, 2 (Spring 2012): 16-28.
In this comparative study, the author examines the reactions of
several Texas newspapers
 to the idea of African-Americans as soldiers. Black soldiers, and
their combat record in a number of engagements, is described in the
papers and then typically denigrated, ridiculed, or condemned as
barbaric. Former slaves were considered to be "an undisciplined
race who would panic as the first signs of combat." Ironically, in
the waning days of the war, and after years of scorn, the *Houston
Telegraph* suggested the time may have arrived when "our military
authorities will be forced to try him [the black man] as a soldier."
The article contains 58 notes; many are based on period Texas
newspaper accounts.

456.   Walls, David. "Marching Song of the First Arkansas
     Colored Regiment: A Contested Attribution." *Arkansas
     Historical Quarterly*, 66, 4 (Winter 2007): 401-421.
This article examines the origination of two song versions
associated with black troops in the Civil War. The first version, sung
to the tune of "John Brown's Body," the "Marching Song of the
First Arkansas Colored Regiment" was "written or at least
transcribed" by Lindley Hoffman Miller, a New Jersey-born captain
in the regiment. It first appeared in a broadside published in
Philadelphia by the Supervisory Committee for Recruiting Colored
Regiments. A similar version of the song entitled "Valiant
Soldiers," published in 1876, has been attributed to Sojourner Truth.
However, the author concludes that the weight of evidence supports
Miller's claim as the originator. Regardless of authorship, "the song

is a vital document of racial pride, confidence, optimism, and the sheer joy in having a hand in the defeat of the Confederacy." The lyrics of the original Miller song are printed in entirety. Except for a few stanzas and word changes, the Sojourner Truth version is basically similar. The article contains 47 notes based on primary and secondary sources.

457. "War Graph." *Civil War Times*, 54, 2 (April 2015): 17.
An illustrated map depicts those black regiments that were present for Lee's surrender.

458. Ward, Andrew. "What Happened at Fort Pillow?" *American Heritage*, 56, 4 (August/September 2005): 22.
This is a one-page essay by Andrew Ward, the author of *River Run Red: The Fort Pillow Massacre in the American Civil War*. Brief though it is, the essay presents several compelling but often overlooked observations regarding the massacre. According to the author, once the murderous Confederate rage against African-American soldiers subsided, "black survivors fared much better than their white comrades. Blacks were valued as recovered property." Likewise, most of Forrest's men, Ward maintains, were not poor whites but men who "owned, or stood to inherit, substantial property, including slaves."

459. "We are Coming, Father Abraham. The United States Colored Troops in Photographs." *American History*, 48, 4 (October 2013): 38-41.
Images of several black soldiers from the U.S. Colored Troops are presented; included is a photograph of Sergeant Major Christian Fleetwood, 4th USCT.

460. Weidman, Budge. "Preserving the Legacy of the United States Colored Troops." *Prologue: Quarterly of the National Archives and Record Administrations*, 29, 2 (Summer 1997): 90-94.
Written over a decade ago but still relevant today, this article discusses the compiled military service records of African-American soldiers maintained by the National Archives and

Records Administration. These records were individually reviewed as part of a project to microfilm the military service records of all Civil War soldiers, both Union and Confederate. They are, as the author indicates, an important but little utilized research source offering valuable information, personal insights, and fascinating details regarding black Civil War soldiers: they "bring to life the service of the African American soldier." Excerpts from the service records are also provided in the form of letters and slave compensation documents.

NOTE:
Individual military service records providing only basic facts regarding a serviceman, white or black, Union or Confederate, can be found online at *Civil War Soldiers and Sailors System*, http://www.civilwar.nps.gov/cwss/. This computerized database system, which is maintained by the National Park Service, provides information from over six million records held by the National Archives and Records Administration (NARA). More complete individual Civil War records can be found by accessing the NARA website; log on to their homepage and, under search, type "Civil War soldiers" which should display you to the appropriate menu for ordering individual service records, both military and pension-related.

461. _____. "'Dear Husband, Please come Home:' Civil War Letters to Black Soldiers." *Prologue: Quarterly of the National Archives and Records Administration*, 35, 4 (Winter 2003): 60-67.
The Civil War Conservation Corps, a volunteer organization of the National Archives and Records Administration, was charged with collecting the service records of African-American soldiers prior to microfilming. Found in the archives were letters sent from the home front which became part of the soldier's compiled service records. The letters paint a compelling and mostly grim description of home front hardship experienced by the wives and mothers of black soldiers. Excerpts from a number of letters are printed; most stress poverty, sickness, a lack of money, and urgent requests for the soldier to come home.

462.   Weinert, Richard P., Jr. "The Battle of Olustee." *Civil War Times Illustrated*, 1, 3 (June 1962): 31-33.
A good but abbreviated description of the Battle of Olustee, Florida fought on February 20, 1864 – the largest land battle fought in the state and a humiliating Union defeat. The article contains several period photographs and a map of the battleground.

463.   Weiss, Nathan. "General Benjamin Franklin Butler and the Negro: The Evolution of the Racial Views of a Practical Politician." *Negro History Bulletin*, 29, 1 (October 1965): 3-4, 14-16, 23.
The author presents a biographical summation of the career of the always controversial Benjamin F. Butler, a politician who began the Civil War as a pro-slavery Democrat and emerged as a radical advocate of African-American equality. Butler's post-war political activities, including, his contributions to the Civil Rights Act of 1866, are also discusses.

464.   Wenzel, Carol N. "Freedmen's Farm Letters of Samuel and Louisa Mallory to 'our absent but ever remembered boy' in McHenry County, Illinois." *Journal of the Illinois State Historical Society*, 73, 3 (Autumn 1980): 162-176.
In 1864, Captain Samuel Mallory of the 64th U.S. Colored Infantry was appointed supervisor of the 800-acre Freedmen's Home Farm at Pine Bluff, Arkansas. These were confiscated or abandoned lands made available to freedmen to resettle and farm. A series of 11 letters written by Mallory and his wife are reproduced. Mallory's letters describe his personal observations about a freedmen's farm, fellow offices, teachers from Northern aid societies, the soldiers under his command, and his responsibilities for administering a "large number of plantations."

465.   Wert, Jeffrey D. "Camp William Penn and the Black Soldier." *Pennsylvania History*, 46, 4 (October 1979): 335-346.
Wert's article is an informative and useful history of Camp William Penn, mustering site and training facility for 11 African-American regiments raised in Pennsylvania. Located eight miles north of Philadelphia, the camp was "especially designed for black

volunteers" and "was like no other military installation during the Civil War." From June 26, 1863 to May 2, 1865, a period of less than 22 months, "nearly 400 white officers and 10, 940 enlisted blacks learned the basic art of soldiering within its confines." Much of the camp's success in training African-American soldiers is attributed to the Philadelphia Supervising Committee for Recruiting Colored Troops. This citizen-founded organization established a school to train white officers while at the same time "diligently protected the welfare of black soldiers." The article contains 51 notes, many from period newspaper accounts.

466. _____. "Rewriting History with the 54th." *Civil War Times*, 46, 1 (February 2007): 7-8.
A very limited account of the formation and early history of the 54th Massachusetts is provided. Recruits for the regiment, according to the author, "hailed from 24 states, the District of Columbia, the West Indies, and Africa." The article is illustrated with period photographs of two soldiers from the regiment.

467. Westwood, Howard C. "Captive Black Union Soldiers in Charleston - What To Do?" *Civil War History*, 28, 1 (March 1982): 28-44.
Using the Official Records and other primary sources, the author examines the confusing and often contradictory Confederate government position regarding the treatment of captured Union black soldiers. The article contains 65 notes.

468. _____. "Lincoln's Position on Black Enlistments." *Lincoln Herald*, 86, 2 (Summer 1984): 101-112.
Early in the war Lincoln opposed the recruiting and arming of African-Americans as soldiers. Instead he advocated a policy of caution and restraint even as he allowed limited recruiting of black soldiers in South Carolina and Louisiana. Mounting Union casualties and political pressure lead to Lincoln's publication of the Emancipation Proclamation. The Proclamation provided that freedmen "will be received into the armed forces of the Union States to garrison forts, positions, stations, and other places and to man vessels of sorts in said services." According to the author, Lincoln's

position on arming African-Americans evolved and changed as black soldiers proved their worth on the battlefield.

469. _____. "General David Hunter and Rufus Saxton and Black Soldiers." *South Carolina History Magazine,* 86, 3 (Summer - July 1985): 165-181.

This article compares the dissimilar approaches to raising black regiments on the Sea Islands of South Carolina. Major General David Hunter, as commanding officer of the Department of South Carolina, Georgia, and Florida, took the heavy-handed approach often forcibly enlisting black slaves. Hunter had no official authority to do what he did; eventually his recruiting efforts ended in failure. Brigadier General Rufus Sarton, as the newly appointed military governor of the coastal islands, took a more nuanced approach. He informed Washington that, pursuant to previous instructions, he was raising a corps of black "laborers" not "soldiers." As directed, these armed laborers could be used to guard plantations and assist in the event of an "emergency." Saxton's approach, and the changing attitude of the Lincoln administration to the idea of arming black slaves, eventually resulted in the enlistment of thousands of African-American soldiers from the Sea Islands.

470. _____. "The Cause and Consequence of a Union Black Soldier's Mutiny and Execution." *Civil War History,* 31, 3 (September 1985): 222-236.

By all accounts, 23 year old Sergeant William Walker of Company A, 3rd South Carolina Colored Infantry was, at least initially, a good soldier. Walker enlisted in the 3rd South Carolina under the assumption, and the Federal government promise, that he would receive the same pay as a white enlisted man. According to the army's pay structure, a white private was entitled to $13.00 per month plus $3.50 per month allowance when clothing was not provided. Non-commissioned officers received more. At first African-American enlisted men in the 3rd South Carolina received the same pay as their white colleagues. However, the War Department interpreted the Militia Act of 1862 to mean all black soldiers – regardless of enlisted rank – were to receive only $10.00

month less $3.00 for clothing. A black soldier's pay was, in effect, $7.00 per month, almost half of what a white soldier received. The Federal government had reneged on its pledge of equal pay and equal treatment. Additionally, rations for the men's families were also stopped. Bitter resentment over the unequal treatment was compounded by excessive manual labor. What Walker found after entering the 3rd South Carolina was long, difficult, and exhausting fatigue duty with little if any instruction as a soldier. Finally, on November 19, 1863, Company A, under Walker's leadership, protested the government's discriminatory policies. Addressing the regimental commander, Walker declared he "would not do duty any longer for seven dollar per month." Charged with leading a mutiny, he was tried at Hilton Head, found guilty, and executed at Jacksonville, Florida, on March 1, 1864. He was the first black soldier to be executed for mutiny in the Civil War. (In fact, 14 of the 19 soldiers executed for mutiny during the war were African-Americans.) Walker's protest may not have been in vain. The 3rd was subsequently relieved of much of its fatigue duties and later, much later, Congress equalized pay between the races. The article's extensive documentation is based exclusively on primary sources.

471. _____. "Benjamin Butler's Enlistment of Black Troops in New Orleans in 1862." *Louisiana History*, 26, 1 (Winter 1985): 5-22.
After the occupation of New Orleans by Federal forces, Union general Benjamin F. Butler, as commanding officer, was desperate for more troops to control the city and its environs. His force was much too small in numbers and essentially isolated from other Federal commands. He was responsible for pacifying the city while encouraging support for the Union without antagonizing local slave holders or disrupting the institution of slavery. Nevertheless, additional troops were acutely needed. An earlier attempt to recruit local white men was only partially successful. One subordinate, Brigadier General John W. Phelps, pressed for arming black slaves. Butler refused and Phelps eventually resigned. Shortly afterwards, Butler enlisted black soldiers. Many historians considered this action as an attempt by Butler, "a self-seeking opportunist," take credit for recruiting and arming black men as soldiers. Not so,

argues the author. To bolster his forces and avoid arming slaves, Butler enlisted "free colored citizens." These were free black men who had been recognized by the Louisiana state government as an unarmed part of the state militia prior to the Union occupation. Butler thus avoided the thorny problem of arming slaves which ran the risk of offending large slaveholders. Ultimately three regiments of Louisiana Native Guards were raised. Nearly all of the line officers were African-Americans. The article is well written and well researched and contains 65 notes, many of which are based on Butler's personal correspondence.

472. _____. "Mr. Smalls: A Personal Adventure." *Civil War Times Illustrated*, 25, 3 (May 1986): 20-23, 28-31.
The author provides a dramatic and entertaining account of the May 19, 1862, escape of Robert Smalls, with his family and several friends, from Charleston harbor via the *Planter*, a hijacked Confederate steamboat. Westwood's article provides considerable details concerning Smalls' careful planning and seizure of the *Planter*, and his subsequent escape to the Union blockading fleet. Smalls' equally remarkable post-war life is only lightly touched upon.

473. _____. "Grant's Role in Beginning Black Soldiery." *Illinois Historical Journal*, 79, 3(Autumn 1986): 197-212.
Though initially indifferent to slavery, U.S. Grant was a supporter of the Emancipation Proclamation and of Lorenzo Thomas's recruiting of freed slaves as soldiers in the Mississippi Valley. Newly recruited black soldiers allowed Grant to free white soldiers for other duties. Moreover, black soldiers provided garrisons at strategic sites along the Mississippi River and protected plantations worked by newly enfranchised slaves. Few Civil War generals, according to Westwood, "contributed more solidly to the ultimate success" of Civil War African-American soldiers than Grant.

474. _____. "Company A of Rhode Island's Black Regiment: Its Enlisting, Its 'Mutiny,' Its Pay, Its Service." In *Black Troops, White Commanders, and Freedmen during the Civil War*, by Howard C. Westwood. Carbondale: Southern University Press, 1992, 149-166.

On St. Patrick's Day 1864, all but one black noncommissioned officer of Company A, 1st Battalion, 14th Rhode Island Heavy Artillery (Colored) refused to answer a roll call. As they stood in the sun on Matagorda Island, Texas, the roll was again repeated and again it was not acknowledged. The causes and consequences of that refusal, a refusal that resulted in the conviction of a number of African-American soldiers for mutiny, are explored. In addition, the author provides a sketch of the regiment's recruitment, its promise of equal pay with white soldiers, its service in the South, and the relations between white officers and black enlisted men. Shortly after the mutiny, the battalion was transferred to Louisiana to join the rest of the regiment in performing garrison duty along the Mississippi River. Later in the century, when a regimental history was published, no mention was made of the Matagorda mutiny. Known locally as the 14th Rhode Island Heavy Artillery (Colored) it was designated, after a few changes by the Federal government, as the 11th United States Colored Heavy Artillery. Well documented, the article includes 72 extensive notes.

475. White, Jonathan W., Katie Fisher and Elizabeth Wall. "The Civil War Letters of Tillman Valentine, US Colored Troops." *The Pennsylvania Magazine of History and Biography*, 139, 2 (April 2015): 171-188.

Several Civil War letters written by Sergeant Tillman Valentine, 3rd United States Colored Troops, are reprinted. Valentine's letters are difficult to understand and are concerned primarily with private and family matters. He only "occasionally commented on the war."

476. White, Lonnie J., editor. "A Bluecoat's Account of the
Camden Expedition." *Arkansas Historical Quarterly,* 24, 1
(Spring 1965): 82-89.
A first-hand account of the Camden, Arkansas, expedition,
including the battle of Jenkins' Ferry, by a white officer of the 2nd
Kansas Colored Regiment. This post-war account appeared in the
Lawrence, Kansas *Daily Tribune* on February 15, 1866.

477. Whyte, James H. "Maryland's Negro Regiment - How,
Where." *Civil Times Illustrated,* 1, 4 (July 1962): 41-43.
This article succinctly discusses the recruiting and military service
of African-American regiments raised in Maryland. Six black
regiments are attributed to the state: the 7th, 9th, 19th, and 30th U.S.
Colored Troops were recruited on the Eastern Shore or southern
Maryland; the 4th and 39th U.S. Colored Troops were both organized
in Baltimore. All six regiment saw hard duty in Virginia.

478. Wickman, Donald. "Their Share of the Glory: Rutland
Blacks in the Civil War." *Rutland Historical Society Quarterly,*
22, 2 (1992): 18-36.
The author provides a capsule history of the 54th Massachusetts
Volunteers as well as biographies of men from Rutland, Vermont
who served in the regiment. Vermont sent 120 African-Americans
off to war; 71 served in the 54th; of that number 20 were from
Rutland. The article also contains a reprint of an April 27, 1865
after-action report to the Adjutant General of Massachusetts
describing Potter's Raid in South Carolina, the last wartime
campaign of the 54th Massachusetts.

479. Wiley, Bell Irwin. "Billy Yank and the Black Folk." *The
Journal of Negro History,* 36, 1 (January 1951): 35-52.
A dated but still valuable study exploring the racial attitudes of
Union soldiers toward the freedmen. Some if not most white
soldiers, according to Wiley, expressed outright antipathy and
contempt toward African-Americans; others were more kindly
disposed, especially after observing first-hand the horrors of
slavery. While most of this well-balanced and careful study

explores these conflicting racial views, the attitude of Union soldiers toward black enlistments is not overlooked. Initially, the majority of white soldiers opposed the enlistment of African-Americans as a threat to white supremacy, or because blacks "were viewed as deficient in soldierly qualities." Opposition to black recruitment decreased as African-American enlistments dramatically increased. However, according to the author, the most important factor influencing white acceptance of black as soldiers "was the simple fact of Yanks growing accustomed to the sight of black men wearing the Federal uniform." This abbreviated study was originally a segment in Wiley's pioneering *The Life of Billy Yank: Common Soldier of the Union Army*. The article contains 47 notes based almost exclusively on personal accounts.

480. Williams, Chad L. "Symbols of Freedom and Defeat: African American Soldiers, White Southerners, and the Christmas Insurrection Scare of 1865." *Southern Historian: A Journal of Southern History,* 21 (Spring 2000): 40-55.
This article recounts the Christmas Insurrection panic that obsessed the white planter class throughout the South during the winter of 1865-1866. Fear of an African-American insurrection in which whites would be slaughtered, and their lands confiscated, ran rampant as rumor fed upon rumor. Most whites believed the insurrection would occur sometime during the Christmas season. White fears were accentuated by the presence of armed black troops serving as an occupational force in the region. Whites, and in particular the planter class, believed that black soldiers were encouraging the supposed insurrection especially since freed people "embraced the troops as heroes, protectors, and liberators." From the white perspective, African-American soldiers were viewed as the final insult and a symbol of the collapse of the old social order; collectively these soldiers embodied the full ramification of emancipation and Southern defeat. Despite widespread white fears, the anticipated violence did not occur. The article contains 34 notes.

481.　Williams, Charles G. "The Action at Wallace's Ferry." *Phillips County Historical Quarterly* 25, 1-2 (December 1986 and March 1987): 46–55.

Based primarily on the Official Records, this is a hurried account of the fight at Wallace's Ferry, Arkansas on July 26, 1864.

482.　Williams, Walter L. "Again in Chains: Black Soldiers Suffering in Captivity." *Civil War Times Illustrated,* 20, 2 (May 1981): 36-43.

An excellent, succinct account of the treatment of captured African-American soldiers by Confederate authorities. According to the author Confederate government policy regarding the treatment of captured black soldiers was often contradictory and confused. Generally, regardless of official policy, captured blacks were summarily executed immediately after capture, sold into slavery, used as forced laborers by the Confederate military, or condemned to prisoner-of-war camps where their chances of survival were minimal. The article is based on the Official Records and is illustrated with photographs and drawings.

483.　Williamson, Jane, editor. "'I Don't Get Fair Play Here'. A Black Vermonter Writes Home." *Vermont History*, 75, 1 (Winter/Spring 2007): 35-38.

This is a reprint of an 1864 letter from Aaron N. Freeman, a black Vermonter serving in the 54th Massachusetts Infantry. In his letter Freeman bitterly complains of living conditions in Jacksonville, Florida, abuse by white officers, and receiving "but 7 dolars a month ... that they paid to colard troops."

484.　Wills, Brian Steel. "A Devil of a Mess in Tennessee." *America's Civil War*, 27, 1 (March 2014): 34-41.

Racial animosity clearly played a central role in the massacre at Fort Pillow. However, according to the author, the massacre was not planned or authorized but resulted from a failure of Forrest to control his men "some of whom killed members of the Union garrison who should have been spared." The article describes the physical topography of the fort, the battle and the battle's contentious aftermath – both during and after the war. The text is supplemented by a superb map that graphically details the events at Fort Pillow as they unfolded. Steel, a professor at Kennesaw State University, Kennesaw, Georgia is the author of *The River was Dyed with Blood*, a first-rate and much to be recommended examination of the Fort Pillow massacre.

485.   Wilson, Catherine. "The 54th and 55th Regiments of Massachusetts Infantry." *The Report: Published Quarterly by the Ohio Genealogical Society,* 34, 3 (Fall 1994): 139-49.
A compilation of men from Ohio who volunteered for service in the 54th and 55th Massachusetts Infantry, two of the three black regiments raised under Massachusetts state authority. Information was extracted from Volume 4, *Massachusetts Soldiers, Sailors, and Marines in the Civil War.* Each individual soldier is listed by regiment, company, name, and Ohio residence upon enlistment. Contrary to the author's assertion, the 54th and 55th were not the first African-American military units in the Civil War.

486.   Wilson, Keith. "Thomas Webster and the 'Free Military School for Applicants for Command of Colored Troops.'" *Civil War History,* 29, 2 (June 1983): 101-122.
This article examines the efforts of Thomas Webster and his Philadelphia-based "Free Military School for Applicants for Commands of Colored Troops." The motivation for the school was the prevailing racial belief that African-American soldiers "needed to be commanded by especially sensitive and intelligent white officers." As a result, the school trained only white applicants and white applicants only, for officer commissions in black regiments. Though the school lasted less than a year, it successfully graduated, according to the school's proponents, a number of future officers considered morally, intellectually, and militarily suitable for command of African-American troops. Webster, a leading member of Philadelphia society and an active Union League member, was the pioneering force behind the school's establishment. The article describes the Free Military School's entrance and screening requirements, curriculum, overall operation, daily training routine, and preparation for officer commission examinations. The school was "a unique philanthropic organization that dispersed aid, not to

the general public, but to the Union army." The article contains 91 notes based almost exclusively on primary source materials.

487. _____. "Black Bands and Black Culture: A Study of Black Military Bands in the Union Army during the Civil War." *Australasian Journal of American Studies*, 9, 1 (July 1990): 31-37.

This well-researched and interesting study, based mainly on primary sources, explores how African-American soldiers culturally adjusted to the "demands of military service" by focusing on the role of black regimental bands in the Union Army. Bands were an essential ingredient in the routine of army life. Bands took part in military executions, participated in funeral services, serenaded officers and men, and accompanied soldiers on marches. They served as a potent recruiting tool particularly in raising African-American regiments. "They drummed in recruits and drummed out miscreants." Bands, both in the military and civilian life, were part of the fabric of American life. African-American music, however, stood well outside the cultural mainstream. Many whites viewed African- American cadence and rhythm – black music – as part of the degrading experience of slavery. They insisted that black regimental bands adopt a musical repertoire more in tune with the likes of white society. This the bands did, but they fused white composition and harmony with their own unique musical traditions. As a result, "black bandsmen gave Union Army music a distinctive African interpretation which was based on their antebellum cultural heritage." Thus, military bands in black regiments allowed African-American soldiers to adjust to army life while retaining their own cultural personality and character. Bands served as a source of unity and pride and "black bandsmen declared their freedom, citizenship and cultural pride in the musical repertoire they performed." The article contains 17 notes.

488. _____. "In the Shadow of John Brown: Colonels Thomas Higginson, James Montgomery, and Robert Shaw in the Department of the South." In *Black Soldiers in Blue: African American Troops in the Civil War Era*, editor. John David Smith. Chapel Hill: University of North Carolina Press, 2002, 306-335.

Thomas Higginson, Robert Shaw, and James Montgomery all played "critical roles in black recruitment and military service" during the Civil War. Though they were abolitionists they carried differing racial preconceptions regarding the African-American soldiers under their command. Higginson was a New England intellectual firmly committed to the cause of abolition; Shaw, born to an elite New England abolition family, had little active involvement in the cause, while Montgomery fought with John Brown in Kansas and waged western style hard war against Southern slave owners. Their individual view of warfare, their opinion of the black troops they commanded, and their command leadership styles are all explored. Montgomery was a religious zealot possessed by a visceral hatred of the slave holding plantation society. He conducted a holy war against slave holders but considered blacks as inferior beings and had little concern for their well-being after the war. "His vision of America was a Christian nation in which white labor was supreme and slavery destroyed." Shaw and Higginson considered the western idea of hard war as uncivilized and were motivated by a desire to improve the lot of the black soldiers they commanded. However, both men professed essentially condescending racial attitudes and considered African-Americans emotionally unstable, lacking in self-reliance, and in need of discipline. This fascinating and thoughtful study contains 57 notes.

489. Wilson, Robert. "Lincoln at Petersburg." *American History*, 48, 4 (October 2013): 32-37.

According to the author, Lincoln, was so moved by his review of black troops near Petersburg in June 1864, that he "showed a depth of emotion" not usually associated with his character. That feeling was reciprocated by the black troops "who crowded around him....some kissed his hands." According to Union General Horace Porter it was an outpouring of devotion that "defies description." Later, in a final act of respect for a fallen president, the 22nd U.S. Colored Troops led his funeral procession from the White House to the Capital.

The article compares Lincoln's emotions before Petersburg with those portrayed in the Spielberg film. Several photographs are included as well as an excellent map.

490. Wilson, Sven E. "Prejudice & Policy: Racial Discrimination in the Union Army Disability Pension System, 1865-1906." *American Journal of Public Health*, Supplement, 100, S1 (2010): S56-S65.

The pension system for Union Civil War veterans was the first large-scale social insurance program in the nation's history. At its peak in 1893 almost 42% of the Federal budget was "being paid out to military veterans." Theoretically, black veterans were subject to the same eligibility requirements as whites and received, if approved, the same benefits. In examining the pension system Wilson analyzed the records of over 40,000 Union Army veterans, both black and white. The data collected came from army service records, pension applications, and Pension Bureau rulings. After careful examination, the author concluded the pension system shortchanged black applicants in a number of ways. As an example, because of poverty and illiteracy, black veterans often lacked the necessary documentation to prove wartime injuries or disabilities. Compared to whites they were less likely to have been hospitalized during the war and thus less able to prove wartime disabilities. In addition, the increasing leniency accorded to white soldiers by pension examiners was often not extended to black veterans. However, "when Whites and Blacks claimed disabilities that were easily verifiable, outcomes were similar, but when verification required a degree of trust, Blacks fared considerable worse than Whites." The article contains two graphs, two statistical tables, and 49 notes.

491. Winsboro, Irvin D. S. "Give Them their Due: A Reassessment of African Americans and Union Military Service in Florida during the Civil War." *Journal of African American History*, 92, 3 (Summer 2007): 327-346.

With ample justification, historians regard Florida as a backwater in the Civil War. Consequently, the role played by African-American soldiers in the state have either been downplayed, misrepresented or, in many cases, deliberately ignored. With the exception of the Battle of Olustee, most wartime accounts of Confederate Florida typically refer to African-American military units only in a tangential sense as 'Colored Troops.'" According to the author, black military participation in Florida's Civil War "has been missing in the literature for almost a century and a half." In order to address this imbalance, Winsboro points out that African-American soldiers in Florida were key to Union success and "participated in at least thirty-two skirmishes, raids, scouting, expeditions, and battles." Additionally, compared to other states, an unusually high percentage of Florida's African-Americans contributed to the Federal war effort by enlisting in either the Union army or navy. Indeed, almost half of all Union troops in stationed in the state during the war were black soldiers. Florida's Civil War African-Americans, either as soldiers or sailors, were instrumental in the liberation of countless slaves, suppressed and countered Confederate guerilla activity, reduced the state's salt manufacturing capability, and hindered the movement of Florida's beef herds that were destined to supply food to a faltering Confederacy. The author emphatically points out that Florida's black soldiers and sailors "have yet to receive their full historical and scholarly recognition." Well written and well researched, the article contains two tables and 55 notes based largely on primary sources.

492. Wood, Larry. "Massacre at Baxter Springs." *Blue & Gray*, 5, 5 (May 1988): 30-31.

The author presents a two-page account of the Battle of Baxter Springs, Kansas, on October 6, 1863. In the battle's opening phase African-Americans of the 2nd Kansas Colored successfully defended the Baxter Springs fort from assault by Confederate bushwhackers. When the guerila force withdrew they fell upon and massacred a nearby column of Union troops. Of limited value for students of the African-American Civil War experience.

493.   Work, David. "United States Colored Troops during Reconstruction, 1865-1867." *Southwestern Historical Quarterly*, 109, 3 (January 2006): 336-357.

Between mid-June 1865 and early 1867 at least half of all volunteer Union troops stationed in Texas during Reconstruction were African-Americans. Initially only one the three army corps dispatched for occupation duties was black; later, African-American soldiers constituted a majority. The last volunteer United States Colored Troops in the state were mustered out of Federal service in August 1867. Black soldiers were dispatched for occupation duties in the Lone Star State for several reasons: To begin with, they were available since most had volunteered late in the war and, as a result, still had a year or more remaining on their enlistments. And, unlike white volunteer regiments, they lacked the necessary political connections for an early release from service. Racism also played a part.

Occupation duties required that black soldiers, and their white counterparts, restore order and enforce the law in what had become, with the fall of the Confederacy, essentially a lawless state. They were also responsible for expediting the French evacuation of Mexico by preventing the flow of supplies to Maximillian, the French supported emperor. Perhaps their most important function, one that was ultimately performed in vain, was to protect the rights of freedmen.

White Texans viewed the use of African-American troops with horror and viewed their presence in the state as a humiliating assault on what was the established social order. During their time in Texas the enlisted men in the United States Colored Troops were often accused of inciting racial incident and were subject to a constant barrage of citizen complaints, slanderous and continual abuse in the local press, and often violent physical attacks. Nevertheless, as the author points out, they did their duty with discipline and "admirable restraint."

This is an important examination of the little-known role United States Colored Troops played in the early stages of Lone Star Reconstruction. Well written, the article is based on newspaper accounts as well as primary and secondary sources. It contains several photographs and 52 notes.

494. Yacovone, Donald. "The Fifty-fourth Massachusetts Regiment, the Pay Crisis, and the 'Lincoln Despotism." In *Hope & Glory: Essays on the Legacy of the 54th Massachusetts Regiment*, edited by Marti H. Blatt, Thomas J. Brown, and Donald Yacovone: Amherst: University of Massachusetts Press, 2001, 35-51.
The 18 month ordeal of the 54th Massachusetts, and its determined refusal to accept unequal pay, is documented in this excellent essay. It was a severe test of the regiment's resolve and it caused great distress for each soldier as well as their dependents. Upon enlistment, the regiment had been promised the same pay as white soldiers. The Lincoln administration, however, determined that the 54th and 55th Massachusetts were enlisted under the provisions of the Militia Act of July 1862. This act paid African-American laborers in the employ of the government. Using these provisions as criteria, the government paid a black soldier, regardless of rank, $10.00 a month minus $3.00 deducted for clothing. A white soldier received $13.00 per month and more depending on rank.

The 54th refused to accept unequal pay, even when the state of Massachusetts offered to make up the difference. The offer, while appreciated, was rejected on principle. The 54th was engaged in a struggle against its own government which caused much dissatisfaction and a number of disciplinary problems. Some white officers even feared a mutiny. Under pressure, Congress finally equalized pay retroactive to January 1, 1864.
The article contains 13 notes.

495.   Yockelson, Mitchell. "Their Memory Will Not Perish: Commemorating the 56th United States Colored Troops." *Gateway Heritage*, 22, 3 (Winter 2001-2002): 26-31.

Yockelson, an archivist with the National Archives and Records Administration, has written a summary history of the 56th U.S. Colored Troops. Raised principally in the St. Louis area, the regiment was mustered as the 3rd Arkansas Volunteer Infantry (African Descent) and, shortly afterwards, re-designated the 56th U.S. Colored Troops. The duties of the 56th, according to the author, "typified all colored troop regiments during the Civil War." They performed the monotonous but all-important guard, garrison, and fatigue duties of occupation troops. The article contains a disappointing description of the fight at Wallace's Ferry, Arkansas, on July 26, 1864. It was the only combat the regiment would see. After hours of intense fighting the 56th, and several other Union regiments, were forced to abandon the field. During the fight the 56th suffered 43 men killed, wounded, and missing; the regimental commander was mortally wounded Following the fight at Wallace's Ferry, the regiment spent the remainder of the "war on garrison duty around Helena." As was the case with most African-American regiments, the 56th lost more men to disease than to battle. Indeed, several days before discharge cholera swept the regiment and carried off some 178 men in a matter of days. Buried on Quarantine Island outside of St. Louis, the bodies were disinterred some 70 years later and removed to the Jefferson Barracks National Cemetery. According to Frederick H. Dyer's authoritative *A Compendium of the War of the Rebellion*, during the Civil War the 56th lost four officers and 21 men killed or mortality wounded in combat, and an astounding two officers and 647 men to disease. Though not the in-depth socio-economic study of a Civil War African-American regiment that is long overdue, the article is still a worthwhile endeavor.

496.   Zalimas, Robert J., Jr. "A Disturbance in the City: Black and White Soldiers in Postwar Charleston." In *Black Soldiers in Blue: African American Troops in the Civil War Era*, edited by John David Smith. Chapel Hill: University of North Carolina Press, 2002, 361-390.

Zalimas examines the experience of African-American soldiers stationed as provost guards and garrison troops in post-Civil War Charleston, South Carolina. During their service, black soldiers encountered innumerable hostile acts by both white army units stationed in in the city and local residents. Frequent acts of white violence, and almost daily street fights between black and white soldiers, eventually resulted in a full-scale race riot on July 8, 1865. The riot continued for several days before peace was finally restored. As a result of the riot, army officials decided to "protect black troops from attacks" by moving them beyond contact with whites in urban areas. As the author indicates, this type of appeasement eventually lead to "the complete removal of black soldiers from the South." The article contains 51 notes, many of which are based on primary source materials.

497.   Zollars, Candice. "They laid down their Lives for the Flag." *Military Images*, 33, 3 (Summer 2015): 25-28.

This article describes the service record of the 6th United States Colored Troops from its training at Camp William Penn, Pennsylvania, until its discharge in September 1865. During the war the regiment suffered 40% casualties. Returning to Philadelphia, the regiment's officers adopted a resolution praising the enlisted men as "brave, reliable, and efficient" and deserving to "be fully recognized as equals." Several *carte de visite* images of the regiment's officers are provided. Included in the photographs is that of Jeremiah Asher, the only African-American chaplain to die in service during the war.

498. Zollo, Richard P. "General Francis S. Dodge and His Brave Black Soldiers." *Essex Institute Historical Collections,* 122, 3 (July 1986): 181-206.

The military career of Massachusetts-born Francis S. Dodge is recounted from his enlistment as a private in the Union Army to his retirement as Paymaster General of the Army. Dodge's Civil War service as an officer in the 2nd U. S. Colored Cavalry is briefly described; however, most of the article concerns Dodge's post-war commands with the 9th Cavalry, an all-black regiment, and as an army paymaster. "Dodge, who had commanded black soldiers from the earliest formation of Negro army units...seems to have escaped the uneasy, not infrequently hostile attitude the United States Army held towards its black soldiers."

CHAPTER 3
SELECTED LIST OF BOOKS FOR FURTHER READING

A number of books describing the African-American Civil War experience are listed below. Most of the works cited are of recent publication. However, a number of 19th Century works are also included; some of which have been reprinted. Collectively the books describe a broad spectrum of the black Civil War experience and range from a collection of letters, biographies, regimental histories, personal recollections, reference guides, and works of a more general nature.

Adams, Virginia, editor. *On the Altar of Freedom*: *A Black Soldier's Civil War Letters from the Front*: *Corporal James Henry Gooding*. New York: Warner Books, 1992.

Addeman, J. M. *Reminiscences of Two Years with the Colored Troops*. Providence, RI: N. B. Williams & Co., 1880. Reprint: Whitefish, MT: Kessinger Publishing, 2007.

An Officer of the Regiment. *Record of the Services of the Seventh Regiment, U. S. Colored Troops*. Providence, RI: E. L. Freeman & Co., 1878. Reprint: Freeport, New York: Books for Libraries Press, 1971.

Ash, Stephen V. *Firebrand of Liberty: The Story of Two Black Regiments that Changed the Course of the Civil War*. New York: W.W. Norton & Company, 2008.

Axelrod, Alan. *The Horrid Pit: The Battle of the Crater, The Civil War's Cruelest Mission*. New York: Carroll and Graf, 2007.

Barnickel, Linda. *Milliken's Bend: A Civil War Battle in History and Memory*. Baton Rouge: Louisiana State University Press, 2013.

Berlin, Ira, Joseph P. Reidy and Leslie S. Rowland, editors. *Freedom's Soldiers: The Black Military Experience in the Civil War*. Cambridge: Cambridge University Press, 1982.

Besch, Edwin W. *U.S. Colored Troops defeat Confederate Cavalry: Action at Wilson's Wharf, Virginia, 24 May 1864.* Jefferson, NC: McFarland & Company, 2017.

Bilby, Joseph G. *Forgotten Warriors: New Jersey's African American Soldiers in the S*

Billingsley, Andrew. *Yearning to Breathe free: Robert Smalls of South Carolina and His Families.* Columbia: University of South Carolina Press, 2007.

Bisbee, John, editor. *Captaining the Corps d'Afrique: The Civil War Diaries and Letters of John Newton Chamberlain.* Jefferson, NC: McFarland, 2016.

Blackett, R. J. M., editor. *Thomas Morris Chester: Black Civil War Correspondent: His Dispatches from the Virginia Front.* New York: Da Capo Press, 1989.

Blatt, Martin H., Thomas J. Brown, and Donald Yacovone, editors. *Hope & Glory: Essays on the Legacy of the Fifty-Fourth Massachusetts Regiments.* Amherst: University of Massachusetts Press, 2001.

Blight, David W. *Race and Reunion: The Civil War in American Memory.* Cambridge: The Belknap Press of Harvard University Press, 2001.

Briggs, Walter De Bois. *Civil War Surgeon in a Colored Regiment.* Berkeley: University of California Press, 1960.

Broadwater, Robert P. *The Battle of Olustee, 1864: The Final Union Attempt to Seize Florida.* Jefferson, NC: McFarland, 2006.

Brown, William Wells. *The Negro in the American Rebellion.* Boston: Lee & Shepard, 1867. Reprint: Miami: Mnemosyne Publishing, 1969.

Burchard, Peter. *One Gallant Rush.* New York: St. Martin's Press, 1965.

_____. *We'll Stand by the Union: Robert Gould Shaw and the Black 54th Massachusetts Regiment.* New York: Facts on File, 1993.

Burkhardt, George S. *Confederate Rage, Yankee Wrath: No Quarter in the Civil War.* Carbondale: Southern Illinois University Press, 2007.

Bryant, James K. II. *The 36ᵗʰ Infantry United States Colored Troops in the Civil War: A History and Roster*. Jefferson, NC: McFarland, 2012.

Califf, Joseph Mark. *Record of the Services of the Seventh Regiment U. S. Colored Troops*. Providence, RI: E. L. Freeman & Co., 1878. Reprint: Freeport, New York: Books for Libraries Press, 1971.

Casstevens, Frances H. *Edward A. Wild and the African Brigade in the Civil War*. Jefferson, NC: McFarland, 2003.

Cavanaugh, Michael A., and William Marvel. *The Petersburg Campaign: The Battle of the Crater, "The Horrid Pit," June 25 – August 6, 1864*. Virginia Civil War Battles and Leaders Series. Lynchburg, VA: H. E. Howard Inc., 1989.

Chenery, William H. *The Fourteenth Regiment Rhode Island Heavy Artillery (Colored) in the War to Preserve the Union*. Providence, RI: Snow & Farnham, 1898. Reprint: New York: Negro Universities Press, 1969.

Christ, Mark K, editor. *"All Cut to Pieces and Gone to Hell:" The Civil War, Race Relations, and the Battle of Poison Spring*. Little Rock: August House Publishers, Inc, 2003.

Cimprich, John. *Fort Pillow, a Civil War Massacre, and Public Memory*. Baton Rouge: Louisiana State University Press, 2005.

Claxton, Melvin and Mark Puls. *Uncommon Valor: A Story of Race, Patriotism, and Glory in the Final Battles of the Civil War*. Hoboken, NJ: John Wiley & Sons, 2006.

Coddington, Ronald S. *African American Faces of the Civil War*. Baltimore: The Johns Hopkins University Press, 2012.

Cole, Jean Lee, editor. *Freedom's Witness: The Civil War Correspondence of Henry McNeal Turner*. Morgantown: West Virginia University Press, 2013.

Cornish, Dudley Taylor. *The Sable Arm: Black Troops in the Union Army, 1861-1865*. New York: Longmans Green & Company, 1956.

Cowden, Robert. *A Brief Sketch of the Organization and Services of the Fifty-Ninth Regiment of United States Colored Infantry and Biographical Sketches.* Dayton: United Brethren, 1883. Reprint: Freeport, New York: Books for Libraries Press, 1971.

Dennett, Georg M. *History of the Ninth U.S.C.T.* Philadelphia: King & Baird, 1866.

Dobak, William A. *Freedom by the Sword: The U.S. Colored Troops, 1862-1867.* Washington, DC: U.S. Army Center of Military History, 2011.

Dobak, William A. and Thomas D. Phillips. *The Black Regulars, 1866-1898.* Norman: University of Oklahoma Press, 2001.

Duncan, Russell. *Where Death and Glory Meet: Colonel Robert Gould Shaw and the 54th Massachusetts Infantry.* Athens: University of Georgia Press, 1999.

Dyer, Frederick H. *A Compendium of the War of the Rebellion.* 2 volumes. Des Moines: Dyer Publishing Company, 1908. Reprint: 3 volumes. New York: Thomas Yoseloff, 1959.

Egerton, Douglas R. *Thunder at the Gates: The Black Civil War Regiments that Redeemed America.* New York: Basic Books, 2016.

Emilio, Luis F. *A Brave Black Regiment: The History of the 54th Massachusetts, 1863-1865.* Boston: Boston Book Company, 1894. Reprint: New York: Arno Press, 1969.

Fox, Charles B. *Record of the Service of the Fifty-Fifth Regiment of Massachusetts Volunteer Infantry.* Cambridge: Press of John Wilson and Son, 1868.

Fox, William F. *Regimental Losses in the American Civil War, 1861-1865.* Albany, New York: Albany Publishing Company, 1889. Reprint: Dayton, OH: Morningside Bookshop, 1974

Franklin, John Hope, editor. *The Diary of James T. Ayers: Civil War Recruiter.* Baton Rouge: Louisiana University Press, 1999.

Fuchs, Richard L. *An Unerring Fire: The Massacre at Fort Pillow.* Mechanicsburg, PA: Stackpole Books, 2002.

Gauss, John. *Black Flag! Black Flag!: The Battle of Fort Pillow.* Lanham, MD: University Press of America, 2003.

Gibbs, C. R. *Black, Copper, & Bright: The District of Columbia's Black Civil War Regiment.* Silver Spring, MD: Three Dimensional Publishing, 2002.

Glatthaar, Joseph T. *Forged in Battle: The Civil War Alliance of Black Soldiers and White Officers.* New York: The Free Press, 1990.

Gould, William B. IV. *Diary of a Contraband: The Civil War Passage of a Black Sailor.* Stanford: Stanford University Press, 2002.

Greene, Robert E. *Swamp Angels: A Biographical Study of the 54th Massachusetts* Regiment. N.p.: Bo/Mark/Greene Publishing Group, 1990.

Hargrove, Hondon B. *Black Union Soldiers in the Civil War.* Jefferson, NC: McFarland, 1988.

Hess, Earl J. *Into the Crater: The Mine Attack at Petersburg.* Columbia, South Carolina: University of South Carolina Press, 2010.

Hewett, Janet B., et al., editors. *Supplement to the Official Records of the Union and Confederate Armies.* 100 volumes. Wilmington, NC: Broadfoot Publishing Company, 1994-2000.

Hewitt Lawrence Lee. *Port Hudson: Confederate Bastion on the Mississippi River.* Baton Rouge: Louisiana State University Press, 1987.

Higginson, Thomas Wentworth. *Army Life in a Black Regiment.* Boston: Houghton Mifflin and Co., 1870. Reprint: New York: Penguin Books, 1997.

Hill, Isaac J. *A Sketch of the 29th Regiment of Connecticut Colored Troops.* Baltimore: Daughtery, Maguire & Co., 1867.

Hollandsworth, James G., Jr. *The Louisiana Native Guards: The Black Military Experience during the Civil War.* Baton Rouge: Louisiana State University Press, 1995.

Humphreys, Margaret. *Intensely Human: The Health of the Black Soldier in the American Civil War.* Baltimore: The Johns Hopkins University Press, 2008.

Jordan, Ervin L. Jr. *Black Confederates and Afro-Yankees in Civil War Virginia.* Charlottesville: University Press of Virginia, 1995.

Kinard, Jeff. *The Battle of the Crater*. Fort Worth, TX: Ryan Place Publishers, 1995.

Kireker, Charles. *History of the 116ᵗʰ Regiment U.S.C. Infantry*. Philadelphia: King & Baird, 1866.

LaBarre, Steven M. *The Fifth Massachusetts Colored Cavalry in the Civil War*. Jefferson, NC: McFarland, 2016.

Lardas, Mark. *African American Soldier in the Civil War, USCT 1862-66*. New York: Osprey Publishing, 2006.

Levin, Kevin M. *Remembering the Battle of the Crater: War as Murder*. Lexington: University Press of Kentucky, 2012.

Levinson, David and Emilie Piper. *On the Other Side of Glory: The Berkshire Men of the 54ᵗʰ Massachusetts Infantry*. Upper Housatonic National Heritage Area, CT: 2011.

Livermore, Thomas. *Numbers and Losses in the Civil War in America, 1861-1865*. Boston: Houghton Mifflin and Company, 1909. Reprint: Dayton, OH: Morningside Bookshop, 1986.

Looby, Christopher, editor. *The Complete Civil War Journal and Selected Letters of Thomas Wentworth Higginson*. Chicago: University of Chicago Press, 2000.

Longacre, Edward G. *A Regiment of Slaves: The 4ᵗʰ United States Colored Infantry, 1863-1866*. Mechanicsburg, PA: Stackpole Books, 2003.

Luke, Bob and John David Smith. *Soldiering for Freedom: How the Union Army Recruited, Trained, and Deployed the U.S. Colored Troops*. Baltimore: Johns Hopkins University Press, 2014.

McCain, Diana Ross. *Connecticut African American Soldiers in the Civil War, 1861-1865*. Hartford: Connecticut Historical Committee, 2000.

McConnell, Roland C. *Negro Troops of Antebellum Louisiana: A History of the Battalion of Free Men of Color*. Baton Rouge: Louisiana State University Press, 1968.

McMurray, John. *Recollections of a Colored Troop*. Brookville, PA: privately printed, 1916. Reprint: Brookville, PA: The McMurray Company, 1994.

McPherson, James M. *The Negro's Civil War: How American Blacks Felt and Acted during the War for the Union.* 1965. Reprint: New York: Vintage Books, 1993.

Macaluso, Gregory J. *The Fort Pillow Massacre: The Reason Why.* New York: Vantage, 1989.

Main, Edwin M. *The Story of the Marches, Battles, and Incidents of the Third United States Colored Cavalry.* Louisville: Globe Print Company, 1908. Reprint: New York: Negro Universities Press, 1970.

Mays, Thomas D. *The Saltville Massacre.* Fort Worth, TX: Ryan Place, 1990.

Mezurek, Kelly D. *For Their Own Cause: The 27th United States Colored Troops.* Kent, Ohio: Kent State University Press, 2016.

Miller, Edward A., Jr. *Gullah Statesman: Robert Smalls from Slavery to Congress, 1839-1915.* Columbia: University of South Carolina Press, 1995.

_____. *The Black Civil War Soldiers of Illinois: The Story of the Twenty-Ninth U.S. Colored Infantry.* Columbia: University of South Carolina Press, 1998.

Moebs, Thomas Truxton, editor. *Black Soldiers, Black Sailors, Blank Ink: Research Guide on African Americans in U.S. Military History, 1526-1900.* Chesapeake Bay, VA: Moebs Publishing Company, 1994.

Morgan, Thomas J. *Reminiscences of Service with Colored Troops in the Army of the Cumberland*, 1863-1865. Providence, RI: Providence Press Company, 1885.

Nalty, Bernard C. *Strength for the Fight: A History of Black Americans in the Military.* New York: Free Press, 1986.

_____, and Morris J. MacGregor, editors. *Blacks in the Military: Essential Documents.* Wilmington, DE: Scholarly Resources, 1981.

National Park Service. *Civil War Soldiers and Sailors System*, http://www.itd.nps.gov/cwss/.

The Negro in the Military Service of the United States: A Compilation of Official Records, State Papers, Historical Extracts, etc. Washington, DC: Adjutant General's Office, 1888.

Ochs, Stephen J. *A Black Patriot and a White Priest: Andre' Cailloux and Claude Paschal Maistre in Civil War New Orleans.* Baton Rouge: Louisiana State University Press, 2000.

O'Connor, Bob. *The U.S. Colored Troops at Andersonville Prison.* West Conshohocken, PA: Infinity Publishers, c. 2009.

Öfele, Martin W. *German-Speaking Officers in the U.S. Colored Troops, 1863-1867.* Gainesville: University Press of Florida, 2004.

Paradis, James M. *Strike the Blow for Freedom: The 6th United States Colored Infantry in the Civil War.* Shippensburg, PA: White Mane, 1998.

Price, James S. *The Battle of New Market Heights.* Charleston, SC: The History Press, 2011.

Quarles, Benjamin. *The Negro in the Civil War.* Boston: Little, Brown and Company, 1953.

Quinn, Edythe Ann. *Freedom Journey: Black Civil War Soldiers in the Hills Community, Westchester County, New York.* Albany: State University of New York Press, 2015.

Ramold, Steven J. *Slaves, Sailors, Citizens: African Americans in the Union Navy.* DeKalb: Northern Illinois University Press, 2002.

Rankin, David C., editor. *Diary of a Christian Soldier: Rufus Kinsley and the Civil War.* New York: Cambridge University Press, 2004.

Redkey, Edwin S., editor. *A Grand Army of Black Men: Letters from African-American Soldiers in the Union Army.* New York: Cambridge University Press, 1992.

Reid, Richard M. *Freedom for Themselves: North Carolina's Black Soldiers in the Civil War Era.* Chapel Hill: University of North Carolina Press, 2008.

_____, editor. *Practicing Medicine in a Black Regiment: The Civil War Diary of Burt J. Wilder, 55th Massachusetts.* Amherst and Boston: University of Massachusetts Press, 2010.

_____,. *African Canadians in Union Blue: Volunteering for the Cause in America's Civil War.* Kent, Ohio: The Kent State University Press, 2015.

Rickard, James H. *Services with Colored Troops in Burnside's Corps.* Providence, RI: the Society, 1894.

Robbins, Glenn, editor. *They Have Left us Here to Die: The Civil War Prison Diary of Sgt Lyle Adair, 111th U.S. Colored Infantry.* Kent, OH: Kent State University Press, 2011.

Ross, Joseph B., compiler. *Tabular Analysis of the Records of the U.S. Colored Troops and Their Predecessor Units in the National Archives of the United States.* Washington, DC: National Archives and Records Service, 1973.

Samito, Christian G. *Becoming American under Fire: Irish Americans, African Americans, and the Politics of Citizenship during the Civil War Era.* Ithaca: Cornell University Press, 2009.

Schmutz, John F. *The Battle of the Crater: A Complete History.* Jefferson, NC: McFarland, 2009.

Scott, Donald, R. *Camp William Penn 1863-1865. America's First Federal African American Soldiers' Fight for Freedom.* Atglen, PA: Schiffer Military History, 2012.

Seagrave, Pia Seija, editor. *A Boy Lieutenant: Memoirs of Freeman S. Bowley, 30th United States Colored Troops Officer.* Fredericksburg, VA: Sergeant Kirkland's Museum and Historical Society, 1997.

Sears, Cyrus. *Paper of Cyrus Sears, Late Lieut.-Col. Of the 49th U.S. Colored Infantry.* Columbus: The F. J Heer Printing Co., 1909.

Sefton, James E. *The United States Army and Reconstruction, 1865-1877.* Baton Rouge: Louisiana State University Press, 1967.

Seraile, William. *New York's Black Regiments during the Civil War.* Studies in African American History and Culture. New York: Routledge, 2001.

Shaffer, Donald R. *After the Glory: The Struggles of Black Civil War Veterans.* Lawrence: University Press of Kansas, 2004.

Slotkin, Richard. *No Quarter: The Battle of the Crater, 1864.* New York: Random House, 2009.

248

Smith, John David, editor. *Black Soldiers in Blue: African American Troops in the Civil War*. Chapel Hill: University of North Carolina Press, 2002.

Smith, John David. *Lincoln and the U.S. Colored Troops*. Carbondale: Southern Illinois University Press, 2013.

Smith, Steven D., and James B. Legg. *"The Best Ever Occupied...": Archaeological Investigations of a Civil War Encampment on Folly Island, South Carolina*. Research Manuscript Series 209. Columbia, S.C.: South Carolina Institute of Archaeology and Anthropology, Department of Archives & History, 1989.

_____,. *Whom We Would Never More See: History and Archaeology Recover the Lives and Deaths of African American Civil War Soldiers on Folly Island, South Carolina*. Columbia, S.C.: South Carolina Department of Archives & History, 1993.

Spurgeon, Ian Michael. *Soldiers in the Army of Freedom*. Norman: University of Oklahoma Press, 2014.

Steiner, Paul E. *Medical History of a Civil War Regiment: Disease in the Sixty-Fifth United States Colored Infantry*. Clayton, MO.: Institute of Civil War Studies, 1977.

Stevens, Michael E., editor.. *As If It Were Glory: Robert Beecham's Civil War from the Iron Brigade to the Black Regiments*. Madison, WI: Madison House, 1998.

Taylor, Susie King. *Reminiscences of My Life in Camp with the 33rd U.S. Colored Troops*. Boston: privately printed, 1902. Reprint: Athens, GA: University of Georgia Press, 2006.

Tomblin, Barbara Brooks. *Bluejackets & Contrabands: African Americans and the Union Navy*. Lexington: University Press of Kentucky, 2009.

Trudeau, Noah Andre. *The Last Citadel: Petersburg, Virginia, June 1864-1865*. Boston: Little, Brown and Company, 1991.

_____, editor. *Voices of the 55th: Letters from the 55th Massachusetts Volunteers, 1861-1865*. Dayton, OH: Morningside, 1996.

_____. *Like Men of War: Black Troops in the Civil War 1861-1865*. Boston: Little, Brown and Company, 1998.

Tucker, Philip Thomas. *Palmito Ranch: The Last Battle of the Civil War*. Mechanicsburg, PA: Stackpole Books, 2001.

Urwin, Gregory J. W., editor.. *Black Flag over Dixie: Racial Atrocities and Reprisals in the Civil War*. Carbondale: Southern Illinois University Press, 2004.

Valuska, David L. *The African American in the Union Navy: 1861-1865*. New York: Garland Publishing Inc., 1993.

War of the Rebellion: A Compilation of the Official Records of the Union and Confederate Armies. 128 volumes. Washington, DC: Government Printing Office, 1880-1902.

War of the Rebellion: A Compilation of the Official Records of the Union and Confederate Navies. 80 volumes. Washington, DC. Government Printing Office, 1894-1922.

Ward, Andrew. *River Run Red: The Fort Pillow Massacre in the American Civil War*. New York: Viking, 2005.

Washington, Versalle F. *Eagles on Their Buttons: A Black Regiment in the Civil War*. Columbia: University of Missouri Press, 1999.

Weaver, C. P., editor. *Thank God My Regiment an African One: The Civil War Diary of Colonel Nathan W. Daniels*. Baton Rouge: Louisiana State University Press, 1998.

Western Carolina Historical Research. *The Battle of Honey Hill, South Carolina, November 30, 1864: An Arrangement of Edited Primary Sources with Attached Appendices*. Charlotte: Western Carolina Historical Research, 1999.

Westwood, Howard C. *Black Troops, White Commanders, and Freedmen during the Civil War*. Carbondale: Southern Illinois University Press, 1992.

Williams, George Washington. *A History of the Negro Troops in the War of the Rebellion, 1861-1865*. New York: Harper & Brothers, 1888. Reprint: New York: Kraus, 1969.

Wills, Brian Steel. *The River was dyed with Blood: Nathan Bedford Forrest and Fort Pillow*. Norman: University of Oklahoma Press, 2014.

Wilson, Joseph T. *The Black Phalanx*. Hartford: American Publishing Company, 1890. Reprint: New York: Arno Press, 1968.

250

Wilson, Keith P. *Campfires of Freedom: The Camp Life of Black Soldiers during the Civil War.* Kent: Kent State University Press, 2002.

_____, editor. *Honor in Command: Lt. Freeman S. Bowley's Service in the 30th United States Colored Infantry.* Gainesville: University Press of Florida, 2006.

Yacovone, Donald, editor. *A Voice of Thunder: The Civil War Letters of George E. Stephens.* Urbana: University of Illinois Press, 1997.

AUTHOR, EDITOR, AND COMPILER INDEX
Names are keyed to the reference numbers found in Chapter 2.

SUBJECT INDEX

Numbers refer to the entry numbers found in the Annotated Article Bibliography.

The terms USCI (United States Colored Infantry) and USCT (United States Colored Troops) are often used interchangeable for the same unit.

Infantry:

1st USCI 117
1st USCT 48, 360, 362
2nd USCI 61
2nd USCT 42, 67
3rd USCT 28, 141, 180, 475
4th USCT 151, 305 459, 477
5th USCT 6, 230, 259, 260, 261, 338, 429
6th USCI 24
6th USCT 320, 396, 497
7th USCT 176, 347, 477
8th USCI 36, 372
8th USCT 166, 293, 394
9th USCT 347, 477
10th USCT 426
12th USCT 294, 338
13th USCT 125
14th USCT 289, 338
16th USCT 289
19th USCT 477
20th USCT 130, 237, 334
21st USCT 161, 338, 388, 392
22nd USCT 489
26st USCT 126, 237, 276, 334
27th USCT 258

28th USCT 229, 312
29th USCI 207, 314
29th USCT 182, 338
30th USCT 477
31st USCT 237, 334
32nd USCI 112
32nd USCT 49, 221, 410, 434
33rd USCT 163, 174, 276, 286, 387, 392
34th USCT 49, 180, 392
35th USCI 112
35th USCT 36, 112, 126, 166, 221, 377
36th USCT 251
38th USCT 129
39th USCT 477
41st USCI 372
42nd USCT 289
43rd USCI 40
43rd USCT 411
44th USCT 120, 289
46th USCT 34, 329
49th USCT 338
51st USCT 34, 329
54th USCI 241
54th USCT 10
55th USCI 25
56th USCI 383
56th USCT 363,495
59th USCI 25, 406
60th USCI 69, 383
60th USCT 363
62nd USCI 17, 304, 335
62nd USCT 227
63rd USCI 8, 298
64th USCI 464
65th USCI 3